Collegiate Republic

JEFFERSONIAN AMERICA

Jan Ellen Lewis,
Peter S. Onuf, and
Andrew O'Shaughnessy
Editors

Collegiate Republic

CULTIVATING AN IDEAL SOCIETY IN EARLY AMERICA

Margaret Sumner

UNIVERSITY OF VIRGINIA PRESS

Charlottesville & London

◆ ◆ ◆

University of Virginia Press
© 2014 by the Rector and Visitors of the University of Virginia
All rights reserved
Printed in the United States of America on acid-free paper

First published 2014

1 3 5 7 9 8 6 4 2

Library of Congress Cataloging-in-Publication Data
Sumner, Margaret, 1972–
 Collegiate republic : cultivating an ideal society in early America / Margaret
Sumner.
  pages   cm. — (Jeffersonian America)
 Includes bibliographical references and index.
  ISBN 978-0-8139-3567-6 (cloth : alk. paper) — ISBN 978-0-8139-3568-3
(e-book)
  1. Universities and colleges—United States—History—18th century. 2. Uni-
versities and colleges—United States—History—19th century. 3. Education,
Higher—United States—History—18th century. 4. Education, Higher—
United States—History—19th century 5. Education, Higher—Social
aspects—United States. 6. Education, Higher—United States—Philosophy.
I. Title.
 LA227.S86 2014
 378.73—dc23

                                                              2013041171

CONTENTS

ACKNOWLEDGMENTS

AS THIS PROJECT traveled the road from dissertation to book, many people provided me with "intellectual and moral" support along the way. As my dissertation advisor, Jan Lewis deserves my highest praise and gratitude for her guidance. From our first lunch together in 1999, she has always been eager to discuss my ideas, question my assumptions, listen to my archival adventures, read multiple drafts of conference papers and chapters, and urge me forward with equal helpings of encouragement and insightful criticism. No graduate student could have had a better critic, colleague, and friend than Jan Lewis. I was also very lucky to have the wonderful team of Nancy Hewitt, Ann Fabian, and Scott Sandage serving as my dissertation committee. These scholars were always on hand, or online, with helpful advice and support.

An American Dissertation Writing Fellowship from the American Association of University Women provided me with valuable time for thinking and writing. I am also a grateful recipient of the Benjamin F. Stevens Fellowship from the Massachusetts Historical Society, and the Jacob Price Research Fellowship from the William L. Clements Library. I would also like to thank the New Jersey Daughters of the American Republic, the Graduate School at Rutgers University, and The Ohio State University at Marion for providing travel and research funding for this project. A special thanks to Professor Ann Gordon at the Papers of Elizabeth Cady Stanton and Susan B. Anthony at Rutgers University for providing me with numerous research assistantships. Under her careful tutelage, I learned essential archival research and editorial skills while paying the rent. Throughout this project, Ann Gordon has been a mentor, critic, and friend. Thanks also to my fellow research assistants, Kimberly Banks, Lesley Doig, and

Ann Pfau, who provided much collegial support as we all worked on our dissertations while "working for suffrage." My thanks to all.

Researching a project that spans multiple colleges would have been impossible without the enthusiasm, dedication, and "institutional knowledge" of a stellar group of college archivists. My deepest thanks to the following archivists and their staff: Sylvia Kennick Brown at Williams College, Chuck Barber at the University of Georgia, Ellen Fladger at Union College, James W. Gerencser at Dickinson College, B. J. Gooch at Transylvania University, Richard H. F. Lindemann at Bowdoin College, and Vaughan Stanley and Tom Camden at Washington and Lee University. Always eager to dig into their vaults for any obscure document or object I requested, and provide me with priceless "insider" information, these scholar-archivists made my study of multiple sites and multitudes of college family papers much easier and certainly more enjoyable.

I owe a debt of gratitude to the many Rutgers University faculty and staff who assisted and advised me during my graduate years: Paul Clemens, Barbara Baillet, Teresa Delcorso, M. Josephine Diamond, Alison Isenberg, Jennifer Jones, Steven Lawson, James Livingston, Phyllis Mack, Meredith McGill, Dawn Ruskai, and Bonnie Smith. My additional thanks to a brilliant circle of graduate friends who listened with patience and good humor as I talked endlessly about the early college world: Kristen Block, Jackie Castledine, Carmen Khair Gitre, Catherine Howey, Kathleen Keller, Danielle McGuire, Robert Nelson, Amanda Pipkin, Louisa Rice, Margaret Smith, and Emily Zuckerman.

I am lucky to have an equally supportive circle of colleagues at The Ohio State University. My special thanks to John L. Brooke for his enthusiastic encouragement of my work as well as his gracious invitation to share my work with graduate students and fellow early American colleagues at the Ohio Seminar. Colleagues Leslie Alexander, Saul Cornell, Margaret Newell, and Randy Roth also deserve thanks for their enthusiastic and helpful comments about my project. My colleagues at the OSU–Marion campus always provided me with generous advice and support when I most needed it. My thanks to James Genova, Derek Heng, Timothy McNiven, Bishun Pandey, and Dean Greg Rose. A special acknowledgement to David Steigerwald, a true mentor whose door was always open, and whose advice was always appreciated. Along with reading chapter drafts, my generous colleagues in the English department at OSU–Marion—Lynda Behan, Sara Crosby, Marcia Dickson, and Cassandra Parente—spent much time with me discussing ways to inculcate the "virtue" of writing, and rewriting, into our work. Our interdisciplinary conversations have greatly enhanced my own approach to teaching, scholarship, and life.

I would also like to thank the early American scholars who read various incarnations of my work as it moved from dissertation to book. Whether on conference panels or over coffee, each of these scholars offered perceptive critiques that were immensely helpful as I revised my manuscript: Catherine Allgor, Jeanne Boydston, Bruce Dorsey, Richard Godbeer, Rodney Hessinger, Nancy Hewitt, Mary Kelley, Cathy Kelly, Martha J. McNamara, Lucia McMahon, Catherine O'Donnell Kaplan, and Peter Onuf. To Kyle Roberts, your longtime friendship, constant intellectual support, and extensive working knowledge of evangelical texts were essential to the completion of this project.

For their steadfast support of a seemingly endless project, my family circle deserves much recognition. My loving gratitude to Neil and Bridget Sumner, Colleen Sumner and John Dennison, and William, Heather, and Grace Sumner. Finally, my love and profound thanks to Roy A. Hampton. Your steady love and affection, enthusiastic support, centered companionship, and expert photocopying skills helped me bring this project to a close so I could start creating a new beginning. I am eternally grateful.

Collegiate Republic

Introduction

WRITING A ROMANTIC NOVEL about a scholar on a journey, a young Henry Longfellow once asked this question of his readers: "Where should the scholar live? In solitude or society?" Where would the scholar be the most productive—and the most effective? Longfellow himself was on a journey when he wrote *Hyperion* in 1839. He had left Brunswick, Maine, where he had spent his formative years as both a student and a professor at Bowdoin College, had studied in Europe, and had then taken up a more lucrative teaching position at Harvard. For the rest of his life, this student who achieved both fame and wealth through the creative powers of his mind continued to wonder if he had truly found the ideal scholarly environment.[1]

Affixing Longfellow's question to the top of her poem for the *Southern Literary Messenger* in 1850, the poet Margaret Junkin answered what one reviewer called Longfellow's "always brilliant, but often misty" speculation. Junkin answered Longfellow's question with an authority forged by a life dedicated to creating the ideal environment of his scholarly dreams. Solitude, she asserted, was definitely not the right environment. As she explained in her poem, the task of learning, with its "wilderness of lore," could easily "dishearten" a lone scholar into depression and madness. Nor was society the answer. In Junkin's opinion, society was a distracting and deceptive place of "passion-whirl'd" crowds among which "eye answers not to eye" and where "fashion" ruined people so badly that "no traces of sweet nature" could be found on them. For Junkin, Longfellow's chosen home at Harvard, in cosmopolitan Cambridge, was such a place.[2]

As the daughter, sister, and wife of professors at Washington College in Lexington, Virginia, Margaret Junkin championed a different kind of space—an ideal world set in "verdant valleys," full of "haunting zephyrs" and "murmuring streams." Her response was a reminder to her colleague Longfellow that there were spaces for true scholars of life. In fact, there existed a "calmer, purer world" due north from Longfellow's Cambridge. In this world, the one he had left behind at Bowdoin College as a student and then a professor, a variety of natural forces—many in feminine form— hoped to teach important lessons about the "ebbs and flows of human life" so that scholars like the uneasy Longfellow would have no need to question their position in life.[3]

For Junkin, this ideal environment was located in her hometown of Lexington, Virginia, the site of Washington College set deep into the Blue Ridge Mountains. It was also in Brunswick, Maine, around Bowdoin College, where, as Junkin might have pointed out, a young Longfellow had once found all the answers to his questions before letting himself get distracted by the problematic society of Europe—or Cambridge. This environment also flourished at Dickinson College in Carlisle, Pennsylvania, Union College in Schenectady, New York, Williams College in Williamstown, Massachusetts, and in the refined "literary villages" of Athens, Georgia, Chapel Hill, North Carolina, and Lexington, Kentucky. These college communities were founded in the 1780s and 1790s as ideal environments dedicated to producing a new generation of republican leaders well trained in a classical, collective form of virtue that would bring about their individual success as well as benefit what college founders often termed the "common good."

Drawing on the published and private writings of those who lived in, worked in, and emerged from this college world, this book explores the charter generation of college families (presidents, trustees, faculty, graduates, and associated "friends") that established an early set of organizing principles and standards for American civil society. Often portrayed by historians as institutions that trained elite white males in Greek and Latin for professions like the ministry, these early colleges were also an interconnected network of families determined to use "our college" as a vehicle in which to rise as an elevated, educated class over the majority of Americans. While creating this new class, however, they attempted to live and work within it. None found it an easy endeavor, economically or emotionally.

Within these new communities, the first set of working intellectuals and educators also established standards of American success for themselves and their students. In their intense, intimate little college world, these families pioneered a set of strategies for categorizing, evaluating, and teaching success (or for divining the potential for future success) that would, through their expanding educational network across the continent, exert immense cultural power over the nation.[4]

The historian Joyce Appleby has studied the "desires, callings, decisions, and reflections" of this post-Revolutionary generation to provide an "intimate view of how the vibrant new abstractions of democracy—the nation, free enterprise, and liberal society—thickened with meaning" during this early era. Analyzing how the nation's first generation of educational theorists and practitioners explored, defined, and enacted such "abstractions" as they attempted to create a civil blueprint for American society reveals why and how such ideals acquired and retained their vibrancy and mythological potency. By focusing on the men and women who created and maintained the nation's early college world, my book attempts to follow these educational principles in action, tracing the interplay between the construction and dissemination of early American knowledge, the institutionalization of college culture, and the creation of society.[5]

This book covers the period from 1782 to 1860, when education and its influence on the nation became a popular topic of debate, analysis, and experimentation among Americans. The "business of instruction," as college-building families called their profession, slowly democratized between Jeffersonian and Jacksonian idealizations of the independent white male citizen, the empowerment of middle-class associational institutions that promoted a "village enlightenment," and the competitive consumerism of a rapidly expanding market economy that included the sale of human beings and their labor.[6]

After 1800, waves of evangelical revivalism transformed and expanded the definition of education—and ideal society—in this era, merging an intellectual world governed by classicism, masculinized reason and virtue, and "common sense," with one that invoked the authority of biblical revelation, feminized emotion and virtue, the essentializing of race, and a mystical, romantic notion of knowledge. College families engaged in all of these transformations, embracing some and rejecting others according to their goal of promoting their distinct definition of virtue and the social ideal of collective harmony.[7]

Forged in the exclusive medieval guild culture of Europe, shaped by a coterie of Reformed and Enlightened gentlemen in Great Britain, and funded by aristocratic patronage, the college was an odd cultural form for post-Revolutionary Americans to embrace so enthusiastically, given the Revolutionary disdain for Old World privilege, aristocratic tradition, and the concentration of elite power. For a war-weary populace, however, the streams of young men returning to traditional educational institutions at Cambridge or Williamsburg or New Haven or Princeton visually symbolized the promise of their newly won free society—an expansive, productive world of opportunity in which students instead of soldiers had the chance to secure the nation's future.[8]

The champions of the new college communities committed themselves to maintaining and cultivating the classical definition of virtue based on self-sacrifice and action for the common good. This ideal was, for many new republicans, the key to their Revolutionary victory and the security of their future. The new republic now needed leaders who could exemplify this virtue by reconciling the demands of self-confidence and self-control within themselves while legislating for an increasingly passionate, rapidly expanding public. The educators of the new nation viewed their new college communities as ideal sites where they could teach this ideal of virtue to the next generation as well as physically model it for their students and the wider nation to observe and emulate.

As Margaret Junkin and her colleagues would assert, the college world provided an essential resource for the nation—a model world that reminded it of the need for collective harmony. Those who promoted these college communities idealized them as peaceful spaces where young minds were being molded and shaped for the future and where the powers of good and evil would not be allowed to "wage" their "strife." These new communities promoted a new and improving form of thought and behavior for the republic—a "moral and intellectual order"—that, college families insisted, would provide a durable template for virtuous activity. College families worked hard at showing their students and their fellow Americans how to follow this order because they hoped, as more and more young graduates left their communities, this template might be adopted by a new generation to temper the wildly competitive social, political, and economic forces emerging around them.[9]

Transylvania College trustee Henry Clay saw that the "main thing" about the educational enterprise at his college at Lexington, Kentucky, would be to "make men live better." Bowdoin College trustee Benjamin Vaughan hoped "tranquility & industry" could "be made to befriend each other" at Brunswick. This new college world would promote a social blueprint dedicated to collective harmony, even if it did not always successfully model this ideal.[10]

Educational historians have long been reevaluating the place of the college in American society, moving past Richard Hofstadter's portrayal of the "old time" college as intellectually isolated in classicism, narrowly sectarian, and stifling to "academic freedom." According to Hofstadter's modernization thesis, these small colleges and their cultural power retreated into groves of conservative elitism throughout the nineteenth century, unable to compete with the modernizing university system that offered more intellectual, social, and professional choices to students, and a professional culture of disciplined, expert knowledge for faculty to cultivate.[11]

Scholars now analyze these early colleges within a wider context, approaching the concept of higher education as a community project, rather than an institutional one. This approach reveals a "multipurpose" nature to the early colleges that provides a new lens through which to analyze them, exploring the many intellectual, religious, and economic resources that a college provided to its town, region, and state. Unfortunately, historians today still tend to focus on a single college or on regional groupings of colleges as representative of a system of higher education. This book is the first interregional study of early colleges positing the creation of a college world by a network of families intent on making their fortunes through the new "business of instruction." Throughout daily rounds of what they commonly called "college work," these families built an intellectual world and a distinct infrastructure to support it.[12]

Actual families embodied these new institutions, like Bowdoin College or "the college at Chapel Hill." Before the Revolution, the leading families living along colonial frontiers had supported institutions of higher education for their sons in need of classical-language training for the Presbyterian or Congregational ministry, or for access to the polished society of gentlemen. After the Revolution, they aspired to see these local "classical schools" or "academies" take their place alongside, and perhaps even rival, the long-established degree-granting colleges of the East and worked together to transform their local schools and academies into colleges fit for their new republic. Through these new institutions, regional elites hoped to gain more political and economic leadership, wider social influence, and a foothold in the new national government. By 1800, many new state legislatures had recognized these small academies as official colleges, chartering them as public institutions granting classical degrees to a new leadership class. In these same regions, many other families feared the new institutions and criticized them as simply new bastions of eastern elitism, sectarian conspiracy, and aristocratic patronage.[13]

These new colleges did indeed become powerful organizational centers for their regions. From the perspective of the families who founded and maintained them, however, they exerted a new kind of power that differed greatly from that prevalent in the larger political or commercial centers of the republic. From towns like Carlisle, Pennsylvania, or Williamstown, Massachusetts, or Lexington, Kentucky, there radiated a new "moral and intellectual" power that was supposed to refine American society and its new generation of leaders. It was hoped that new college graduates, imbued with this moral and intellectual power after four years of training, might do something to calm the increasingly competitive, unstable world of politics and commerce that surrounded them.[14]

The new colleges produced a small, select cohort of male graduates who were expected to exert a new form of collective virtuous power. According to early educational advocates like Benjamin Rush, it took a different sort of mind (and manner) to rule a republic, and a set of colleges far away from the eastern cities to produce them—like Rush's own post-Revolutionary project, Dickinson College. A republican citizen needed to know how to lead in government affairs and to live by the rule of law and merit rather than that of arbitrary power and wealthy patronage. A republican also had to be a confidently knowledgeable yet self-controlled guardian and skilled developer of the republic who would love, protect, and oversee its peaceful expansion. These new men were not to be authoritative patriarchs, but the paternal leaders of powerful, rising families who through virtuous connections with other families would create a "common body of social happiness" for all. This transformation from "subject" to "citizen" could only take place, as Margaret Junkin had pointed out in her poem, in an environment that was protected from the temptations and distractions that commercial or political power attracted—in short, in a place like Lexington, Virginia.[15]

The post-Revolutionary age of college-building was also the age of academy-building, and many new colleges began life as small academies. Both the college and the academy offered "instruction beyond rudimentary literacy and computation." Both were, for most students, boarding institutions where students and teachers lived in close proximity. Until the late 1830s, when some "radical" colleges like Oberlin in Ohio and Berea in

Kentucky, began experimenting with coeducation, the colleges traditionally limited admission to white men only. Many of the academies, however,
were coeducational. Some, like Emma Willard's Troy Seminary in New
York or Mary Lyon's Mount Holyoke Seminary in Massachusetts, actually
specialized in the higher education of young women.[16]

At the academies, the curriculum was varied and flexible. Students often
had a wide range of choice among subjects. Along with English, history,
arithmetic, the "modern languages" like French or Italian, and sciences
like chemistry or physics, or even bookkeeping and engineering, some students could also choose to follow a "college preparatory course" of Greek
and Latin. Young men regularly attended these academies to prepare themselves in these languages for college. The focused study of these "sacred
languages" marked the primary difference when it came to differentiating
academies from colleges. In their famous defense of the classical curriculum in 1820, the professors at Yale made this difference well known—and
well publicized, characterizing the academy as offering "a little of everything," whereas the college focused on training men in a "uniform course"
of classics. To distinguish their own institutions from the many other post-
Revolutionary institutions of higher education (academies, institutes, seminaries, and schools), the new colleges promoted a standard seemingly set
in stone: a "regular" and mandatory course of Greek and Latin. Only certain men— those destined for leadership—were judged eligible and capable
of mastering the body of learned traditional knowledge that made up the
colleges' classical curriculum.[17]

But forced to compete with the academies for students, and also
responding to the interests of their students and professors, the new colleges did, over time and in haphazard ways, add to their offerings. New
scientific subjects like chemistry or physics, or new languages like French
or German, became common in college catalogues. Yet, no "regular" student who expected to receive a diploma could escape the core curriculum
of classical subjects—no exceptions.[18]

The academies were nevertheless central to the expanding college
world. Indeed, many college family members had been educated in the
academies, or began their teaching careers there, or sent their sons to them
to prepare for college. Still, for college families, the academies were merely
basic training grounds for the young men who would be admitted to the
new college classrooms, or for the young women who would be admitted
to their society. According to Benjamin Rush, the academies were part of

the growing collection of "inferior schools" sprouting up in the republic. They were "like so many nurseries of trees, where the young plants may grow promiscuously, and from which those who distinguish themselves by superior abilities, may be transplanted to the more favourable situation of the college." Only after ascending to a college could students be "cultivated to bless their country with the fruits, which a benevolent providence has enabled them to produce"—the fruits of classical learning and leadership. College-trained men were expected to lead rather than merely participate in the republic, unlike the majority of academy students, both male and female.[19]

Additionally, it was the academy teacher, not the college professor, who was expected to act as a surrogate parent to students. In some academies, male students still encountered corporal punishment. As one graduate of a local academy near Athens, Georgia, who would later matriculate at Franklin College, remembered ruefully, Greek and Latin were "literally whipped into the boys." College families, on the other hand, insisted that their students should be viewed as adults in need of training instead of as children in need of discipline. Instead of corporal punishment, college professors preferred to rely on the practice of public lectures or private conversations as well as a system of demerits that punished students through monetary fines, parental notice, suspensions, and, in the worst cases, expulsion. Indeed, professors bristled at parental assumptions that they were duty-bound to correct their sons' "child-like" behavior. Professors would act as family members toward students, but they and their colleagues would develop a very different definition of family as they constructed their college world.[20]

Historians have long theorized about the transforming role of the early American family—a "cradle" of class and gender formation, as Mary Ryan coined it, in which family members practiced collective strategies to help negotiate an unstable market economy and achieve at least an appearance of gentility. Using the categories of race, class, and gender, social and cultural historians have added to our understanding of the formation of the middle class by exploring its cultural parameters: how, for example, the emerging middle class—or, as Peter Gay has theorized, an assembly of "middle classes"—forged and enacted their notions of public and private spheres, masculine and feminine citizens, laboring and leisured classes, and white and "colored" bodies. This book draws on social, family, and intellectual history to explore the underpinnings of this "cradling" process.[21]

College families were deeply enmeshed in working out these familial strategies as they tried to sustain not only their own families but also the larger collection of individuals that embodied their collegiate institutions—the "college family." They thought in larger, more expansive terms about the nature of the family as being more than merely an institution made up of authoritative parents and dutiful children. This notion of a large network of associates connected through more than blood resembled the Jeffersonian "consciousness" of generations that "suggested an organic, quasi-familial conception of the nation." To Jefferson, such a nation was not made up of a single centralizing force, but was an "expanding union of republics held together by ties of interest and affection." Similarly, these families imagined their colleges as part of an expanding network of like-minded Americans that emphasized the collective goals of self-sacrifice, collective action, and voluntary association. This "thickening weave of family connection, interdependent interest, and affectionate fellow feeling" would help perpetuate a "decentralized union" and facilitate the structuring of the antebellum nation. The new colleges that were founded in the more-distant regions of the republic only appeared to emulate their eastern counterparts. But according to the families that founded and maintained these new institutions, they were much more distinguished. As Margaret Junkin would point out, their new world of virtue and harmonious collectivity, deep in the interior of the republic, was where the most effective and most successful thought and action existed.[22]

Yet, the fact that Margaret Junkin had to remind her colleague Longfellow about its existence reveals the difficulties faced by those who would promote this new world and its ideals. Once someone left the college world and got caught up in "passion whirl'd" society outside, there was always the fear that they would forget about their formative training. Even Longfellow—a consummate Bowdoin family insider as the son of a trustee, a graduate, and a professor—had seemingly forgotten his roots, as Junkin reminded him. The "college work" of Junkin and other members of the college family involved educating a future elite, but it was also preoccupied with reminding the forgetful or the neglectful about the essential importance of their world and its ideals for the success of the new nation. In their words, their texts, and their communities, Junkin and her colleagues worked continually to promote a set of important ideals to a nation that always seemed more determined to figure out its own version.

◆ ◆ ◆

My first chapter, "Cultivating the College World: 'The Generous Purpose,'" follows the newly elected Washington College president, George Baxter, in 1805 as he solicits "the people" for financial donations for his new enterprise in Lexington, Virginia. He discovers along his route east that his fellow Americans are determined to create viable futures for themselves by taking advantage of the expanding opportunities of a commercializing economy. Yet he also discovers that this endeavor has led to a troublesome new redefinition of virtue as an enthusiastic pursuit of self-interest. In response to his calls for donations, many of his fellow citizens believe they do not have enough money, time, or even patience to support the president's "virtuous" cause. The ideal of virtue, assumed to be permanently fixed in the hearts and minds of the American revolutionaries, now had to be cultivated in an increasingly forgetful and, in Baxter's view, corrupt society. Moreover, the presidential trip reveals how the traditional classical and Christian definitions of virtue promoted by the college world are no longer based on consensus. College families will have to develop new strategies in the name of virtue in order to once again attract the interest of the people.

My second chapter, "Organizing the College World: 'All Various Nature,'" focuses on the families of Bowdoin College in Maine and explores the ways that coeducational sociability between "ladies and gentlemen" shaped training in the college world. As one professor described it, a college town—like his own Williamstown in western Massachusetts—was an ideal "society in miniature." This chapter explores the creation of that society. The collective understanding of a specific and "appropriate" gender order strengthened college families' attempts to position themselves as an elevated class in American society. The influence of women in the college world through the social and educational power of "college ladies" is examined in particular. Such refining strategies, performed in every college community by the college families, shaped the social and intellectual foundations of the college world and provided a model for social advancement and economic success for the outside world to observe, acknowledge, and emulate.[23]

My third chapter, "Building the College World: 'An Elegant Sufficiency,'" follows the families at Franklin College in Athens, Georgia, who, like their colleagues around the nation, used both real and ideal constructs (buildings, educational and religious associations, religious revivals) to create communities of "virtue and knowledge" that would enlighten the "gloomy" interiors of the republic. As they built and inhabited these educational structures, college families resisted the growing cultural tendency to perceive society as divided into public or private domains with distinct forms of production and gendered behavior assigned to each. As spaces were divided and gendered, so was the already fragile definition of virtue. Determined to retain a "standard" and stable notion of virtue, college citizens idealized and practiced structural unity in their buildings and in their families. From their classrooms to their parlors to the local tavern, they insisted that all social structures and spaces should be designed for educational purposes and thus devoid of division and partisanship. In an improving republic, there were no public spaces or private spaces—only virtuous spaces. In this chapter, we see college families determinedly living according to these principles, moving through (or breaking through) bounded space to retain unity and collective harmony in the face of diversity and division.

In chapter 4, "Working in the College World: "Ease and Alternate Labor," the college families confront a new world of work and assume new identities as different kinds of workers. Exploring how one college family at Williams College in Massachusetts harnessed both mental powers and manual labor to carry out their "college work" reveals how these new "brain-workers" consolidated their economic and emotional position in the commercializing republic. Those who lived and worked in college communities hoped to use the "furniture of their mind," as they would say, to support their families and furnish their homes. As men moved from the agricultural fields and artisanal workshops into the classrooms and offices of the college world, and as women were encouraged to pick up their pen and publish or to stage debates in their parlors, as well as to care for children or perform housework, college families became deeply engaged in the changing "notions" of labor in their lives, exploring various ways to measure, evaluate, and perform it. Their experience reveals the complicated ways that the nation's first class of working intellectuals created new standards for labor performed by the mind.

Chapter 5, "Leaving the College World: 'Gentle Spirits Fly,'" focuses on the "dark" minds of the college world, which is how college families identified the "colored students," servants, and slaves who lived, worked, and learned within the college world. Following the experiences of John Russwurm, the first "colored" graduate of Bowdoin College, and Jenny, a slave woman owned by the daughter of a Washington College trustee, as they engage with the moral and intellectual order of the college world, this chapter explores how a distinct racial and class order strengthened and maintained the cultural power that the college world asserted. Most college families were colonizationists—enthusiastic supporters of the American colony of Liberia on the west coast of Africa. College families were fond of imagining Liberia as one more educational community for their world, a distant place where "black" genius might be cultivated. As part of their "college work," college families filled the ships departing for the west coast of Africa with black emigrants whom they had "educated," along with the money, books, and supplies they assumed a black colony would need. The African career of John Russwurm after his graduation from Bowdoin College reveals the long-lasting ties, ideal and real, between college families and Liberians—as well as the college world's commitment to strengthening and purifying a white republic by supporting and educating leaders for a (very) distant black one. While some "dark" minds were allowed into the classrooms of the college world to be trained for leadership in exile, others were to be found among its serving class—both free servants and slaves. College families kept their domestic class busy serving the college world. Servants and slaves kept themselves busy observing the workings of this world and its "moral and intellectual" logic, learning how to improve their mental and physical "condition" and then working out a way to escape their servile position for a more-elevated place in the world. The example of Jenny, a slave living in the Lexington, Virginia, college community, reveals that this new college world was more apt to produce "impudent" servants well trained in the skills of observation, speculation, and self-determination than in any lessons about eternal servility.

◆ ◆ ◆

In my reading of the many letters and diaries of college families, I found, time and again, excerpted quotations from the poem *The Seasons*, written by the English Whig poet James Thomson. Some lines became veritable colloquialisms of the college world. Families were always fond of noting, earnestly or sarcastically, how education was a "delightful task" that involved teaching "the young idea how to shoot." Thomson had completed this long poem, divided into four parts by season, by 1730. A revised edition appeared in 1744. Like many of Thomson's works, it is full of classical references, Virgilian pastoralism, and, even more importantly, the critical

Whig ideology that many Revolutionary Americans embraced with enthu-siasm. After the Revolution it made sense that the poem remained a favor-ite among well-read families intent on creating new worlds of "retirement, rural quiet, friendship, books"—worlds that would train young, impres-sionable minds in classical subjects as well as warn them about the dangers of concentrated power, passionate ambition, and moral corruption. Each of my chapter titles borrows a phrase from Mr. Thomson, all of them from the section most dedicated to youth: "Spring."[24]

Cultivating the College World

"The Generous Purpose"

IN 1805 GEORGE BAXTER rode out of his mountain town of Lexington, Virginia, on a borrowed horse. Newly elected to the presidency of the "college at Lexington," the young Presbyterian minister intended to solicit funding for its future success. The cities of the eastern seaboard were to be the prime coordinates on his "begging" tour. As a graduate of another new college, Hampden-Sydney, as a minister, and as a former academy principal, Baxter was no stranger to the advocacy of religion and education. In the past, he had found that the two traditional pillars of post-Revolutionary society—virtue and knowledge—had sparked much enthusiasm and financial generosity from fellow Presbyterians. On this tour, Baxter hoped to cast a wider net for his new institution, determined to find even more friends and even more funding.[1]

The new president wanted more than sectarian supporters. His institution had recently gained a national friend, and he hoped to cultivate a few more. Originally founded as a school that taught the languages of the ministry, Greek and Latin, to the chosen sons of Presbyterian families, Baxter's institution had once been known as Liberty Hall Academy. It received its first national exposure when it gained the attention of George Washington. Lexington families were thrilled when the "asserter of the liberties of his country," the "illustrious Washington," donated funds to support the little school that survived the Revolution. They promptly renamed their institution after the president, and Washington Academy quickly turned into Washington College—chartered, like all new colleges, by a state legislature that allowed it to give out college degrees. As he prepared for his fundraising trip in 1805, Baxter envisioned "people of first rank" emulating their former leader, eagerly sharing friendship and funding with an institution worthy of Washington's notice.[2]

Confident in his expertise at fundraising, experienced as an advocate of virtue, and bolstered by Washington's support, Baxter was optimistic that his fellow Americans would want to follow their first president's classical ideal of virtue: the tradition of self-sacrifice for the common good. President Baxter was only one of hundreds of educators involved in building the college world, and they all undertook similar fundraising tours. By following him, we can see the challenges they faced as they tried to promote their favored definition of virtue—self-sacrifice and collective effort in the name of education—in a rapidly transforming nation starting to embrace less-sacrificial definitions of virtue.

In his history of Dickinson College, Charles Sellers observed that the "American mania for college founding" revealed two cultural needs haunting post-Revolutionary society: the desire to speculate over founding ideals like virtue, and the desire to speculate over all the new economic or political opportunities emerging after the Revolution. Underlying this mania was the republican fear of self-interest and the extent of its influence on the new republic. This is the dilemma that George Baxter and his colleagues confronted whenever they solicited funds for their institutions. Their attempts at cultivating their college world compelled Americans time and again to ponder the place of classically defined virtue in their new society. Were Revolutionary ideals based on self-sacrifice and collectivity still relevant in a republic increasingly characterized by intense competition, the individual search for opportunity, and the vehement contestation of opinion? Did a classical definition of self-sacrificial virtue have a place anymore in the increasingly commercialized and politicized nation?[3]

Baxter and his colleagues firmly believed that it did. They believed that all Americans were capable of practicing self-sacrifice for the common good; they simply needed to be reminded of this Revolutionary duty to be generous. After 1800, it took a more potent blend of traditions—both classical and Christian—to rouse the people to prioritize the collective good above their own self-interest. College families considered it part of their new "business of instruction" to issue these reminders.[4]

Baxter was an eyewitness to the potential power of this combined call for civic and Christian action. Hearing about the religious revivals along the Kentucky frontier, Baxter traveled there, where he saw "professed infidels" transform into model citizens who expressed "friendly temper," "sobriety," and a deep love of God after listening to sermons on salvation, charity, and brotherhood. Baxter was most impressed with the widespread "liberality" he observed among the settlers, and he lingered over the details of what he had seen as he wrote to interested friends back East. To accommodate the crowds flocking to the revival grounds, both "public and private houses" had been opened, and "free invitations given to all for lodging." Before the harvest, farmers willingly "gave up their meadows" so horses and wagons could be accommodated. Groups of rowdy settlers, notoriously divided by "private animosities and contentions" and "petty lawsuits," were moved to settle their differences out of court. Feuding families talked out their differences and then, to Baxter's amazement, promised to "forbear all mention of the past." This precipitate culture of "liberality" made a deep impression. Defending the transformations he saw on the frontier to skeptical friends, Baxter insisted that what he had witnessed among the settlers was not mere "enthusiasm" or "animal spirits," but a veritable transformation of society after a call to duty. To Baxter, the experience proved that self-sacrificial virtue could be forgotten or abandoned for a time, but once the people were collectively reminded of their civic and Christian duties, they remembered the true meaning of virtue—and then acted on it.[5]

Baxter and his colleagues thus took on the task of reminding Americans about this civic and Christianized version of virtue, one that hearkened back to the Revolution but borrowed heavily from the more-recent evangelical movement that had emerged after 1800. The builders of the college world believed their new educational institutions would provide their fellow Americans with actual "brick-and-mortar" reminders of their duty to support such virtue. Along with providing classical knowledge, college families offered Americans a classical world, one studiously set apart from commerce or politics, in which republicans could demonstrate that they remembered the old self-sacrificial brand of virtue. Out of their own economic and social needs college families worked to cultivate any and all donations of money, time, and friendship that helped them expand their new world. It did not matter if these gifts came from private citizens or public legislators. All gifts were welcome, since each was proof of the public's commitment to the older, classical definition of virtue.

Donating to colleges—and befriending the families who maintained them—became a favorite way for Americans caught up in a competitive, commercializing nation to prove they still had what it took to make a sacrifice. Any donation to a college was a chance to pledge again, in a very public way, their commitment to transmitting to future generations such a laudable founding ideal as self-sacrifice for the public good.

When George Baxter arrived in Lexington with his family to take up the post of president, he saw what he expected to see as a member of the college world: a veritable orgy of "liberality" inhabiting the space around his college buildings. There, his family found a circle of instant "friends" who were happy, even anxious, to donate to the new presidential family and to "our college," as the locals tended to call the institution. Families gave freely of their time, socializing and providing emotional support to the newcomers. They were also generous with financial support. After a fire suddenly burned down the original Academy building, the community jumped into action. Some citizens donated buildings in town so classes could resume immediately. Others opened their homes to homeless students. A wealthy widow exchanged her land for that of the college's smoking ruins, offering extra acreage on generous terms. White Lexingtonians donated cash, land, and the labor of their slaves, as well as "a hundred bushels of corn," toward the reconstruction effort. These families in Lexington, Virginia, were not unique in offering such support. Every new college community had a group of "friends of education," as they called themselves, who assisted their local institution and the families who worked there.[6]

The success of a college not only depended on the efforts of the president and his faculty. Circles of associated families worked for the fortunes of the colleges. George Baxter shared every detail of his fundraising trip with his wife Anne. While always requesting she kiss the children for him, he was also aware that there were more people than those in his fireside circle who were interested in his activities. Local families and "friends" in Lexington avidly followed his progress and made suggestions—through Anne's letters—about social contacts to develop, houses to lodge in, and easier routes to follow. One of them loaned him his horse. As he moved from Richmond to Petersburg to Norfolk, Baxter lodged with the "agreeable and friendly" relations of families from Lexington, making sure to compliment their hospitality and interest in his letters home. He was always careful to identify everyone who gave him assistance along the way, plotting out a web of potential friends from the mountains to the seacoast. Just a few days after his departure from Lexington, he wrote that he had already had an "opportunity of seeing something of mankind" and that he expected "some advantage from my trip." Baxter's confidence in the success of his tour had much to do with this supportive network of friends—and their promises of funding. He expected to meet like-minded people farther up the road who would sympathize with his institution's needs in the same way. If they did not, or seemed uninterested in his project, he planned to use the examples of Washington and Jesus to remind people about the need for self-sacrificial giving.[7]

From the Kentucky frontier Baxter tried to convince a group of ministerial friends at Princeton that traditional virtue had truly reappeared in American society. The Princetonian skepticism he encountered was not surprising. There were many doubts among the elite even during the Revolution over the ability of the American people to sustain the strict discipline of classical virtue. The postwar decades had only increased these fears. After the Revolution, new republicans confronted a whole set of puzzling social, political, and economic problems. The nation was plagued with economic instability, class tensions, spiritual controversies, and racial and gendered transformations.[8]

For such a fundamental element of American identity, the classical virtue of the Revolutionary era proved to be highly unstable material upon which to build a nation. As Noah Webster observed in 1788, new Americans proved shockingly adept at changing this fundamental notion so that it better fit the commercial and political opportunities arising in a post-Revolutionary world. As he described his view of the world from New Haven, Webster observed that the "scene of ambition is opened" and that a celebration of self-interest instead of selflessness motivated society. Commercial regions "swelled with innumerable merchants," and any person with a new scheme would find "a speculator at his elbow" interested in supporting any cause that promised financial profit. As many began debating the implementation of the new federal system, he noted, some Americans were already "feeding on the expectation of a new congress and federal government." This enthusiasm for private interest at the expense of the common good seemed to reverse any Revolutionary gains. The former revolutionaries were actually embracing new forms of elitism, patronage, and monarchy. Webster mocked these "independent Americans" who identified themselves as forward-thinking, enlightened people. In his opinion, they were simply moving backward, with their dreams of being "courtiers, gentry, and great men." Instead of remembering to sacrifice some of their fortune for the public good, these new republicans actually embraced and welcomed back into their lives the Old World culture of corruption, luxury, and patronage that they had just spent years fighting against. As he observed, "The liberty and property of the common people are in some danger." The aggrandizement of the self, a growing admiration of private enterprise, a celebration of individual aspiration—all of these values became the central features in a new, increasingly popular definition of virtue."[9]

Amidst all of these challenges, Revolutionary leaders like Washington clung to the hope that Americans would remember that virtuous self-sacrifice alone had provided victory over Great Britain. This brand of virtue needed to be preserved and exhibited for future generations to learn about, emulate, and preserve. His donation to Washington College was part of this elite concern about preserving such notions of virtue. Throughout the 1780s and 1790s, newspaper and periodical contributors expressed a mixture of surprise and relief that beneath all of the perceived chaos after the Revolution, there was evidence of some sort of order, and the order was distinctly educational. The people had a rage for founding educational institutions of all kinds: schools, seminaries, academies, institutes, and, specifically, a whole new generation of colleges in developing regions "at the west." One periodical writer in 1787 praised the virtue of those families who worked to found and fund such institutions. They proved that the "first care" of Americans was not their self-interest, but the common good. The ultimate vindication of the Revolution, the writer observed, was not only a citizenry "lavish in praise of learning," but people lavish in funding it. Writers pointed out repeatedly that the continued support of educational institutions would allow Americans to reap the most important benefit of their Revolution—a secure future dedicated to the expansion of virtue. Educational institutions would produce never-ending generations of young republicans who would go on to secure, and then expand, the new nation.[10]

Families settling developing regions of the republic quickly seized upon educational institutions as the main channel through which they could secure a stable future for themselves and their communities. They founded and maintained educational institutions for their children, who they wished to be educated closer to home rather than at institutions "back East." Based on this private family need, such families created a public good, promoting their home regions and educational institutions as ideal sites for settlement as well as for learning for all. Fond of criticizing eastern commercial and political urban centers as corrupting and confusing, western elites promoted their regions as protected from urban corruption, full of unimaginable opportunities for pursuing happiness, and, of course, as the home of true virtue. As one commentator observed, it was better for young minds to become "vulgarly right" within the virtuous "orders" of a rural village than to become "politely wrong" through exposure to distracting city experiences. Many leaders in developing communities acted on this belief. When families in Schenectady, New York, realized that the city of Albany might trump them in their bid for the location of Union College, they wrote newspaper articles and circulated petitions to highlight the "comparatively few fashionable vices" that might infect young minds to be found in their village, in contrast to what was to be found in the more cosmopolitan parlors of Albany. Likewise, the citizens of eight separate villages in Maine petitioned the trustee families of Bowdoin College, who were searching for a site for their new enterprise. One village described itself as the least "exposed" to the "many Temptations to Dissipation, Extravagance, Vanity and various Vices" found in "great seaport towns" like Portland. The village of Brunswick, Maine, eventually won the trustees' favor.[11]

Similar to Baxter's Washington College, Dickinson College in western Pennsylvania began its existence as a small Presbyterian academy. With the support of concerned Revolutionary veterans like Benjamin Rush and John Dickinson, local families eagerly turned it into a degree-granting college shortly after the war by legislative act. Like many of his college-founding colleagues, Benjamin Rush envisioned Dickinson as a virtuous outpost that would offer a purer environment for learning and living, a marked contrast to his own college at Philadelphia that was continually plagued with religious partisanship, political wrangling, and, in his opinion, moral vice. In 1784, Rush traveled to Carlisle, Pennsylvania, with John Dickinson to attend the first trustee meeting for the college. Recording all of the events in his diary, he provides a glimpse of the excitement the local families felt when they realized they would soon have a college in their town. Like George Baxter, Rush was quick to notice and record the numerous displays of "liberality" exhibited by the Carlisle families. Local families from all over the county invited Rush and Dickinson, who was the "president" of Pennsylvania at the time, to dine in their homes and converse with them over tea. They were even entertained one evening by ladies playing the harpsichord. A collection of local men accompanied Rush and Dickinson on a tour of buildings that had been donated freely by leading citizens "for the Accommodation of the pupils and professors." Throughout his trip, Rush recorded his conversations with a diverse group of people—artisans, farmers, merchants, and "genteel sensible young ladies"—who expressed much enthusiasm for the college and promised their full support, financial or otherwise. He was pleased to find that the "principal inhabitants" of Carlisle were "agreeable" to his educational enterprise. On his and Dickinson's last evening in town, a large crowd gathered at the tavern, where they all ate an "elegant dinner" that was "provided by the Citizens of Carlisle." Rush was pleased that the new college had such a friendly, generous group of supporters—"friends" well schooled in what he and his generation viewed as the essential Revolutionary lesson: a desire to support the public good over private interest.[12]

To Rush it seemed that many in Carlisle had learned the Revolutionary lesson well. The struggle with Britain had imparted one important maxim about attaining and maintaining a free society. Only an "informed citizenry" could recognize their natural rights and work together to liberate themselves whenever the slavery of "foreign tyranny" and other forms of darkness threatened to oppress them. Benjamin Rush predicted that the inhabitants of Carlisle were on the path to national success due to their enthusiastic support of Dickinson College. As long as they supported educational institutions, leading elites like Rush hoped, Americans would reap the blessing of a free society—a secure future. Since the public seemed committed to making sacrifices in the name of education, they would also bring about another ideal from the Revolution: social harmony.[13]

In stark contrast to the sectarian bickering that disturbed the state legislature and his own college back in Philadelphia, Rush was happy to report to his wife Julia that the town of Carlisle was amazingly harmonious. During his visit he marveled at how the town's families (all from rival religious sects) gathered together at the Episcopal Church to hear a sermon on "the Utility of Seminaries of learning." As the approving Rush looked on, a fellow Dickinson trustee served as minister, using a line from Corinthians I, "For knowledge puffeth up, but charity edifieth," as the starting point for his sermon.[14]

Benjamin Rush approved of this sermon because it linked the two post-Revolutionary pillars—knowledge and virtue—together. While college towns and their citizens might "puffeth" up in knowledge, benefiting from the economic and social opportunities that a college would bring to the region, they would also experience the call for virtue. Their charitable duty of financially and socially supporting Dickinson would temper any corrupting influences brought about by economic or social success. Supporting a college in town would, it was hoped, protect inhabitants from such vices as class rivalry or selfish luxury. Education advocates like Rush hoped that collective support of any educational institution would naturally "edify" Americans, reminding them of their Revolutionary commitment to self-sacrifice for the public good.

For leading members of the elite like Rush, the support of the new colleges offered the opportunity for a diverse group of people divided by varied interests and varied definitions of virtue to learn again how to focus on a common goal—education. This chance to work together would, they hoped, establish social harmony. After the trustees founded Union College in Schenectady, New York, they invited John Blair Smith to leave the presidency of Hampden-Sydney for the leadership of Union. He accepted, praising his new institution in frontier New York as a model of religious and social harmony. Union College was truly a union—its trustees comprised of "men of diverse religious convictions" (Dutch Reformed, Presbyterian, and Episcopalian) who "set aside faction and divisions" to petition the legislature for funding and a charter to transform their local academy into a degree-granting college. President Smith joked of the "Excellent rivalry" between religious sects in town, which fought to "contribute most to the general welfare by devising plans through which the best education could have its birthplace and dwelling place here." Soon, Smith predicted, this spirit of cooperation sparked by a college in town would bring "refinement, civility, and culture" to New York frontier society, an atmosphere that would rival the "famed Lyceum at Athens." Those who worked to build the college world hoped that support for their efforts would provide the nation with a union of purpose that would facilitate collective prosperity and general cultural advancement.[15]

The Trustees

At the highest level of college "friends" were the families who founded and patronized this new generation of colleges—the trustees. Some were wealthy members of the elite and former revolutionaries like Benjamin Rush or John Dickinson; they hoped to promote and preserve order in the developing regions of the republic but were too old or settled to move there themselves. Other trustees had served as officers in the Continental Army or in local militias and now moved their families west, hoping to take advantage of the developing territories. Many were young professionals educated in eastern colleges and hoping to make their fortunes in medicine, law, or divinity in the new regions. These new trustees represented a class of rising regional elites who chose to settle far from the eastern urban centers but who expected higher education and high status for their children. They championed self-sacrificial virtue because, as they saw it, the ideal helped secure social cohesion in frontier regions awash with rampant competition, class tensions, and, at times, outright violence. Social disorder threatened their plans to position themselves as the "elevated" class in the region, dedicated to providing economic, political, and social leadership for their new states and their new nation.

As one such enterprising settler complained, "the want of good schools" in his new home of Georgia was a major economic and emotional barrier to his family's ability to pursue happiness—and lucrative futures for his children. He informed a professor at the new Franklin College at Athens that he had been forced to send his son to the new University of Vermont for a classical education. He was wealthy enough to afford this great cost of both travel and education, but he knew "thousands" of fellow settlers who "cannot afford to send their children abroad for education." Thrilled to hear that the "college at Athens" had opened, the father inquired about the possibility of his son transferring there from Vermont. He had never been able to "reconcile" his mind to his son's New England education because it seemed useless to do so. Since he expected his son to build his future in Georgia, or farther west, the father wanted him closer to home, learning how to be a gentleman among fellow Georgians, as well as a dutiful family member. By attending nearby Franklin College, he would gain membership into important developing regional networks and quick access to knowledge of any sudden opportunities for advancement. An education in classical virtue at Athens would teach him how to seek out success in connection with other young Georgians, as well as secure it for the benefit of his family.[16]

Most of the first graduates of these new colleges were the sons, brothers, nephews, and cousins of such settler-trustee families. Trustees intended to protect virtue for the public good, but they also desired to protect their sons by keeping them close to home. Their founding of institutions of higher education along the frontiers of the republic depended on this blend of private and public need. At state legislatures, where many of the men of these trustee families frequently served, the lawmakers regularly recognized the private need for higher education as a public interest to promote the common good. Legislators from Maine to Georgia announced their willingness to give "aid and encouragement to seminaries of learning" because of the collective desire to spread the Revolutionary legacies of virtue and knowledge. They were eager to promote any new enterprise that marked their transformation from dependent colonists to independent citizens. Due to the lobbying of trustees, state legislatures issued charters for "public institutions," creating degree-granting institutions like Bowdoin College, or, as was the case for Dickinson or Washington College, transforming academies into degree-granting colleges. In the case of the new Southern institutions, like the University of Georgia or North Carolina, or for new states like Vermont, the legislatures were chartering their state's first institution of higher education. These new "public institutions" satisfied the educational demands of new regional elites intent on developing the fortunes of their new home regions.[17]

College charters outlined expansive yet vague powers for the new trustees, encouraging them "to do all such things as to they shall appear requisite and necessary" to "forward" the "establishment and progress" of their colleges. Some legislatures donated initial gifts of land to the new colleges, which trustees either sold off in speculation deals for cash or rented for income. There were never any firm promises of permanent financial support from legislators, however, and funding always depended on the political whims of the party in charge. As the builders of the college world would discover, state legislatures (and the people they represented) could be incredibly "liberal" or they could be forgetful when it came to supporting educational institutions. The only surety was that the support was unpredictable and that a whole range of alternative fundraising strategies had to be planned.[18]

Based on the familial nature of their enterprise, trustees often insisted on personally supervising their new colleges, assuming that the charters gave them the supervisory powers that a father might exert over his own children. Indeed, trustees often spoke of their new collegiate institutions as entities in need of parental care: as "nurseries of literature, piety, and virtue," and as a "child of hope and heir of fame"—or, as the busy Benjamin Rush once called the always financially struggling Dickinson, as a "brat" that demanded constant attention. Adopting a paternalistic mode, trustees attempted to supervise everyone who lived and worked within their fledgling enterprises.[19]

Interactions with these educational patrons could prove to be both overwhelming and reassuring. When the trustees of the new Transylvania University in Lexington, Kentucky, elected him president, the Bostonian minister Horace Holley decided to pay a visit before accepting the post and relocating so far west with his wife Mary and their infant daughter. Even before he reached Lexington, Holley wrote Mary that he was constantly surrounded by "quite a collection of lawyers, judges, and gentlemen." At Paris, Kentucky, he met up with a group of trustees and they all had "a good deal of conversation on the subject of the college." The men talked about his future presidency and their plans for Transylvania's success. Many assured him that the rumors he heard about Presbyterians and Baptists opposing his election because of his Unitarianism were untrue. In any case, they insisted, they would smooth over any local tensions. Happy with his collective and cordial welcome, Holley informed Mary that "thus far they promise everything." When he finally reached Lexington, Holley found that his trustees were indeed virtuous. Their enthusiasm involved more than words. They also possessed much "liberality." The "new college" they had built on a rise in Lexington was, according to the Yale graduate, "the handsomest brick building of the sort in the United States." One of Transylvania's more politically prominent trustees, Henry Clay, invited Holley to stay at his home, dine with the family, and personally escorted him around Lexington on a series of social calls to the town's various leading families—"friends" to Transylvania. Some of these families had opposed Holley's nomination, but all seemed "cordial" as Holley strolled the streets with the influential Clay. This experience with the trustees dispelled any worries about the new enterprise in Kentucky, and Holley wrote excitedly to Mary that she needed to prepare herself for a great change. They were moving to Kentucky to take up the "business of instruction."[20]

Under the paternalist influence of the trustees a form of educational commerce was initiated that looked a lot like the other commercial exchanges taking place in the new republic, but was to its practitioners in the college world of a completely different nature. Virtue was the precious commodity transacted in these new trades, an ideal offered in exchange for freely given cash, goods, and services. The profits of this new commerce were made through acts of self-sacrifice rather than self-interest. Its business plan involved the constant cultivation of generous donations from the public (indirectly through state legislatures) or from private individuals. All such economic activity was carried out in the name of the common good, and the continued "liberality" of the people was its only form of insurance. Without such "liberality," the fledgling college world would disappear.

Trustees pioneered this ideal commerce by being the first to donate to the colleges, receiving nothing of commercial value in return. Along with land and cash, trustees donated supplies, or collected them from friends and family—the beginnings of an ever-widening circle of college friends. The trustee Benjamin Vaughan sent numerous boxes to Brunswick, supplying Bowdoin College in Maine Territory with mineral samples, scientific equipment, books, and "some old pamphlets from my brother in London." Coordinating a wide range of transatlantic friends, Vaughan informed Bowdoin's president that he should expect "various other parcels which will equally be shared with the College." There were also generous patronesses. Angelical Campbell of New York sent a "donation" of books to Union College, informing President Eliphalet Nott of her "respect" for him and for the new institution's promotion of the ideal of sectarian union at Schenectady. Early presidents and their faculty at these new colleges accepted any gift that came their way. After Joseph McKeen accepted the presidency of Bowdoin College, he was alarmed to discover that the trustees had not thought of providing a library or scientific equipment. One trustee assured him that they planned to "collect donations" for these materials, because "literature and science has always lived on patronage & surely we need not blush to beg for it for the public institution." In this new college world it was not shameful to beg for public support. In fact, college officials thought people should consider it an honor to be solicited—to be given the chance to donate and exhibit the extent of their commitment to true virtue.[21]

There were soon many enthusiastic donors to these fledgling colleges. Thanks to the suggestions of the trustee William Jenks, Hannah Crocker, a descendent of Cotton Mather, decided that her ancestor's library would be best preserved at Bowdoin. When a "gentleman of great respectability and science" decided to donate a "splendid collection of books belonging to the department of Natural History" to the new University of Georgia, the president made sure to publicize this gift in newspapers nationwide. Through the cultivation of such public donations, trustees ensured their colleges of an ever-expanding interconnected network of friends.[22]

On his road trip in 1804, George Baxter met with a particularly friendly and powerful trustee who decided to accompany him on the road for a while. Baxter was thrilled to be accompanied by General Porterfield, a veteran of the Revolution. He reported excitedly to Anne in Lexington that the "General's influence may be of use to me." The General proved to be "very clever," offering to take some of Baxter's subscription papers around to all of his wealthy friends in Albemarle County so that Baxter could visit more towns and then perhaps start for home earlier than he had planned. The General also promised to "make an effort" to win Cincinnati Society Funds for the college. As he informed Baxter, he was determined to use his military status with the state legislators to convince them to transfer the funds of Virginia's now-defunct Society of Revolutionary War Officers to the College's treasury. Sensitive to the unpopularity of this elitist hereditary fraternal brotherhood, Baxter was not optimistic, but he wished the General luck. This offer revealed Porterfield's very public friendship to the college. He not only accompanied the college president through the Virginia countryside, but he donated money, solicited funds, and introduced Baxter to his friends. Baxter expected that many from the General's circle would emulate this very public act of patronage and "liberality" to Washington College.[23]

Through the work of trustees, the new colleges became familiar as institutions of higher education, favored recipients for donations, and important coordinates in a highly effective network of educational opportunity. When Daniel Dana, a friend to Bowdoin College, wrote to congratulate President Jesse Appleton on his institution's "flourishing state," he also shared the news that he had recently become a trustee of a new institution. As a patron of a new theological seminary in his Maine village, Dana enclosed his institution's "Constitution" and requested that it "be deposited, if it should be thought proper, in the library of Bowdoin College." Dana and his fellow seminary trustees planned to send the constitution to "all the Colleges in new England, and to the principals, in the Southern States," shrewdly linking their new enterprise to an educational network that was "flourishing" across the republic. Linking his village seminary with this expanding college world would bring it status as well as open up the possibility of attracting students and donations from a wider network of "friends."[24]

After a month on the road, George Baxter had become familiar with any number of definitions of "virtue." He was not pleased. In his letters to Lexington he described how many of the people he met were quick to agree with him that institutions like colleges were essential to the survival of their republic, and he went on to note that he had received "very polite and friendly treatment" and heard much vocal enthusiasm for educational causes. The people he met very quickly changed their tune, however, when he turned the conversation from the general importance of educational expansion to the more particular financial needs of his struggling college.[25]

Confronted with an array of excuses, complaints, and outright resentment at his requests for money, Baxter—the expert on cultivating virtue—was shocked to find himself treated more like a despised creditor than an honored advocate. Not only did the president find that he now had problems making friends, he also discovered that he could make enemies with his requests for donations. Initially worried over raising enough money to make his college a success, Baxter now discovered that he and his colleagues in the college world had an even larger problem: with competing definitions of "virtue" floating around the republic, Baxter now had to explain and defend his classical definition of the term.

The root of the problem, according to Baxter, was the alarming spirit of competition he found among his fellow citizens. This competitive environment prompted even him, a college president, to question his basic assumptions about virtue. Writing from Richmond, Baxter informed Anne that he found "people more reluctant about giving money on account of the contributions they made to Princeton and other seminaries." This was troubling. As he talked to people and heard about other donations they made, he began feeling worried, angry, and even envious of the success of these other institutions. That did not feel right. What happened when two or more institutions dedicated to virtue were forced to compete for support from the people? Baxter remained optimistic; he wrote that he had "set a subscription on foot and have collected about 300 dollars," and that he thought he would "have it in my power to collect a good deal more" before leaving Richmond. What was the source of this confidence? Baxter leaned heavily on his Presbyterian contacts, relying on the influence of Washington College trustees and their friends. His institution also had a unique distinction in having been patronized by Washington as the first of its "friends." No other institution could claim that kind of kinship. To his friends in Lexington he reported that he was "indebted to the activity and politeness of Mr. Alexander Stuart" as well as "Messrs Preston, Mims, and Edwards Johnson," who seemed "very anxious to give me every aid in their power" despite the competition from other institutions. As trustees, they were duty bound to help him. As regional elites, they wanted their little college at Lexington to succeed. As Baxter moved on to Petersburg, the men gave him "introductions to several gentlemen" in that place who "appear very polite and friendly." It was Baxter who kept track of these "gentlemen," sent their names on to Lexington, and evaluated their friendship factor. Were they simply "friendly," or would they be a true friend of the college, a person who would freely donate services or money? Collecting and connecting with such true friends would be the key to surviving the culture of competition Baxter had discovered along his trip.[26]

The Faculty

Sources of friendly assistance could come from anywhere, and the families of presidents and professors hired by trustees to live and work in the colleges took up the duty of identifying potential sources of virtuous generosity, and cultivating them. These families also became experts at evaluating and cultivating a circle of like-minded "friends." While trustee families relied on their commercial or political ties to further the interest of their colleges, faculty families used the tool of their trade: educational expertise. In exchange for supporting their college, they offered to potential friends the valuable commodity of knowledge and, of course, access to books.

When a young woman in a small Maine village bereft of a school faced the "arduous" burden of educating her children alone, she turned to her friend Elizabeth Appleton, the wife of Bowdoin College's president, to discuss this "business of education." As she observed to Appleton, "The dispositions of children are so varied that they cannot be treated alike." She asked for advice, because "you know as well how to manage them as any one that I am acquainted with." Appleton sent her an educational book by Maria Edgeworth, urging her to read it so that they could discuss it. Strongly approving of Edgeworth's program of daily instructional chats with each child, the woman despaired whether she could find time in her busy household to carry out the plan effectively. "I wish I was capable of giving my child instruction by means of conversation," she mourned, but she was too busy. She agreed with Appleton that a "well informed mother might do much towards implanting a taste for knowledge in the breasts of her children." Elizabeth Appleton sent more educational books and advice, which the woman fully appreciated. As she told Appleton, the more she read, the "more & more interested on the subject of education" she became. She hoped to be "enabled to practice as well as read" on the topic. After this exchange, the woman and her husband, a Harvard graduate who had spent a postgraduate year as a college tutor at Brunswick, became firm friends to Bowdoin. Her husband later served as a trustee, and the family donated money. The woman became an avid college recruiter, sending two sons to Bowdoin and nudging likely young men in her family and town toward an education at Brunswick. She also sent young women from her social circle to spend a season at the president's house under Mrs. Appleton's wise tutelage. With book exchanges, conversations, and friendly letters of advice, Elizabeth Appleton merely carried out what numerous faculty family members felt was an educational duty: convincing people to become virtuous supporters of their college world.[27]

Faculty families assiduously cultivated the "liberality" of anyone who came to visit or study with them. Anyone could become a potentially powerful and useful friend. When young Andrews Norton, recently graduated from Harvard, arrived in Brunswick to work as a tutor to Bowdoin College students, a common postgraduate activity for young men, the faculty families living around the college buildings warmly welcomed him into their society. Norton developed a great "regard" for those who ran the new institution. Returning to Harvard to take up an administrative job, he offered himself and his services to Bowdoin's president: "I shall be much pleased if you should employ me in procuring books either for yourself or the library at Brunswick or if you should make use of my services in any other way." His time in Brunswick among the faculty families cemented a bond of both affection and profession with the new college. The faculty families had done well, the bond they created promising future offers of free service and, even better, free books. The creation of a broad, ever expanding educational family, connected through affectionate relationships based on the exchange of educational "liberality," facilitated the social and economic survival of these fledgling institutions.[28]

The other duty of faculty families was overseeing the daily workings of the "business of instruction." Yet this involved more than simply teaching the classical curriculum. After his meeting with Transylvania trustees, Horace Holley reported to his wife that when it came to scheduling classes, organizing college activities, interacting with townsfolk, and overseeing the buildings of the college, "everything is to be done," and according to his trustees "almost the whole is proposed to be left to me to arrange." Holley and his fellow faculty families were in charge of the everyday business of the college world, but securing potential sources of generosity to keep the business going was, at times, their most important task. Trustees provided the basic infrastructure, financial resources, and important connections, but they had other interests to cultivate. Holley soon found it a challenge to direct the trustees' attention to the many pressing needs of his fledgling college. According to faculty families, their distinctive managerial function was what made them different from trustee families. Their attention never swerved from the needs of their colleges, because their own fortunes and that of their families were inextricably linked to the fortunes of these new colleges.[29]

Trustees had multiple identities beyond just being "friends of education." They were also merchants, planters, or professionals intent on making money in the commercial world and gaining influence in the political world. They could be powerful patrons for colleges, but they were easily distracted. Even as he stayed in their homes and socialized with them, George Baxter realized he could easily lose the attention of the college's trustees and their friends. At Lynchburg he discovered he could do nothing for the college because, as he grumbled to Anne, "the gentlemen all went to the Campbell election" and were blatantly uninterested in conversing with him about educational matters. Baxter's presidential colleague at Bowdoin College learned quickly that trustee assistance could never be taken for granted. When Bowdoin president Joseph McKeen asked a trustee for some new books for the library, the man sharply told him he was too busy and that McKeen had to solve this problem himself: "Have you no brother Academitician or nabob acquaintance who would contribute to these objects to oblige you?" Prompted by trustees who were often unconcerned with the tedious details of college maintenance and administration, faculty families became experts at discovering alternative sources of "liberality." They took up the trustee network of "friends" and expanded on it, including anyone who believed, like they did, that anything done "for the good of the college" was an act for the public good—an act of self-sacrificial virtue.[30]

Since their family fortunes depended on the decisions of the trustees who hired them, fired them, and decided their salaries and raises, professors and their families equated their prospects for personal prosperity with those of their college. This first generation of faculty families rarely had "nabob" acquaintances. They were not as wealthy as the trustee families, who often lived in nearby cities or inhabited impressive homes near the college. Contrasting themselves with the distracted, wealthy trustee families, faculty families saw their position in the college world as the more focused and, of course, the most committed to cultivating virtue. Many faculty members believed that they and their families had sacrificed the pursuit of private interest for their colleges—and for the common good.

The longer he stayed on the road, the more George Baxter pined for his family at Lexington. "I can assure you madam," he wrote to Anne, "I would rather be at home than any where else, and the more new faces I see the happier I am that my fortune is made." Like all college families, the Baxters linked their fortunes to their college, a strategy that allowed them to deflect charges of personal ambition or selfishness. Any move they made to cultivate their family's prosperity had to benefit their "business of instruction." Their dedication to their college absolved them, in their minds, from any charges of personal ambition. With their family fortune dependent on their institution's fortunes, faculty families saw themselves as a peculiar entity—members of a distinctly elevated class, and pioneers in a new business that promoted profits from self-sacrifice and demanded collective rather than individual prosperity.[31]

After George Baxter's death, his daughters came to regret this enthusiasm for self-sacrifice. Baxter had ignored the need to protect their mother's inherited "valuable lands in Kentucky," deciding that rather than "securing a merely secular good," his "time and talents" should be focused on his presidency of Washington College and on his role as the town's Presbyterian minister. Publicly praising her father for his "entire devotion to his work," Louisa Baxter also acknowledged that the family had hired an "eminent lawyer" after her father's death, who informed them that "much valuable property has passed from us for want of attention." The Baxters had been left with few resources to maintain their genteel social status as a college family. George Baxter did bequeath one important legacy to his children: a thorough knowledge of the classics, which his daughters put to use immediately. Louisa and her sisters opened an academy in Lexington that prepared young men to enter Washington College and trained young girls to teach the same classical subjects. Bereft of their mother's legacy because of the demands of Washington College, the Baxters could easily point out the importance of education as a tool for self-support, as well as demonstrate, albeit a bit regretfully, how one family enacted pure virtue, sacrificing its personal fortunes in order to support a college.[32]

In the 1780s on his trip to Carlisle as a new trustee the optimistic Benjamin Rush believed that many of the Carlisle families he met were just as willing to sacrifice their fortunes to support Dickinson College. Given all of the donations of goods, services, and time that were eagerly promised to him by the people he met, Rush expected nothing but success for the new institution. Not all of Carlisle's citizens, however, viewed their support of Dickinson in such a self-sacrificial fashion. For many, their donations were simply speculative investments, and they expected Dickinson to provide them with a future full of benefits and rewards. In return for their support, Carlisle families expected their sons to matriculate at the new college, attain a classical education, and find sure success in the professions. Supportive farming families also expected to make large profits from Dickinson, as they hoped to sell their products to a growing college town with its continual waves of hungry students. One local craftsman, John Fisher, was only too happy to accept Benjamin Rush's commission to engrave the college seal. He assured the trustees that he would also be available for the institution's future engraving needs, already expecting his business to expand. Rush also had numerous conversations with local women of "good Sense & valuable improvements of mind" who looked forward to supporting the refining atmosphere of a "literary village." One elderly woman informed him that she could "not live without books," and that she expected that her support of the college would bring more books into her life, and, perhaps, free access to the college library. Instead of cultivating a self-sacrificial ideal, as Rush and early advocates hoped, many early supporters of Dickinson College had their own expectations about future private rewards. They were not going to give something for nothing. It was faculty families who tended to correct this misunderstanding about the true meaning of virtue. Supporting the college world, they argued, should be a commitment to the pursuit of self-sacrifice, not self-interest.[33]

A decade after Benjamin Rush's first visit to Dickinson, the college president, Charles Nesbit, issued a reminder during his commencement address to students and local families about the correct way to support Dickinson. After an initial burst of support, local families had focused more on how the new college would "puffeth up" their own interests rather than spend much time or money on the college itself. By 1792, the community's charitable donations of land, money, and time had petered out. Trustee interest had lagged. The town of Carlisle had also become less harmonious, with the college tending to spark the conflict. Some local families disliked that the college was run by a Presbyterian president, and they made their opinions known in the newspapers. Other factions called for the college to close completely, arguing that it was too exclusive. Why should only the sons of rich local men receive an education? As parents heard of the tensions plaguing Carlisle, fewer students applied for admission. Fewer students meant less tuition money collected. The prospects for Dickinson did not look good, and President Nesbit and his faculty were worried about the future. On Commencement Day, Nesbit thus addressed his graduating students and their families by issuing a "solemn and weighty charge" to his listeners. He challenged his graduates to continue in their search for knowledge, but, more importantly, to renew their "zeal for the public." Without a collective enthusiasm for supporting such a public institution as Dickinson, the college would close, there would be no more institution that would "edify" the public about its duty to support virtue, and Carlisle would descend into complete disharmony.[34]

Ten years after Nesbit's address, commencement audiences at Bowdoin College in Brunswick, Maine, heard a similar warning. Bowdoin's president, Joseph McKeen, reminded his audience that their little college on the eastern frontier had been founded to foster the public, not private, interest. He recalled the college's original purpose: "It ought always to be remembered that literary institutions are founded and endowed for the common good, and not for the private advantage of those who resort to them for education." As with many faculty families, this address, with its preoccupation with the ongoing problem of "private advantage," was as much a warning to McKeen himself as to the graduates, parents, and townspeople he was addressing.[35]

Had the desire for "private advantage" motivated Joseph McKeen to accept Bowdoin's presidency? When the college's trustees had offered him the job, his nephew had urged him to take it, reminding him that in contrast to a ministerial post, Bowdoin would provide him with the "power to educate your sons much cheaper, than where you now live" (the sons of faculty often attended their colleges for free). There was also the possibility that McKeen could "have a sallery double what your present living is" and that life in Brunswick, therefore, would be more "pleasant" than his present situation as a New Hampshire minister. How could McKeen be sure he was not acting merely for himself out of personal ambition? Linking his fortunes to those of Bowdoin College was the ideal answer to this question for all faculty families. Like the Baxters, the McKeens constantly asserted that their family was part of a much larger college family. Any benefits or opportunities they received as members of the college family were used to strengthen Bowdoin College interests. Whoever was "aided by a public institution to acquire an education," McKeen reminded his audience, was "under peculiar obligations to exert his talents for the public good." Graduates needed to constantly look out for ways to increase the advantage of the public good. If not, they could abandon all hope of exhibiting true virtue.[36]

All of the McKeens viewed their private interests as a college affair, their identity as a Bowdoin College family helping to assuage their fear of exerting self-interest or personal ambition. After their father's early death, the McKeens continued to live in Brunswick near the college. The president's daughter Alice became a social leader in town, her letters to friends living outside of Brunswick full of college news—and solicitations for college needs. Since the McKeen sons attended Bowdoin for free, they were, according to family dictates, duty bound to work for the good of the college their whole lives. They chose occupations outside the field of education but remained strong "friends" to Bowdoin, socializing with faculty families, serving as trustees, sending their sons to Bowdoin, and acting as official "agents" for the college. When a building on campus burned down, one McKeen son headed to the wealthy parlors of Portland to solicit donations for a new structure, using his commercial ties made as a merchant. Another son relied on his medical contacts as a pharmacist to help attach a medical school to the college. Members of faculty families like the McKeens and the Baxters always championed the self-sacrificial form of virtue promoted in their world, defending it at every opportunity. This defense of virtue became a family *and* a public duty. College biographers noted that it was the "conservative care of the McKeens" that had helped the college expand its borders in the early years and that helped protect its property rights—and stretches of lucrative pine forests—in later years.[37]

To the public, the actions and words of college families were important indicators of their institution's "character." In 1804, the editor of a New York paper published extended extracts of the inaugural speech of Eliphalet Nott, the new president of Union College, so that "the public may be better enabled to judge of the present situation of the Institution and of the system of Instruction and government." As the leader of a new institution that promoted itself as a representative of varied religious and social interests, Nott's character became a matter of public inquiry and scrutiny. No member of a college family could afford to appear ambitious or partisan. Individually and as a group, families wished to exhibit a virtue that transcended private interest. This disinterested strategy would win them more friends. College families (and their fledgling institutions) could not afford to limit their friends.[38]

When it came to early American politics, for example, college families quickly learned to embrace a neutral stance. The new colleges soon provided a contrast to the nation's original colleges, founded in the colonial era and deeply enmeshed in early factionalism. These more-established colleges tended toward supporting Federalism. When "Harvard presented her children to the world" in 1796, the commencement audience heard a distinct political and educational message: "Federalism and Science walked hand in hand and never was a union more lovely or more interesting." Many in the newer college families were hesitant about revealing their own views in such an open, public way, even if many also tended toward Federalism and, in a later era, Whiggism. They were quick to criticize educators, college presidents especially, who advocated for specific parties, playing political games instead of calling for more-virtuous play. An angry editorialist in 1816 revealed how playing politician in the college world could lead to a public relations disaster. The critic was irritated by "College Doctors" who taught students "to admire their systems not only of Moral and Logic, but of Politics too." Especially in the developing regions of the republic, the friends of the new colleges might quickly become enemies if they believed that the "heads of our Colleges" were "almost without exception, Tories." This was a "lamentable" fact for a new republic, according to the editorialist. Becoming enmeshed in politics was a problem that the new college world worked hard to avoid.[39]

When his uncle was elected to the presidency of Bowdoin College in 1802, Levi McKeen sent him a letter from western New York recalling the recent "imprudent, violent, and unjust part" that the presidents of Princeton and Yale had taken in "our Political struggles" over Federalist and Republican tensions. Their openly Federalist position threatened newer institutions like Bowdoin, or his own local enterprise, Union College. According to this young settler, the Federalist leaders of Princeton and Yale had "laid the foundation of a jealously which may prove very detrimental to Learning and Learned men." When republicans inevitably controlled state legislatures, as he believed they would, they would initiate a vengeful "purge" of "seminaries" with an "undiscriminating hand." He hoped his uncle would protect his new job and his new institution by remaining neutral. His uncle's character—his personal ideals of "Charity and moderation"—would go far in keeping Bowdoin neutral amidst the "turbulent scenes" of the political world. While the established colleges, surrounded by cosmopolitan controversies, took partisan stands, new colleges on the frontiers of the republic had to learn how to work with everyone. As Levi advised his uncle from the New York frontier, the families running Bowdoin College must learn how to win the "applause of all parties" or they and their new enterprise would not survive.[40]

This need for neutrality was based on the ideals of college families, but it also reflected the real-life necessity of building successful institutions along the frontiers of the republic. Many college friends hoped the new colleges they supported would remain above the political fray, offering a rare neutral space in a fractious republic. There needed to be someplace that was protected from angry words and social strife. Maybe this new college world would provide that space.

As advocates for self-sacrificial virtue, it was bad for business to appear politically ambitious. Although they were determined to survive in an increasingly competitive educational landscape, college families were also hesitant to appear commercially ambitious. George Baxter was highly attuned to avoiding the appearances of ambition whenever possible— whether for himself or for Washington College. When he learned that the construction of a nearby academy had been halted due to insufficient funds, Baxter was quick to make a move. Through his letters to Anne he directed one of his professors to contact the trustees of the failed institution and work out with Washington College trustees how to "divert the funds" to the college at Lexington. If this did not work, Baxter suggested that someone travel to the nearby village, make a speech about Lexington's needs, and collect subscriptions. This potential source of funding needed urgent attention. As president of Washington College, however, Baxter felt he "could not with propriety" act so openly against the fortunes of another educational institution. He was the public representative of Washington College and the advocate for virtue and knowledge. He could not act in such an overtly ambitious manner. He merely sent the information to Lexington in a letter, calling it a "prospect of doing something handsome" for the college.[41]

In his attempt to take the funds of one academy to build up his own college, George Baxter never referred to the cash involved. Faculty families steered clear of ever portraying their "business of instruction" in the same light as the business transacted on Wall Street. In his letters Baxter alluded to cash as a natural resource, like a stream of water to be diverted or a living object that he "set on foot" toward Lexington, as if the money naturally made its way to educational institutions like his without human intervention. In a short postscript to one of his letters, Baxter merely hinted about the failed academy. He knew his friends at Lexington would ensure that such a windfall would benefit their collective enterprise.

As men who patronized education but cultivated other interests as well, trustees were free to act with less "propriety." Pledged to further the success of their institutions, it was ultimately the trustees who handled the money transactions in these early college communities. Trustees oversaw the land transactions that provided the initial endowments, and a trustee often acted as treasurer, collecting tuition from students and doling out cash as "sallary" to professors. Faculty families certainly handled cash in their own households. Some acted as treasurers on campus, handing out pocket money per parental request to their students. Yet, faculty often did this with distaste or annoyance. They preferred to leave to the trustees the trial of handling what more than one professor called "filthy lucre." Along his route, George Baxter pointedly collected what he called "subscriptions," promises of money to be paid sometime in the future. He did not return to Lexington with a bag full of cash, but a list of potential donors or "friends." His trustees would, he hoped, collect on all those promises of virtue.

Baxter's veiled hint about a nearby opportunity for Washington College ensured that a collective of educational patrons like his trustees, not an individual, would be the catalyst that closed an educational institution. In the name of virtue the trustees would deposit funds in Washington College's treasury, and Baxter and his faculty would, on the strength of this new source of funding, improve the college with more buildings or more faculty. While Greek, Latin, and higher mathematics would always remain at the core of the early colleges' curriculum, new subjects like chemistry or physics, or French or Italian, would appear, a result of student interest or, more commonly, the curiosity and interest of the faculty. New courses incurred new costs, whether it was for the "scientific apparatus" that helped demonstrate the wonders of chemistry or physics to students, or for an entire laboratory building in which to impart these new lessons on the natural world, or for the extra salary for a "modern language" instructor. There was always the possibility, too, that the failure of a neighboring educational institution would prompt its students to consider Lexington as the place to finish their higher education. But any influx of new students would demand more dormitories and the need for more classes. For faculty, success secured their future, but it also brought with it a whole new set of problems.

In spite of his attempts to avoid looking competitive, Baxter was actually haunted by competition throughout his tour. The popularity of the new academies had become a widespread problem for those interested in promoting the new colleges. As Baxter observed on his trip, the academies were "every where on hand" and stretched people's "liberality" to their generous limits. Some families in Richmond refused to give him money because, they proudly informed him, they were already supporting an academy in their city. Petersburg's Presbyterians were more interested in financing "an Academy of their own" than in supporting Washington College in Lexington. According to Baxter, this mania for academies was a wasteful form of competition. After seeing a few failed academies on his travels, and helping himself to the funds of at least one, he noted that "none of them will come to any thing." None of them could claim George Washington as a patron. More importantly, he could argue, none could award their students with a degree. He could not understand why so many people championed these new institutions when his own enterprise at Lexington offered so much more. After a series of unsuccessful and "very tedious" meetings with merchants, Baxter announced to Anne that "the present seems to be an unfavorable time for my business." No one seemed impressed enough with his advocacy of virtue to choose to support his college over their local academies.[42]

Baxter felt that the environment in the port cities especially, actually restrained his work. In contrast to Lexington, the families of Norfolk were "entrenched in such a multitude of forms" that he was unable to call on them "with propriety" unless during "certain hours and those too the hours of business." Forced to plead the case for his college in shipping offices, counting houses, and other commercial locations, Baxter was unable to attract any interest through his favorite channels of Revolutionary or Christian appeals to virtue.[43]

Solicited on commercial territory, mercantile Virginians viewed Baxter's appeal as an invitation to invest, not as a Revolutionary call to charitable duty. Many turned him down flat, arguing that a struggling little college deep in the mountains was not a good investment for the future. Some may also have been skeptical of supporting a self-proclaimed "public" institution that was, due to its early history as a religious academy, dominated by Presbyterians. Restricted to commercial spaces and hours, Baxter soon viewed his efforts at cultivating virtue in Norfolk as fruitless. He received fewer promises of money there than in Richmond, and he resolved never to return.

As he moved along the coast, Baxter's letters grew increasingly full of complaints about greedy, acquisitive, selfish planters and merchants and their misunderstanding about virtue. "Liberality" seemed to be fading fast everywhere, and Baxter's complaints reveal where he thought virtue actually existed in 1805. It was definitely not in the counting rooms of merchants. It was not even in their parlors, where city ladies, traditionally receptive to charitable requests, were now more interested in fashion and rich living. Meeting a variety of Virginians along the road, he found that those from the counties "just below the Blue Ridge" and "more in our vicinity" were "more disposed" toward helping the college. Living in the mountains, away from the distractions of the cities and close to such a true repository of virtue, Baxter believed, these Virginians were more receptive to his call to virtue and possessed a sympathy characteristic of family ties. They were true friends.[44]

Upon his return, Baxter had much to ponder as he took up teaching classes once again and prepared for the annual commencement season in August. The Baxters questioned the value of his taking another trip in the fall, but many in Lexington suggested that his appearance in the nation's capital at the opening of the new congressional session might be advantageous—the college was, after all, named after President Washington. Baxter agreed.

Baxter's trip that fall did not begin well. He started out by describing his experience as annoying and "uniform." At Staunton, he reported to Anne, he would "shew my papers," describe his college's needs, and ask for a donation. People "sometimes decide to give liberally," and then "sometimes penuriously," and then "sometimes not at all." Solicitations for funding sparked such an unpredictable array of responses that Baxter doubted the trip would bring any chance at success. Trying to make new friends was not as easy or natural as he expected, especially when he was confronted with resentment or outright lies about the poor state of their personal fortunes from the people he was soliciting. He found it "strange" to hear what he considered "independent and rich men talk of their poverty," and he considered all of their excuses a waste of his time. Their litanies of financial woes were, in his opinion, done "all for an off put" of his request.[45]

One complaint that especially annoyed him was a donor's excuse that he could not give much to the college because he had to support his family. According to Baxter, who visited the prospective donor's wealthy home, the man was as "rich as a jew, but feels himself poor because he cannot get richer as fast as he desires." The man donated twenty dollars, but Baxter assumed he could give more. Baxter had no sympathy with the man's worry that he had to provide for the future of "so many poor Grandchildren." Baxter sent a sermon home in his letters to Lexington, in which he congratulated his parishioners for their support of the college in spite of the hard times. Rich people had a harder time being so virtuous. While the afterlife would be hard for them to achieve, the present life was also hard: "How unavailing is riches, for it does not lesson our anxieties about the world." He believed that such rich men also lied to preserve their fortunes. At Winchester, Baxter heard from planters that crops had been bad and business was "extremely dull." They also informed him that money was "(they say) most uncommonly scarce." Baxter did not believe them. How could there be no money left to support virtue?[46]

Baxter's gloomy, critical outlook on the world perked up a bit when he entered the paved, well-lit streets of Baltimore. He reported to Lexington that the city lights produced a "fine effect to a stranger" but "the noise and bustle is inconceivable." Like Norfolk, the city environment was not conducive to his need to hold persuasive conversations about virtue. The "rattling of carriage, wagons, drays, the hurry of passengers, the prancing of horses &c &c make it difficult to hear one another speak." The commercial noise of Baltimore, like the social forms of Norfolk, drowned out the important conversation that inhabitants needed to hear about virtue. After missing a meeting with a trustee who would have introduced him to potential friends, Baxter truly felt himself alone in a world of strangers. Hoping to be "busily employed in attempting to raise subscriptions," he soon pronounced his Baltimore efforts "futile."[47]

Baltimore once again brought up the problem of competition among educational institutions. Baxter heard constantly from people who "profess to be friendly, and tell me that my want of success is entirely owing to the many previous application which have been made in this place." Again, he tended not to believe that there was not enough money to support all of the academies and colleges in the region. Ultimately, he collected only three hundred dollars in Baltimore and was "not pleased" with the families he had met. They were "kind in their way but they flatter too much." There was much vocal support for Washington College but few real financial offers of assistance. At Baltimore, he informed the families at home, there were "so many Irish, so much *blarney*, I could not relish it." According to Baxter, Baltimore may have been paved, well lit, and even more modern than Lexington, but its society was found wanting when compared to the generous circle of friends flourishing in their "liberality" around the college at Lexington.[48]

Upon his arrival in Washington, Baxter was frustrated to discover that he had missed another meeting with a trustee, and he found himself again "entirely among strangers." He was not hopeful—and he was no fool. Without letters of introduction or a connection with "any other person to influence characters here," Baxter now knew that he and his cause would be treated with indifference in the political world. He did make one friend, a "very obliging" gentleman living in Georgetown, who helped secure some time with one of the most notorious skeptics of Presbyterian influence in Virginia, President Thomas Jefferson himself. Baxter came away from the meeting with fifty dollars, given by a man that he would have categorized as an "infidel." Yet, the two men shared a belief in the importance of education—and educational institutions. A few decades later, the families at Lexington would watch suspiciously as Mr. Jefferson's new university, with its own secularized definition of virtue and a campus planned without a chapel, inserted even more educational competition into their world.[49]

After starting with the executive branch, Baxter turned his attention to the assembling Congress and began making enquiries on his own about potential donors. He soon learned that congressmen were "not very rich, not making much by their office." Competition again haunted his fundraising attempts. The congressmen were "tied to a great number of subscriptions" and, he was warned, will "perhaps not give much." His sources proved correct. Baxter came away from the capital with Jefferson's donation and the opinion that the new capital was "most unlike a City of any place

I ever saw." He had been invited to preach at Congress and was surprised to see a "great many people" in attendance, "expecting some one to preach, not knowing or perhaps caring who." The detachment, even indifference, among his listeners during the religious service shocked him. He informed Anne that there was nothing for Washington College in Washington City and he "would not stay long." The only evidence of virtue he found in the capital was a letter from Lexington at the post office, full of college news and inquiries about his health. He was fine, and he was glad to hear that the family and the college were "all well."[50]

Contemplating his return to Lexington, Baxter decided that for all his feelings of personal failure at raising cash and subscriptions, he had "gotten something and seen a little of the world." What Baxter had "gotten" was confirmation that there was a growing difference of opinion between those organizing a college world for the nation and those organizing the nation for themselves. Such "begging trips" to political and economic centers would always occupy the time and efforts of trustees, college presidents, and their faculty. They would never give up on their vision of popular support for their institutional network. Presidents and their professors especially would view such visits away from the college as sojourns into a different, distracted world in need of their friendly reminders about the Revolutionary commitment to true virtue.[51]

In Baltimore Baxter had received news from Anne that the families in Lexington wanted him to continue these fundraising trips to cultivate virtue. He objected to this plan. "You say," George responded to Anne, "the people talk of my taking another trip next Spring, but I am determined to make this the last." In spite of his hesitance, however, Baxter would travel again for Washington College, as would many college presidents and faculty. Trips out of their college world for fundraising purposes, however, would become only one strategy in a wide repertoire of economic, social, and intellectual practices that college families would perfect. They would become experts at coaxing outsiders to enter into their virtuous network of generous "friends."[52]

As the historian of education Laurence Cremin observed, the practice of creating social identity in the early republic did not involve a "retreat from the world," but a search for a "new relationship with it." Relieved to turn his horse toward home, Baxter did not consider retreating from the world. All of his experiences from his "begging tour" would now be brought back to his colleagues and students at Lexington to be discussed and debated. College families used all of this "intelligence" to plan the best ways to forge new relationships with the world through their vision of educational enterprise.[53]

On his way to his new position as president of Transylvania University in Lexington, Kentucky, in 1818, the Reverend Horace Holley of Boston shared a coach with an engaging lady named Selina Nichols. Nichols was the principal of the Ann Smith Academy, the female academy at Lexington, Virginia, down the road from George Baxter's college. Nichols eagerly informed Holley of the impressive range of educational activities that flourished around Washington College. Hopeful of making Transylvania a similarly influential force in the West, Holley took notes as Nichols lectured. His travel journal is full of "intelligence" about the college that was, according to Nichols, "endowed by Washington & called after him." With sixty young men at the college, and thirty young women at the academy down the road, Lexington was a bustling educational hub for the Blue Ridge region. It was also a moral hub. Holley learned that all students attended morning and evening prayers at these institutions and underwent public exhibitions of their intellectual and moral knowledge. Nichols proudly added that the college was a "candidate for the university of the state" that year as well. Much to the chagrin of Lexington families, Thomas Jefferson's educational enterprise at Charlottesville would eventually take that prized position.

In contrast to his own alma mater of Yale, Holley saw Washington College as a modest affair. For a newer institution, however, it was still impressive, and Holley was particularly fascinated by George Baxter, the reigning president until his death in 1830. Although Holley's coach did stop in Lexington to change horses, the new president of Transylvania University did not have time to tour the college as he had wished. He did, however, meet a "collegian" who was just as eager to talk about the local educational activities as Selina Nichols had been. The student boasted about Baxter and of the vast influence of his college. "You know that all towns, little towns as well as others, all have each their great man, as great as any man in the Unites States," wrote Holley to his wife Mary a few days after his visit. Baxter, he believed, was Lexington's "great man." When Holley asked the college student about the "learning and talents" of the college's president, the young man answered "promptly" that Baxter was "remarkably distinguished in mathematics, languages, the belles letters and theology, and that his reputation reaches as far as that of any man in the United States."

Priding himself on his cosmopolitanism, Holley was "amused" at what he considered the young man's naive provincialism. Since Holley had never heard of Baxter, he assumed that "nobody out of Virginia is acquainted with him." He was impressed, however, by the student's love and respect for Baxter, and hoped such a "novice" would make the same statements about him someday.[54]

Baxter and his circle of families around Washington College learned quickly about the power of making friends. As Horace Holley quickly discovered as he moved through their town, their educational enterprise produced a set of "friends" who easily and eagerly promoted their educational activities to anyone they met. Such friendly interactions through "educational intelligence" would, they hoped, exert some moral and intellectual influence in the name of Washington College.

• • •

After 1800, a collection of trustee and faculty families working together built a network of new colleges along the frontiers of the republic. Their first goal in this new college world was to train an ideal class of leaders for the new nation, teaching them how to define virtue properly, exert its powers for the public good, and disseminate virtuous thought and actions through an educational network spanning the whole republic. Their second goal was to "edify" their fellow Americans who were increasingly obsessed with "puffing themselves up" and in need of reminders about the common good. How well this new class, dedicated to the "business of instruction," preserved their own definition of virtue while engaged with those from a less-than-virtuous world depended on their talents at finding and making enough friends with just the right amount of "liberality." It would take a lot of like-minded people working together to reclaim and refine the country in the name of true virtue.

Organizing the College World

"All Various Nature"

ON A WINTER'S DAY in 1808 Martha Cleaveland sat by the fire in her parlor near Bowdoin College and answered a letter from her brother John. Ensconced in her new home in the eastern territory of Maine, Martha was a determined collector of what her sister in Boston jokingly called "all the proceedings of the western World." Her correspondents ranged from families in port cities to country villages throughout New England, and her contacts were always glad to hear news about how her family—and the family business at Brunswick—was faring.[1]

Two years earlier, this merchant's daughter had taken a huge risk by accepting the marriage proposal of Parker Cleaveland, a Harvard graduate determined to build his fortune through the new "business of instruction." After his graduation in 1805, Parker had dutifully tried out each of the established paths open to a young college graduate. He read law. He studied medicine. He even engaged in literary aspirations, publishing some rather effusive poetry. Nothing seemed to hold his attention for long. A man of diverse interests and talents, Parker confused and worried his family with his desire to explore everything. They wanted him to pick a future path quickly. The only position that finally sustained his attention was teaching. To support himself, Parker had begun teaching classes in a number of academies in Massachusetts. He found that he liked to teach, that the students liked him, and that their parents noticed. This flair for instruction soon earned him an invitation to return to Harvard to work as a tutor. In this assistant teaching position Parker began to envision a future for himself as a college professor. He grew more confident in this decision once he met the encouraging Martha, a woman who was more open to the possibilities of the teaching profession than his own family.[2]

Parker Cleaveland. Passing through Maine in the 1830s, the artist Thomas Badger hoped to "put on canvas the face of many" promoting the new state and its first college. Displayed in the Boston Athenaeum in the 1830s, this image of Parker Cleaveland promoted his popular geology studies and his patron, Bowdoin College. The image was used again in the college's first institutional history in 1880, Cleaveland continuing to promote Bowdoin College long after his death.

Courtesy of George J. Mitchell Department of Special Collections and Archives, Bowdoin College Library, Brunswick, Me.

When the Bowdoin College trustees, in search of a mathematics professor for their new college in the Maine Territory, offered Parker the post, with a salary of $800 a year, he gladly accepted. It was then that he finally felt free to propose marriage to Martha, who accepted. As the young couple settled in Brunswick, built a house near campus, and began their own family (baby Moses appeared in 1807), the Cleavelands joined an emerging class of men and women who hoped that the new "business of instruction" would provide their family with economic success and emotional satisfaction. At the same time, this new class had to make their "business of instruction" and their colleges relevant (and profitable) in the expanding market society of the early republic. The whole project was risky, especially when success hinged on the willingness of parents to send their children to new, untried educational outposts on the frontiers of the republic.[3]

Martha's merchant family had never sent any of its young men to college. After her marriage to Parker, however, some relatives took a sudden interest in acquiring a classical education. She was pleased to answer a letter from her brother John, inquiring about his chances of admission to Bowdoin. In her response, Martha spoke as a loving sister. She was also just

The Cleaveland House, ca. 1900. The Cleavelands lived in their home as Bowdoin's rent-free tenants during Parker's lifetime. After a number of faculty owners, Bowdoin bought the house in 1991 as a presidential residence. It now serves as a reception space for the traditional college "sociable."

Courtesy of William D. Shipman Scrapbook, Cleaveland House Papers, George J. Mitchell Department of Special Collections and Archives, Bowdoin College Library, Brunswick, Me.

then learning how to speak as a professor's wife, practicing how to provide one of the new products of her new college world: educational advice and direction.

Having learned that John was studying Greek, Latin, and mathematics under the guidance of a minister, Martha consulted with her neighboring families at Bowdoin College about her brother's chosen tutor. She was pleased to report to John that the minister had "the reputation of being a pious and literary character," was a confirmed "friend" to Bowdoin, and would be a good influence on his chances of admission. Martha urged him to take full advantage of his teacher's influence. This was an important point because John could not just depend on his blood ties to Bowdoin for admission. He had to learn how to work hard at his studies—and direct his passion toward achieving this new future he had chosen. "You must love study if you are desirous to be distinguished in the world," Martha informed him, adding that "it is folly to conceive that knowledge can be acquired without application." This "folly" was a popular notion that college families like the Cleavelands worked hard to dispel. Acquiring higher knowledge was hard work. It was also hard work, they would point out, to prove oneself worthy of acquiring this knowledge. Martha would keep a close eye on her brother as he prepared for admission. She identified herself as "one who feels interested in all your pursuits," and demanded more letters detailing "how you progress in your studies." She was not, of course, the only one interested in John. Her husband Parker added his own scribbled postscript to his wife's letter, urging the young man to remember that "another person" would be reading his letters and would be "no less happy to hear from you." In his dual position as professor and brother-in-law, Parker wished John "no discouragement in your studies" and sent "love and good wishes."[4]

With a single letter of inquiry, John found himself on probation as a potential member of a new family. Admission would only take place on certain terms and after proof of hard work, because this family—the college family—was too new and unstable to rely on mere blood ties. In 1806, choosing to marry a professor or work for such an unstable enterprise as a new college was a pure gamble. Not only did faculty families like the Cleavelands have to establish their own economic stability in new college communities like Brunswick, but they also had to defend the cultural importance of their collective enterprise. John was loved and accepted by Parker and Martha as a brother. In order to gain the acceptance, support, and helpful "friendship" of the wider college world, however, John and his fellow applicants had to apply on its classical terms. Was he capable of handling all of the higher knowledge that Bowdoin College offered?[5]

By 1800, early American colleges were both celebrated as repositories of virtue and denounced as nests of vice. Many Americans were undecided on the actual benefits of a college education. The frequency of student riots, vandalism, and "infidelity" in the more-established college centers like Cambridge or New Haven prompted many to doubt the worth of founding any more such institutions in a nation increasingly concerned about maintaining order. For some skeptics, a whole new generation of colleges emerging in distant regions like Brunswick, Maine, or Lexington, Kentucky, or Athens, Georgia, promised only wilder examples of disorder.

Even some "friends of education" proved skeptical about the ultimate success of these new colleges. Hearing the news that his former Harvard roommate had accepted Bowdoin's presidency in 1807, Jonathan Ward, a minister, sent a letter of condolence rather than congratulation to Jesse Appleton. He feared his friend's new job would be "uncommonly difficult," and would require much "labor, anxiety, and regard" with very little compensation. The newspapers reported that Brunswick was a "place of lax morals" and that the students were "rude and ungovernable." He would have been "afraid" to have accepted the job. There was, he allowed, some real potential for his friend to establish himself in society. The "station" of college president could become "honorable," he mused, but only if Appleton could "establish and maintain your authority." This, he believed, was "rather difficult at any College." It seemed more profitable, even easier, to be a minister in 1807.[6]

After 1800, new waves of evangelicals called for social reform, targeting colleges especially as degenerate spaces in need of intense moral monitoring and Christian purification. For those like Noah Webster who worried about the unstable state of virtue in American society, colleges in the former colonial centers of Boston or Philadelphia offered "scenes of dissipation and amusement" that threatened to "corrupt the hearts of youth and divert their minds from literary pursuits." It would be "extremely dangerous," Webster warned, to allow male minds to spend their youth—a period "when the passions are strong, the judgment weak, and the heart susceptible and unsuspecting"—in such educational sites where, according to some reports, "there is not the least restraints upon their inclinations."[7]

Religious periodical writers repeatedly spun tales of college students dying young and unregenerate, corrupted by the "bad company" to be found in college dormitories in the turbulent 1790s. It seemed that a blend of atheism, laziness, and loose morals—all foreign imports, of course— was destroying the minds of American youth. Many periodicals echoed a republican critique that condemned long-established institutions like Harvard that were still promoting, according to its critics, the aristocratic manners and corruptions of the colonial era. According to one tale, a father who sacrificed everything to send his son to Harvard received the news that the college had taught his son to "surpass the most accomplished cox-comb" in fashion, "run a man thro' with as little remorse as Arnold," and "swear the whole college out of countenance." He was now a gentleman, the young man informed his father, and was not obliged to work—or repay his father: "Thus have the college lads made me a new creature." This new creature—the "college rake," or "college blood"—quickly took his place as a literary villain at the side of the libertine, the atheist, and the effeminate fop in literary works of the early national era. By 1800, it was a common suspicion that time (and money) spent at a college could just as easily ruin, rather than refine, a young man.[8]

To faculty families like the Cleavelands, such notions were bad for business. They countered these popular fears with the offer of a new college world with its ideals drawn from the collective Revolutionary legacy, the everyday realities of their developing regions, and their own professional aspirations. Using the same republican imagery as the college critics, faculty families reminded their fellow Americans that virtue did exist, that it could be transmitted to the next generation, and that it was to be found in their new, improved, and growing college world along the borders of the republic. It was not cosmopolitan Cambridge or New Haven that provided the ideal training ground for the nation's next generation of leaders, observed Noah Webster, but institutions in the "country," on the outskirts of the republic, "where there are no great objects of curiosity to interrupt the studies of youth or to call their attention from the orders of the society." In these developing regions, far from the former colonial power centers and expanding urban regions full of vice, instructors could more easily occupy the "time and attention" of students and ensure that "a proper bias may be given up to the tender mind" and that they be "trained up in the way they should in future walk." A blend of Whiggish "country party" positioning, the proverbial wisdom of Solomon, and pastoral romance became important rhetorical pillars in the new argument set forth by faculty families as they defended and promoted their new college world.[9]

The Cleavelands and their colleagues offered special benefits, even privileges, to those who took the risk and sent them their children to instruct. In exchange for their "friendship" to the college world, families received a distinct educational blend of virtuous protection, patronage, and promotion for their children. This trio of benefits—a package deal in virtue—became the most important attraction of the new colleges. Families like the Cleavelands promoted themselves as an ideal class dedicated to self-sacrificial service to the public, their only interest being the cultivation of a world in which youthful training in virtue could take place safely without distraction or vice. From their new communities they brashly offered a guarantee of success to their students, but only under certain virtuous terms.

In these new college communities students did indeed find a highly regulated, intimate, microscopic world designed to mold their minds and manners in ways that, they were promised, would bring about their improvement and ultimate success. Those at Union College were fond of calling their community a "little world." At Dickinson College, one student echoed this idea, proclaiming the town of Carlisle to be a "miniature of the whole country." At Williams College in western Massachusetts, one professor pronounced Williamstown a "society in miniature." Those living and working in the new college centers believed that the virtuous power inherent in their intense little worlds—the world of the "virgin" province, full of developmental potential and uncorrupted virtue—would one day regulate the troublesome, corrupting powers emerging in the more-populated urbanized regions. It was hoped that the students who emerged from this college world would then set about improving the world at large. A virtuous kind of "new creature" would then enter the worlds of commerce, politics, and society in waves, and they would work together to redirect the republic's path toward a more virtuous and regulated definition of success.[10]

Viewing themselves as examples of virtue on display, professors and their families imagined themselves as role models to the young people coming to their communities for higher knowledge. They believed their refined society offered the key to how to interact as leaders in a republic. Their chief pedagogical goal was to refine and redirect youthful passion and selfish ambition toward a more elevated, classical form of leadership. Thus, college families focused much of their energy on strategies of refinement, always searching for the best way to organize the younger generation into a tightly fused class of educated, socially elevated, interconnected youth who, like their instructors, would know exactly how to work together and run a republic. Families like the Cleavelands hoped that all of their hard work on this class-construction project would provide a secure and stable future for themselves and, most importantly, the solution to their country's greatest social problem: how to create a more perfect union. The answer was to create a perfect class to supervise it.[11]

Since they viewed themselves as role models, college families had to first establish that they could successfully refine and redirect their own passions. In the two years that she had lived at Bowdoin College with Parker, Martha Cleaveland had watched as her husband worked at focusing his diverse interests and passions toward the demands of the college world. Her husband's quest for virtuous success, as well as his definition of it, proved very different from the kind of success pursued by her merchant family.

Faculty families like the Cleavelands always viewed their personal successes and ambitions in tandem with the success of the institutions they ran. Any profit made by Parker or his family members would always be defined, somehow, as a gain for Bowdoin, not Parker. Faculty families constantly followed this strategy, trying to direct the corrupting influence of individual passion and personal ambition away from their individual selves and toward a more public, collective good. In their case, this larger good was often the trustee and faculty families that lived and worked together at their college—their "college family." To Martha, Parker exemplified the ideal man of virtue—one who strove successfully to direct his mind and manner toward collective rather than individual goals. His ability to analyze personal situations to collective advantage was a skill that Martha hoped her brother—and all students—would one day acquire. As Martha knew, Parker had not started life as a paragon of virtue; he had worked hard to achieve a state of self-sacrifice. As Martha would have explained, it was always more of a struggle for men to maintain this virtuous state. It went against their very nature.[12]

Parker was once like any other young man, full of selfish passion and individual ambition. When they were first married, her husband proved too ambitious about his future prospects. He speculated, buying land from the region's largest landlord, Bowdoin's board of trustees, and paying a local architect to build a stately house for his new family next to the campus. One year later, Martha arrived as a new bride to live in a home they could not afford. With their new professor now awash in debt, Bowdoin's trustees offered to purchase Parker's land and house and, in effect, make the Cleavelands their tenant as well as their employees. The young professor agreed to this new relationship, part of his salary now offered up as rent to Bowdoin College. He and his family also began repaying their debt through a series of "improving activities."[13]

The new couple forged another tie with Bowdoin College. Like many early faculty families, they began feeding Bowdoin's students for a fee. At many early colleges there were no communal dining facilities. It was common for students to eat and, due to a lack of dormitory space, sometimes to sleep at nearby homes owned by college faculty and local "friends." Like many faculty wives, Martha found herself responsible for the care and feeding of an assorted array of young men and boys each term. This new "family" expanded quickly to include the Cleavelands' actual children. After her eldest child, Moses, was born, Martha had six more children in quick succession, thereby becoming the manager of an ever large academic household.

Augusta McClintock, the wife of a Greek and Latin professor at Dickinson College, experienced the same situation; her husband bemoaned the fact that she had to be "lady, cook, and housemaid" all at the same time and had little time to talk to him. Writing to her sister-in-law, Augusta apologized for her late letter, explaining that she did not "have much spare time." She had recently had her first son, Emory, and currently cared for "8 in family" with only a "poor stick" of a servant girl, Maria, for help. After Maria contracted the measles, Augusta cared for the girl and took over the care, "week in and week out," of the infant Emory. She was cooking, sewing, cleaning, and focusing much of her direction on one boarding student whose "manners at table" had been "much neglected" by his parents. She reported that the other students were "doing well in their studies." In spite of all her work, Augusta thought there was "nothing but dirt and growling from morning till night" in her college home, the growling mostly from her husband who wished they could afford more servants to help her. Augusta felt her "life almost worried out of me." Writing her letter with "Emory in one hand and the pen in the other," Augusta announced she had "boys enough" in a home supposedly filled with young gentlemen. If one of her sisters-in-law came to help her, she hinted, everyone could have more time for the real work of the college world—"study and improvement." Until she could figure out how to manage her new academic household effectively, that part of her work had to be postponed.[14]

Like most faculty wives, Martha Cleaveland figured out how to manage such a household through trial and error and the assistance and advice of fellow faculty wives. She was proud that she and Parker had successfully navigated their way through the web of his passionate enthusiasm and embarrassing debt. Just a few years later, Parker urged his father in Massachusetts to visit and see the "wonders" his family performed at Brunswick, "living on love & a crust of bread." He informed his father that he had now acquired a useful passion for "economy" and that his family, now deeply enmeshed in the collective workings of Bowdoin College as faculty, tenants, and food-service providers, now prospered in a more regulated, collective manner.[15]

Parker also worked on redirecting his professional ambition toward more collective ends. From the very bedrock of Brunswick, he cultivated another passion, one that would establish his scholarly reputation as well as that of his college family. Digging a section of river bed in order to float logs from one of Brunswick's new sawmills, laborers discovered a cache of colored rocks. They brought them to Parker hoping he would confirm that they had found precious stones. The mathematics professor could tell them nothing and was embarrassed by his lack of knowledge in front of people who had sought him out as the local "man of science." Spurred by such a public failure, Parker sought out works on geology and mineralogy. He discovered there was a lack of English texts on the subjects and began translating French and German treatises that had been donated by the college's trustees. He became fascinated with the hidden materials to be found beneath the surface of the uncharted republic, realizing that there were lucrative links to be made between the new science of chemistry and the practice of mineralogy, and he was soon obsessed with studying all of the "elements" of chemistry.[16]

The wider world soon learned about Parker's passion, as well as the existence of Bowdoin College, when his *Elementary Treatise on Mineralogy and Geology* appeared in 1816. If studied by a "citizen and the scholar," he promised in his preface, chemistry and mineralogy would yield "individual wealth" and a stimulation to "arts and manufactures" that would "promote the public good." He had written the book for "the use of pupils, for persons attending lectures on these subjects, and as a companion for travelers in the United States of America." Parker not only intended the book for students; he hoped it would attract others who might join the network of educational friends. When writing their textbooks, professors at the time envisioned their readership in very broad terms; anyone with an interest in the subject might pick up the book and through such an anonymous connection an intimate friend to the college might be made. Thus, even the books written by faculty members promoted their strategy for success. As Parker made clear in his preface, he hoped that any "individual wealth" made in the pursuit of his new subject should be used to "promote the public good."[17]

The public responded enthusiastically to Parker's invitation to explore a new subject. Some citizens were truly interested in chemistry. Some citizens were interested in Parker's pioneering categorization theories about various rocks and minerals. Many more responded to his idea that there was "individual wealth" to be made by mining the land beneath their republican feet. In any case, the book made Parker a celebrity within the college world and outside of it, and Bowdoin College shared in this celebrity. During his vacations Parker discussed his discoveries in public lecture halls from Portland to Boston. Before a curious public, he gave lectures, displayed mineral samples, and performed chemical experiments.

The contents of the *Treatise*—its theories, practices, and knowledge—began to form "the general subject of conversation" in many other classrooms and parlors around the country. Harvard's chemistry professor expressed surprise at "how suddenly the taste for mineralogy has sprung up among us," with "every body" now "collecting a cabinet" of local minerals for their own parlors or "engaging in mines" in search of treasure. *Cleaveland's Mineralogy* became a standard text at many colleges and could be found on private family bookshelves, a national advertisement for Parker's pioneering scholarship and Bowdoin's patronage of it. Both his name and Bowdoin's were displayed prominently on the title page, an example of how individual and collective ambition could be made into one virtuous act.[18]

Parker established the college's reputation though his new passion for science. His lectures helped spread scientific knowledge to the public and also acquainted him with many new friends who shared his passion. The lectures also helped him hone his passion for economy, one of his constant concerns, as Martha regularly presented him with little Cleavelands throughout the 1810s. Informing his brother-in-law John that he had made "about $500" in ticket sales for one set of chemistry lectures, he wryly described the windfall as "much to the *credit* of the Ladies and Gentlemen of Hallowell—and quite to the satisfaction of the *Lecturer*." He was quite happy to give the people of Hallowell, Maine, full credit for their efforts at educating their individual minds while also supporting the Cleavelands.[19]

Parker's move to direct his professional ambitions toward the more collective goal of building up Bowdoin's reputation yielded impressive emotional and economic profits for both. The extra cash from lectures and book sales helped the family pay some of their debt to the trustees, and the trustees were now also indebted to the Cleavelands. After 1816, they added Parker's innovative scientific offerings to the college catalogue and Parker abandoned math to teach chemistry and geology. These new subjects became very popular among young men bored with their daily recitations of Greek, Latin, and mathematics, and more students appeared at Brunswick eager to share in this new scientific excitement. The trustees, like the scientifically minded Benjamin Vaughan, were also enthusiastic; Vaughan introduced Cleaveland to his own transatlantic collection of scientific friends. The trustees raised funds for the construction of a laboratory on campus, which Cleaveland happily designed and ran. They also presented him with a $200 bonus, which increased his salary to $1,000 a year.[20]

With Cleaveland now running the science courses, a space opened up for a new math professor. The Bowdoin trustees soon expanded their circle of faculty families by hiring William Smyth, a recent Bowdoin graduate, who arrived with a young family in tow. Smyth received a starting salary of $600 per year. He had a reputation for genius in both Greek and mathematics, and the trustees hoped he would follow in Parker's footsteps by producing influential work that would further enhance Bowdoin's reputation. Smyth did just that, publishing popular textbooks in the higher mathematics. He also (reputedly) introduced the use of the chalkboard to the college world, constructing his own. He also worked on establishing a graded elementary-school system at Brunswick, and then itinerated around Maine encouraging other towns to follow the Brunswick model of successful public education. A year after Smyth was hired, Parker urged the trustees to raise his new colleague's salary, and after much negotiation Bowdoin's new mathematics professor eventually earned as much as Cleaveland: $1,000 a year.[21]

Bowdoin College was becoming known as an institution that produced success. By the 1820s, it was hard to differentiate between the individual success of its teaching staff and the success of the college. However it was perceived, one thing was certain. This brand of collective success had made family life for the Cleavelands, Smyths, and their colleagues more regulated, predictable, and profitable.

To Martha and her family the achievement of economic prosperity and intellectual authority began when her husband determined to control himself, focusing his diverse individual passions on cultivating collective principles based on economy and chemistry. This process was how faculty families like the Cleavelands defined the route to success. This carefully plotted, highly focused route was proof to many in the outside world that faculty families in the new college world were truly ideal models for young people to emulate.

As relations between Martha, Parker, and John reveal, the "college family" often began as a real family related by blood. Yet the builders of the college world began expanding this traditional notion of family, creating a new class that spoke in the language of familial affection but also behaved in a more professional manner that depended on merit.

As the hiring of William Smyth at Bowdoin reveals, college families were fond of hiring from within, practicing a form of educational patronage. Yet they also championed the ideals of merit and hard work. Smyth was one of Bowdoin's "own sons," but he had started out as a poor student, the son of a blacksmith, who had worked hard at his studies. Hired for his talents in Greek and math, Smyth was an ideal Bowdoin College success story, a boy from the artisan class who had been transformed by the classics into an educational leader. Just as Cleaveland's success symbolized the transformative power of scientific knowledge, Smyth's success confirmed that classical knowledge had this same power of transformation.

The experience of another graduate of the college world revealed the effectiveness of this familial yet professional form of patronage. After graduating from Washington College in Lexington, Virginia, this young man moved to Richmond where he tried to navigate the overwhelming world of opportunity he found there. College trustees and alumni of Washington College helpfully shepherded him through training in the law. Their well-connected families invited him into their parlors. With such professional and social support, the young man was able to begin a successful law practice of his own and achieve a leading position in Richmond society. He once joked to a friend back in Lexington that "I always claim kin with everybody that comes from the mountains," but he and many graduates like him studiously practiced this strategy of kinship, and always helped perpetuate it. The young lawyer eagerly helped anyone affiliated with Washington College, from finding jobs for recent graduates, to hosting faculty families as they traveled through Richmond, to speaking at commencement. He became an accomplished lawyer and statesmen who the college family around Washington College was only too happy to offer up as yet another example of virtuous success produced by kinship with the college world.[22]

Learning how to "claim kin" in the college world was one of the most important and valuable skills a young person would ever possess. Blood ties could bring one far in a republic, faculty families thought, but one's honor and true abilities would always be suspect. Relying on the ties of a "college family," however, provided the more ideal way to rise (with a degree of merit in hand) amidst a very broad group of regulating and supporting "friends." For college families, this was the virtuous path toward success that their students needed to follow.

Many historians have ascribed the in loco parentis status to early faculty and their institutions, especially since many new colleges admitted boys as young as ten or twelve. Professors always refused this title of surrogate parent and constantly complained about the extreme youth of the students who tried to gain admission to their institutions. With their growing networks of contacts, and the collective knowledge they brought, professors considered themselves patrons to young people, not parents or nurses. They always maintained the position that students needed to master the basic moral and intellectual knowledge offered by their families, primary schools, and academies before attempting to enter the college world. Academies, for example, were always idealized by professors as institutions where young men should master the basics of classical grammar and arithmetic before seeking admission to college. Intent on highlighting their profession and their institutions as different from the many educational projects emerging in this early era, professors argued that their institutions initiated students into a world of higher moral and intellectual knowledge that, they believed, would help the next generation of leaders secure the republic and help it prosper. Professors therefore did not want to waste precious time going over the basics. There was too much higher knowledge to impart.

As Transylvania's president, Horace Holley, clarified to his wife, they were not students' parents or servants, but public servants—"aids to others in the nation's 'career of improvement.'" At their community in Lexington, Kentucky, they and their fellow academic families would "give form and symmetry to as good materials as can be found in the world." Professors and their families would provide students with the advice, the role models, the correctly stimulating environment, and the connections. If students had not fully mastered the basics, they would have problems understanding how to use all of this new knowledge. If a student did not learn how to take advantage of this collective offer of patronage, protection, and promotion to "claim kin" with the college world, then he would fail himself and his country. He would be, according to the college world, blinded by ignorance and left on his own.[23]

Parents always disagreed with professors on this point about student preparation. Their letters to college officials reveal the reasons why they expected faculty to be surrogate parents. They were absolutely panicked about sending their children into a world of strangers without someone they could trust to be truly interested in their children's welfare. Because there was no other common supervisory position than parent, parents insisted on this role for their children's professors. "We are perfect Strangers," a woman informed President Eliphalet Nott of Union College in Schenectady, but "what I have heard of your character I feel intire confidence that my dear boy will meet with kindness and affection from you. . . . I do not feel at all uneasy." An "extremely anxious" father had heard that Franklin College in Athens, Georgia, had reopened under the supervision of a new presidential family. Relying on the "character" of one of its professors, he informed the man that "should your account of Athens be any way flattering," he would send his eleven-year-old son to Athens, and requested the man's personal supervision of the boy. Another "anxiously enquiring" parent in search of "the most eligible situation" for her twelve-year-old daughter wrote to the preceptress of the classical Ann Smith Academy, founded alongside Washington College in Lexington, Virginia. She demanded that the girl be placed "entirely under your care in every respect, not only for instruction in the various branches of polite female education, but to board her also with yourself." It was evident that parents expected college families to take on the parental role whether they wanted it or not.[24]

College families countered parental fears with their unique definition of family, offering themselves as merely one of many friendly advisors that students would encounter in their college world. They spoke in the language of affection and sentiment, but acted along their notions of professional patronage and extended kin relations. To parents they always insisted that in their college world their children would no longer be children, but ladies and gentlemen in training who needed to learn how to interact with a broader set of carefully chosen acquaintances and to exercise their free status in the republic. College professors and their families felt as responsible for monitoring and judging these social interactions and exercises in local parlors, streets, and dormitories, as they were for hearing Greek recitations in their classrooms.

Historians have always emphasized the conflict between male professors and their fractious male charges, portraying the relationship between students and teachers as one of constant intergenerational conflict—of opposing definitions of manhood or ideals of power. The personal letters between students and professors also reveal many moments of cooperation and support. Writing a note of thanks to a favorite professor, one Williams College graduate noted how important the professor's friendship had been in his transformation from awkward, passionate boy to socially adept, self-controlled man: "Many things I said and did then [were] not the results of my judgment but the effect of certain uncontrollable circumstances." Fellow students and townspeople had made him "the object of ridicule and contempt rather than of kindness and sympathy." The professor, however, acted "towards me the part of a friend." The alumnus informed him that his "friendly offices," even if the professor considered them "trifling," were "more than sensibly felt and shall ever be remembered with gratitude and affection." Professors did make an impression on some students. It was part of their job, they would argue, to transform students from awkward outsiders to knowing insiders.[25]

Professors played favorites, however, and students commonly complained about it. Student slang at the time had numerous words for professorial pets. The term "bootlick," for example, described a student who "sits in the first bench" or lingers after class to "have a little chat with the Prof." Whether looking for a better grade or currying favor for some other reason, these students were the ones learning how to "claim kin." Winning favor with professors (and their families) was a smart strategy for young men whose own families did not have influential contacts. Professors had personal access to an extensive network of "friends" who could provide countless opportunities for their young protégés in search of entry-level professional positions in the teaching, ministerial, or book trades.[26]

Whether they had been "pets" or not, alumni returned to the college world in great numbers to attend the annual commencement. Diaries and letters contain endless evidence of alumni eagerly visiting the campus or stopping by faculty homes, alone or with their own families. Professors were always interested in noting what former students were doing (and thinking) out in the world. Besides their own personal curiosity, they were always attuned to discovering any future benefits this growing network of graduates could contribute to the college family. Of course, the sons of alumni were always encouraged to apply to the college for admission.

Long after they handed out degrees, faculty monitored their students. Sidney George Fisher, a Dickinson College graduate, experienced this postgraduate scrutiny firsthand, surprised at finding continued affection and direction from a former instructor. A wealthy Philadelphian, Fisher had no economic need to curry favor from Dickinson families. He was quite certain of his elevated place in society and rejected much of his education at Carlisle as useless and tedious. Yet, when he bumped into the college president in a Philadelphia bookstore one day, he was surprised that William Neill recognized him. He was shocked even more when Neill recalled his talent at writing poetry and asked if he had continued his writing. Fisher presented Neill with his recent book of poems and was pleased to later receive a "very friendly letter" from him praising his poetry but also "expressing great anxiety lest I had strayed from the right path in religious belief." Apparently, Fisher's poetry did not reflect the virtuous thinking that the Presbyterian Neill expected from his students. Fisher disagreed but "answered his letter as kindly & politely as I could," amused (and also a bit impressed) that his old instructor remembered him and wanted to engage in his ongoing literary work. Once indifferent to his time at Dickinson, Fisher grew nostalgic in his diary, recalling how Neill had "been very kind to me" when a student. Later, Fisher attended a commencement ceremony and addressed one of the student debating societies, taking an interest in "Old Dickinson" again after hearing that mostly Methodist families were now running it. Meeting and enjoying the company of this circle of families at the president's house one evening, Fisher became a "friend" to the college again. Neill and the Methodist families had done their job well. They all knew there would only be future benefits for Dickinson College if one of its wealthy Philadelphian graduates decided it was high time to "claim kin."[27]

In order to prepare himself for admission to Bowdoin, Martha Cleaveland's brother John spent much of his time memorizing mathematical theories and lines from classical texts. To faculty families he (and hundreds of other young men like him) had to prepare himself fully to inherit a traditionally masculinized power—a set of traditional ideas that would strengthen him as he took on the mantle of freedom. A liberal education was defined in this era as the "instruction, or training up of freemen," and faculty families appointed themselves leaders in ascertaining the eligibility of male minds for taking on this free status and using it for virtuous ends. The prime educational challenge for faculty families was how to redirect the passions of young men in the same way they tried to redirect their own.[28]

In a note on one of Martha's letters to John, Parker carefully outlined the admission requirements of Bowdoin to his brother-in-law, pointedly noting that, in Latin especially, he had better be prepared for harsh scrutiny about his classical knowledge: "Our examinations are more lengthy and more minute than at Cambridge." Beyond translating various sections of Virgil and biblical passages from Latin and Greek, as well as demonstrating his familiarity with the "common rules of arithmetic," John also needed to produce a letter from his tutor confirming his "good character for regularity of deportment." For college families this behavioral "regularity" was as essential as the mental mastering of the classical curriculum. In fact, it was the same thing: proof of a young man's eligibility to carry an important element of virtue—a free mind. An effective leader of the republic would have to expose himself to all kinds of knowledge, pure and impure, yet also have the power to remain free from corrupting ideas or the "slavish commands of others." When John appeared before the trustees and professors of Bowdoin College to apply for admission, he would have to prove that he had the potential to exercise the broad, wide-ranging, discriminating freedom of thought that only a gentleman of true virtue could possess.[29]

Since John's tutor was a "pious" Congregationalist minister, the clergyman's letter of recommendation would carry much weight. For college families, reformed Protestantism was an equal partner with the classics in their work at molding minds and manners at early American colleges. Their teachings assumed a "synthesis of faith and fact—the synthesis of traditional Christian values and Enlightenment premises" that would strengthen young minds and hearts. While pagan writers had begun the search for the good life in their philosophical writings and should be read, professors allowed, it was a different text that would outline the correct route to truth. As Parker's colleague Samuel Newman, a professor of rhetoric, explained to a student, the Bible revealed "the course which it is the duty of every rational being to pursue." By "what it unfolds & places before the view," a Protestant brand of Christianity provided the best "system designed . . . to affect & form the character of men."[30]

For college families, harnessing both classical and Christian traditions into one educational system was a guarantee that either one or the other (and ideally both) would inculcate virtue in the new generation destined to lead the republic. The young men sent to these new communities for training symbolized a great deal of potential power of mind that if not harnessed and directed into a well-established system could easily bring about disorder and chaos. Obsessed with regulation and systems, the supreme concern of those trying to guarantee virtuous success for their college world was establishing a mechanism for control.

Eschewing the corporal punishment meted out by parents and academy teachers, faculty championed a new technique for maintaining order among their students that borrowed heavily from John Locke's political and educational ideas. As institutions founded by charters from "the people" in state legislatures, these new colleges extolled the principles of the social contract and mutual consent as the basis of their educational and social order. Professors rarely referred to their students as children or boys. They addressed them collectively as "gentlemen," whether they were listening to them recite the classics in class, socializing with them, or trying to quell their rioting. Assumed to be consensual members of a contracted "society in miniature," such "gentlemen" had to learn how to think and act under the terms of their admission. They were not free men yet. They were freemen-in-training, supervised by patrons and guides who would help them learn how to carry out the full terms of their contract as free men in a republic.

For early Americans the idea of the contract defined more than a political or commercial connection. It was also a social connection. For the many Congregationalists and Presbyterians who founded and ran these early colleges, the contract-like covenant provided a rational and righteous way to explain God's relationship with humans. College families relied on the ideal of mutual consent in the daily workings of their educational institutions, a contract between students and teachers as the basis of their ideal society.[31]

"On entering college," lectured Bowdoin's president, Jesse Appleton, to his students, "a student does, in fact, form a contract with the governors of the institution." He and his faculty promised "to instruct and guard" each student. The student, "on his part stipulates obedience to the laws, docility, application, and correct habits." Appleton portrayed students as gentlemen-in-training who were learning how to rule themselves rather than live under a set of laws. Ideally, all "laws, whether of a college or of a civil community," should be "few in number, easily understood, reasonable in themselves, and punctually executed." If not, "the authority of the whole becomes enfeebled." When fair laws existed and consequences for "every transgression and disobedience" were swiftly carried out, "there is no cause of complaint: nothing takes place, but what, at the time of entering into an agreement, it was understood should take place." With this "view of the subject," the college president pointed out the "high value of good government" as well as its "object"—to "promote the literary and moral character of those who acknowledge it."[32]

Following the principles of good government and consistently living according to the rules of civil behavior would actually make all laws unnecessary. At some point, college families hoped, students would learn how to regulate themselves without sets of rules. They would then enjoy a well-regulated life that would help them carry out the duties involved in being free.

Receiving a copy of Jesse Appleton's "suggestions reflecting Locke," one Harvard president suggested that it was "desirable to have a textbook for our colleges on the Science of Mind" that would point out to the world these important connections between the college world and ideal, virtuous society. Building and living in their "world in miniature," faculty families consciously set out to design a blueprint for the larger world—a template in which civil interaction among individuals was a firm foundation for a regulated, constantly improving Union.[33]

Faculty wives like Martha Cleaveland claimed an equal responsibility with their husbands in this collective social endeavor. For professors' wives and the many other women associated with college families, "Woman" and her special feminine powers had an intellectual and social role to play in the new college world. It would take more than a contract between men to create a perfect Union. The contract would also need the consent and cooperation of women. A whole new generation of young men and women needed to be trained to lead because they now had "an empire to raise and support." There was now a new "national character to establish and extend" via "wisdom and virtues." In order to extend a republican form of government over the whole continent, an elevated class would have to learn to work together.[34]

For Dickinson College trustee and women's educational advocate Benjamin Rush, the education of women "must concur with all our education for young men, or no laws will ever render them effectual." While he called for women to learn the "usual branches of female education," he also added the "the principles of liberty and government; and the obligations of patriotism" to their curriculum—similar to the subjects that he desired young men to study. Yet, because the "opinions and conduct" of men were "regulated" by women, and because women served as the primary instructors of young children, according to Rush, their "mode of education" had to be "separate and peculiar." The college world explored this odd educational proposition intensely, studying how the female mind could be trained in equality yet retain what they viewed as woman's essential difference.[35]

Pleased that her brother was preparing himself intellectually to enter Bowdoin, Martha was equally concerned with his social preparation. She demanded details about the environment in which he prepared for Bowdoin. It had to be full of improving opportunities that promoted success, not stagnation or distraction from focus. She peppered John with questions. Did he board with the minister's family or with strangers? With whom did he socialize? She wanted to know "in what manner your time & attention are at present employed" when not studying. She informed him of nearby relatives and college "friends" he should meet in the area. In Martha's estimation, her brother needed to devote as much "time & attention" to discovering his exact position in society, and to what extent others might help him improve that position, as he did translating Greek and Latin verse. He needed to learn how to become "advantageously situated" so that he, like Parker, could easily recognize any opportunity or possibility for advancement that came his way.[36]

Martha was intensely interested in one particular component of his environment. A "close applicant" like himself needed "occasionally & prudently to indulge in some recreation," and Martha informed him that she had heard from her colleagues that there was much "good society" circulating around his tutor's ministerial home in New Hampshire. Noting how *"emphatically"* John had spoken of the literary talents of some village girls, Martha enthusiastically approved of his "associating with ladies of refined taste & correct sentiment." These connections "will undoubtedly have great influence on your manners & you will in this way naturally acquire those sentiments which are requisite for a gentleman who wishes to be distinguished in polite society." Worried that her brother's impressionable mind might misinterpret her enthusiastic praise of "ladies," Martha Cleaveland clarified her thoughts: "Think not that I wish you to form a *particular* friendship or acquaintance with any lady." Any focused attention on one girl might distract both of them into a passion that would create irregular thoughts and actions. Any such passion could ruin his chances for the future, "giving a deadly blow to all literary eminence." If he wanted to socialize with ladies, he needed to remain polite, friendly, and maintain a certain platonic distance. This refined interaction between "ladies" and "gentlemen" was the cornerstone of the college world.[37]

In the new college world, male students divided their time between recitations halls, dormitories, college chapels, town streets and spaces, and the homes of college "friends." It was in these elevated homes especially that young men encountered women, young and old, whose society was meant to offset the long periods of unnatural isolation needed for "abstraction of study," as well as the overwhelming weight of the "rivalship of genius and those contraries of opinion, which too often impair, not to say poison the enjoyments of male society." As one University of Georgia alumnus fondly recalled as an old man, it was the women in college families, the *"femina Atheniensis,"* who "sustained the character" of society and students in Athens—and made it enjoyable. Such "intelligent females," one writer observed in 1803, were a natural resource for the republic that could be discovered and developed, like Cleaveland's minerals. They were "precious metals," he observed, rare and priceless in value but "seldom to be found." Martha Cleaveland believed that a critical mass of these "ornaments to society" could be found throughout the new college world.[38]

"College ladies" like Martha Cleaveland and her three daughters, Martha, Anne, and Elizabeth, were expected to possess a particular blend of natural and learned knowledge. They were expected to exert a natural intelligence that mixed easily with male thought and action. Such ladies were "agreeable tutoresses," endowed with "a peculiar aptitude to please" and a "wonderful facility in adapting themselves to the tempers of others," chiefly men. The female mind possessed a natural talent, it was assumed, for "insensibly, and yet effectively" imparting important lessons, "as people in general catch the sentiments and manners of those they esteem." The refined female minds of the college world exerted a "secret power over the conceptions of their scholars," imparting social lessons "without appearing to teach." Thus, being in the female presence and engaging in conversation with them was an education in itself. Alpheus Packard, Bowdoin's professor of rhetoric, believed that his wife's first duty in life was not to have children or even run a household. These were important duties, but Alpheus prized Frances Packard for much more—for her knowledge of how to "educate & develop the social affections." She worked hard at creating and maintaining society at Brunswick. The "sound and instructing conversation" of Frances Packard, Martha Cleaveland, and other college ladies echoed throughout the college world, their natural knowledge of "female" advice and guidance helping to shape the college "world in miniature."[39]

Along with this guiding natural knowledge, "college ladies" were expected to acquire and improve upon traditional learned knowledge. Many professors' daughters were encouraged to learn the same classical curriculum as their brothers. Wherever a population of young men followed a "classical course" of knowledge in these college communities, a population of select young "ladies" lived and learned close by at "sister" academies or seminaries. Visitors to Lexington, Kentucky, were impressed with the "fine female academy" that sat alongside Transylvania University. In this institution young ladies learned the same "ancient languages" as the young men, the instructor hoping "to improve the education of woman and place her in this respect, upon the equality of men."[40]

College professors often gave instruction at both the college and the female academy. At the Ann Smith Academy in Lexington, Virginia, one professor's daughter took classes in Latin, French, and science, taught by nearby Washington College professors "who were willing to extend their labors and add to their emoluments in this way." A professor's daughter at Dickinson College described similar training. At the Ladies Academy down the street from Dickinson College in Carlisle, Pennsylvania, she informed a friend, she studied English grammar, astronomy, drawing and painting, French, Italian, and music with a "lady preceptress," but the

Dickinson professors came to teach her classical languages, moral philosophy, and mathematics.[41]

Schooling college ladies in the same subjects as college gentlemen led to inevitable comparisons between the minds of "Woman" and "Man." According to college families, the female mind often proved superior to the male mind when it came to speed of comprehension and power of speech. John McClintock, professor of classical languages at Dickinson, was shocked to find that his academy ladies mastered their Greek lessons faster than his college gentlemen, and with much more enthusiasm. He worried privately in his diary about this peculiar sluggishness of male comprehension. At times, women's minds seemed better than men's. Wasn't it true, he mused in his diary, that his wife Augusta was the quicker wit at college parties than himself? He decided to inform his students about this evidence of feminine superiority as a "spur" to their eventual improvement. One wonders if it worked.[42]

"College ladies" often served as this "spur" to male improvement. A teaching corps of "agreeable tutoresses" emerged from these early college communities, trained to interact with and influence their male students. While college families expected young men to ponder a professional future, they expected young women to ponder the young men—and think of ways to redirect the unfocused, wild, and overly ambitious male mind toward more virtuous goals. This intellectual project, the direction of the male mind, was supposed to vindicate the higher education of "college ladies." As one Dickinson student pointed out to the ladies of Carlisle, setting a male mind on the "road to excellence" would "convince the world of your capacities—you would improve your own minds—and at the same time assist in rendering those of the male sex more accomplished."[43]

While they allowed that the female mind might be more brilliant than that of men, college families also believed that nature had created each sex for specific futures. While feminine thought served as a "spur" to the male mind, it could not be allowed to compete with male thought and action. This would disrupt the natural and divine plan. The mind of "Woman" should gently, even "insensibly," nudge the male mind toward true virtue and the "road to excellence." Thus, college ladies had to learn the skill of how to be complementary rather than competitive. In their social interactions with one another and with students, women practiced various "forms of politeness" that mitigated the seemingly inevitable social conflict and social tension that appeared in groups of ambitious young people whose minds were, according to their instructors, made to be equal and different in a natural and divine plan.[44]

The college families at Athens, Georgia, proved full of such "amiable tutoresses" dutifully carrying out their college work. One student recalled that he was "afraid of female society" when he arrived as a freshman at Franklin College. He had not grown up with sisters and "lacked that ease and freedom and self-poise of manner and ability to converse on ordinary topics, which are such a necessary part of a boy's education." When his friends suggested he accompany them on their regular visits to the president's house to visit his daughters, he at first refused. They were "beautiful and accomplished," he remembered, and, like all his fellow students, he knew them "very well by sight" because he "saw them nearly every day." Concerned, however, about his lack of social skills and his fear of "failing in conversation," the student "determined to begin with them." He found their tutelage immensely helpful. The young women were "quite skilled in drawing out young men," and after an hour filled with "kindness" the young man felt he had "crossed the Rubicon" and began to frequent even more faculty parlors to talk with the "ladies of the college town." Thanks to the college ladies of Athens, he had learned how to "claim kin." He was soon ready to graduate and take up his new socializing skills within the Athenian network of "friends."[45]

College ladies were deeply involved in the intellectual world of male students. They were the judges, evaluating students at college festivities, on the streets, or in the parlors. Attending a "quite crowded" performance of Transylvania student speeches in Lexington, Kentucky, Maria von Phul sent her estimation to a friend in Louisville. One student "had an elegant speech and delivered it very gracefully; yet there was an affectation and something too confident in his manner to be quite pleasing." Another student "spoke charmingly, and looked as well as he spoke." It was not only the speeches that Maria was judging, but manners and appearance. How persuasive, and thus influential, would these young men be in shaping the future nation? Could he appeal to both men and women? Did he overestimate his talents by choosing the wrong speech for his voice and manner? Did he seem too confident or ambitious? Three memorable performances, according to Maria, were not of the students' own writings, but speeches of well-known men whose ideals the students admired: "Nott's oration on the death of Hamilton" (the Union College president's anti-dueling warning to students about the dangers of misdirected passion), a "celebrated speech of Emet's, the Irish Patriot," and a piece written by a Transylvania trustee. All had been "spoken very handsomely," and some students possessed a "mind of more than ordinary ability." On the second day, Maria and her friends were so unimpressed that they "took the liberty to retire." While she feared their collective exit out of the hall was viewed as "rudeness" by some, it was "precidented." When young men were not worth their attention and appreciation, college ladies let them know they had failed. It was their public duty.[46]

The words, actions, opinions, and judgments of "college ladies" like Maria and her friends possessed strong authority and influence in the college world. They were the chief critics for college orations, busy fundraisers for college financial needs, and friendly student companions for botanizing and mineral collecting trips. They hosted social events, always selecting certain students who needed improvement. Frustrated with the hesitance of a shy student, one trustee's daughter informed her friend that when she returned to town she would make sure "he should take more part in the affairs of" the Lyceum "than he did that evening at your house." When one student loudly declared in their presence that he was "dissatisfied" with Bowdoin College, Parker Cleaveland's daughters Ann, Elizabeth, and Mary thought there was "room for improvement" in his attitude. They invited him to visit their parlor "almost every eve" for conversation. His attitude improved, and they soon proclaimed him a "constant beau." They favored another student because he came "politely" to their home to render services without being asked, ready to discuss, borrow, and share books. Any student who willingly involved them in intellectual conversations and debates became a quick favorite. A Cleaveland daughter approvingly noted the transformation of one painfully shy student as he made his way through the Brunswick parlors. In one year, she marveled to a friend, he had "grown quite tall," and she was impressed that he "can dance." Most importantly, she was pleased to report after a few visits with him that he could now "talk fast enough."[47]

Along with claiming kin, talking "fast enough" was another skill that the college world demanded from its young men and women. College ladies proved essential to this skill because, they assumed, when "Woman" participated in conversations, she introduced a certain "ease" among men, who could then engage in "agreeable & instructive conversations" without descent into heated, competitive arguments that might lead to blows or duels. The president of Union College, Eliphalet Nott, used the death of

Hamilton as a moral lesson to his students about the problems of passion and ambition among men, a lesson that circulated around the college world quickly—as it's appearance at the Transylvania event reveals. College officials were some of the first Americans to protest the practice of dueling.

In the college world, the way toward success involved practicing one's debate and conversation skills in the company of wise, controlled teachers: professors, of course, and also a group of ameliorating, calming, noncompetitive ladies. After commencement, which was, in effect, one final round of student speech-giving and debates, faculty families hoped that their graduates would leave their world well trained in the tenet that conflict and disagreement were better resolved through civil discourse than combat.

The problem of passion haunted the college world. Individual passion in the form of romantic attachment, sexual competition, or even personal enmity had to be monitored, deflected, and redirected during the many coeducational encounters between young people. Such displays of "self-love," or passionate pride, as college families called it, threatened their ideal of a broader, collective family and the harmony that it was supposed to establish. The college world relied on its "ladies" to help deflect these passions, and faculty families like the Cleavelands worked hard at promoting and exhibiting the many benefits and advantages to be gained from coeducational cooperation and the demand for sexual harmony.

There were both economic and emotional costs to promoting this vision. Anyone judged guilty of passionate "self-love" by the college world was threatened with exile from the college family, cut off from its system of support and patronage. As a professor's wife, it was Martha's duty to watch vigilantly for any young people who overstepped the college world's promotion of broad, platonic friendship and moved too far into that fatal realm of passion.

"Nothing but sad experience," Martha Cleaveland's sister once concluded, would ever teach young people to rein in their natural passions and live by the principle of "prudence." As her warning to John against focusing his affections on any particular New Hampshire girl shows, Martha demanded that male students learn how to exercise the principle of prudence. As she warned her brother, any "passion" would distract his young mind and "disturb its tranquility & incapacitate it for intense application." Martha thus directed him, even before arriving at Bowdoin College, to cultivate her broad definition of friendship, making friends only with those who "merit your approbation & esteem." Indulging in early passions limited the range of privileges and possibilities that a wider "acquaintance" might offer a young man later in life.[48]

As she trained her daughters and other "college ladies" to be "agreeable tutoresses," Martha was more strident in her demands for prudence. For John and his fellow students, a few wrong decisions could be corrected—and forgiven. As Martha well knew, her own husband Parker had had an early problem with a speculative passion and had plunged the family into debt. After a few mistakes, he was able to recover with stunning success. For "college ladies," one rash decision or passion could destroy any chance for a secure future in the college world.

One young woman circulating through Brunswick's parlors learned about the high stakes for college ladies-in-training. As a young unmarried schoolteacher, Sallucia Abbott's livelihood depended on her maintaining a reputation of prudent judgment. Opening a school for children in Brunswick with the patronage of the college, Sallucia mingled socially as a "college lady" with professors' daughters and Bowdoin students. Her flirtatious, assertive behavior with one student was so outrageous to "Mrs. Cleaveland" and other ladies that Sallucia learned they had spread a "humiliating story" speculating about whether she had secretly eloped with the young man. According to Sallucia, the untrue story "alienated my affections for them so that I fear I shall never overcome it." The story also alienated the college family from Sallucia and she was shunned. Without the patronage of Bowdoin College, her school was in jeopardy. While angry at the gossip that threatened her emotional and economic security, Sallucia was actually more upset that the faculty families had thought so little of her power of judgment that they had linked her to such a student. He had a "fickle" character that she could "never value or accept had it ever been offered to me." She was horrified. The young man would be "the reverse of my choice," she asserted to a friend. Her urgent desire to correct, rather than ignore, the views of Martha Cleaveland and the other Bowdoin ladies reveals their success at insisting that the principles of broad friendship and prudent behavior be maintained. After defending herself and clarifying the issue with some professors' daughters, Sallucia regained the good graces of the college family. She continued teaching and socializing—albeit with a bit more caution.[50]

This collective scrutiny and discipline was an important part of the training of college ladies, one difference that set their education apart from their male companions'. Feminine minds, doubly empowered by nature and society to "spur" male minds in virtuous directions, needed to feel such shameful moments of "sad experience" as well as the intensity of social scrutiny before they could be trusted to direct male minds toward virtue.[51]

Martha had one more point to impart to John as he continued to sit in a minister's house in New Hampshire memorizing lines of Latin, Greek and mathematics and, thanks to Martha's advice, thinking about the organization, communication, and relationship skills that would facilitate virtuous success. Fearing that John might still choose Harvard over Bowdoin, Martha had Parker make the case that the choice of Brunswick was superior, and he listed all of the various benefits to be gained from membership in the new college world: "I think you will spend your College life in Brunswick with great satisfaction to yourself. *Your* advantages will be superior to which they could possibly be in any other Institution, when we take into consideration your residence in my family and the *greater opportunities* you will consequently enjoy with regard to the Experimental part of Chemistry and natural philosophy. Your classmates can only *see experiments* performed—you can have the benefit of assisting me in the *preparation* of these *experiments*."[52]

In the promotion of their institution over others, Martha and Parker joined many other college families in creating a new language that consistently linked "advantages," "privileges," and "benefits" to the intimate, familial interactions taking place in their communities. A classical education gained in their distant, provincial, and developing communities would be more virtuous. It was also a better investment in a young man's future, since an education at Bowdoin or other new colleges was less expensive than at established institutions like Harvard or Yale. More importantly, life at Brunswick was not "so dissipated as at Cambridge," Martha observed. Thanks to college family discipline, the community was "well calculated for students as it affords but few amusements—our society is improving & is at present very good." John would receive even more benefits than the average Bowdoin student. He would be a privileged member of the Cleaveland family and he would enjoy the benefits offered by the wider Bowdoin college family. How could he say no?[53]

Martha and Parker promised John that he would only achieve emotional and economic success through an education at Brunswick. They made this promise to many others. The relatives of many faculty families soon followed John into the college world, receiving a classical education in virtue. John's training took place in the Cleaveland laboratory (where many students worked for free as Parker's assistants), in Bowdoin classrooms, and in Brunswick parlors. Encouraging any eligible young man to join the Bowdoin family also helped Parker. He acquired an array of cheap, eager assistants for his scientific endeavors. This continuing scientific work attracted increasing numbers of tuition-paying students, adding more money to Bowdoin's treasury, more money to Parker's salary, and more capital on which to expand Bowdoin College. With the increasing numbers of students arriving in Brunswick, the trustees soon arranged for a medical school to be attached to the college. As Bowdoin's preeminent "man of science," Parker happily took on the task of organizing the medical lectures, and increased his salary again. By the 1830s, he could happily point to an important affinity between his two favorite principles—chemistry and economy.

John Bush proved an apt pupil, becoming a favorite example of Bowdoin success. After graduating, John's chemical experiences in Parker's laboratory led him to study medicine. He soon opened a successful medical practice in Maine. The refinement he learned from Brunswick society led him to navigate the parlors of Boston, where he successfully courted and won a wealthy wife. While John eagerly took advantage of the many "privileges" offered to a young, successful college graduate, Parker constantly reminded him of his "peculiar obligations" to Bowdoin. John continued to receive letters from his family at Brunswick—his college family. Parker requested that John return to Brunswick regularly to visit. He was always welcome, Parker informed him, because they heard "good accounts of your practice and success" from many college friends. John's presence at Brunswick, especially at commencement, would be an ideal chance for the Cleavelands and their colleagues to display the effectiveness of their strategy for attaining virtuous success. Trained by both Parker and Martha, John was living proof that the college world was full of influential guides who taught young men the best way to direct themselves toward a successful future.[54]

The appearance of Martha's younger sister in the Cleaveland household coincided with the publication of Parker's new textbook. Hannah, John's sister, arrived just in time to help Martha with her domestic duties. In tempting Hannah to her home, Martha revealed the trick to managing such an unwieldy project as an academic home: collective assistance. Her household eventually contained eight Cleaveland children, various extended family members, visiting and boarding students, and domestic servants. In exchange for her unpaid domestic labor, Hannah received the "advantages" offered by the virtuous environment of the Cleaveland home.

Trying to juggle her own academic home in Carlisle, Augusta McClintock also hit upon success, wooing her sister-in-law to give up Philadelphia city life and discover the more virtuous benefits of being a college lady in the countryside. Augusta promised the young girl a home in a refined household where she could learn both Greek and piano. In return, the girl had to help her with her new baby. She would also have the chance to hone her social skills. Augusta needed someone to "keep the parlors in order and see the company."[55]

Just as John's unpaid assistance in Parker's laboratory facilitated Parker's production of his scientific research and textbook, Hannah's unpaid domestic work allowed Martha time to hone her skills as a professor's wife. The authoritative presence of "Mrs. Cleaveland" appeared all over her neighbors' letters. At a social event, Sallucia the schoolteacher had already learned one of her painful lessons about prudence. Martha Cleaveland's baked goods earned high praise at college festivities and fundraising events. She was also a notorious haunt at local auctions, where she loved to discover bargains that would furnish a home that was once awash in debt. Like her husband, Martha had learned to exercise much caution in "economy." Attending auctions furnished her with plenty of "intelligence" about local families that did not practice this Cleaveland principal of economy and might be in need of guidance. Martha was also known for her continued connections with her mercantile family. She often traveled to Portland and Boston with her daughters to purchase items (at a family discount rate) for the Cleaveland home—items that were only available in these more-cosmopolitan markets. For Martha, these excursions into the commercial society of the larger cities provided much material for the social lessons she would impart to the college youth upon her return to Brunswick.

Whenever Parker left home on his lecture tours, he relied on his wife to be the chief source of information about "college news." In her letters Martha was always careful to record how many calls the president had made at their home and whether he requested any task from Parker. Detailing the many visits from college families, trustees, local villagers, and students to their home, Martha assured her husband that this constant activity proved that Bowdoin College was running smoothly. "I assure you, my dear," she wrote to Parker, "our friends are all attentive." As long as the college family visited, socialized regularly, and engaged in civil conversations, their "little world" at Brunswick remained stable.[56]

Upon her arrival at her sister's faculty home, Hannah was instantly admitted into the usual round of educational activities. Cleaveland "ladies" led reading circles, organized parlor interactions with students, and learned how to manage an academic household. Parker engaged a music teacher from Boston for his three daughters, and Hannah benefited from this training in harmony. The young teacher, Mary Brown, received her wages in cash, along with some priceless virtuous benefits. As her father wrote to Parker, the Brown family was happy Mary had the chance to live and board with the Cleavelands, gaining access to Brunswick society. Mary Brown's father hoped that Mary would "considerably improve" herself by living with "a family of your standing in society." Time spent teaching at Brunswick would also be "conducing to her worldly emolument." A year later, the more-refined Mary Brown wrote from Boston to remind Parker Cleaveland to pay her bill quickly because she had "several things to purchase" before she began her new teaching post. She sent her "best love to Mrs. Cleaveland and tell her I shall always feel myself greatly indebted to her, for all her kind attention and politeness during my residence at Brunswick." The improving environment of the college world, and the influence of those like Martha and Parker who championed its benefits, became a desirable commodity for many like Mary who hoped to refine themselves in the eyes of the wider world—and thus gain worldly "emolument."[57]

While assisting her sister and her household, Hannah worked hard at improving herself. Along with all of her literary activities, she learned to play the piano from Mary. She was also "much engaged in a singing school" that opened in town. According to Parker, Hannah was "making rapid improvement in singing." These lessons were part of her training as a college lady, as she was expected to spur male minds with her musical knowledge. As Parker warned John, Hannah would not "condescend to sing with you" on his next visit to Brunswick unless John could "read music well" and "slide down the appropriate notes, with delicacy & grace." Even after graduation, the college world expected its students to keep on improving themselves. Without continual efforts at improvement, Parker warned, John would lose the approval, or even the attention, of the ladies.[58]

Like John, Hannah heard about the problem of passion. Like Sallucia, she had her own painful lesson in the principal of prudence. In her social-izing with students, she came to an understanding with one who would soon graduate from Bowdoin and begin studying law in a nearby town. He proposed marriage. College family members "thought it one of the best matches" because both parties seemed rational and controlled, will-ing to wait until the young man had established himself in the law. When the young man abruptly "deserted" her, all the college family was irate to learn that it was his father who had facilitated the break, objecting to the engagement because Hannah was not wealthy. College lady Alice McKeen pronounced the break as "strange" and a "sad experience" for the young Hannah. Indeed, Hannah provoked pity rather than criticism from the col-lege families. She had followed the rules of prudence—unlike the flirty, prideful Sallucia (even if they now acknowledged that their original per-ception of Sallucia may have been wrong). Hannah received sympathy and support from the college families, who thought she "must feel a great deal" over the humiliation. Alice admired her because her "spirits are said to be very good" and she was spotted with the Cleaveland daughters attending a "famous Ball" with all of the other "young ladies" of Brunswick. In spite of her recent disappointment, reported Alice, she determined to have "a fine time."[59]

An ideal college lady, Hannah appeared self-controlled and indiffer-ent toward her own self-interest, whatever her private passions. She con-tinued on in her training for the future, soon taking on the management of a local primary school. There, she dealt with managing a passion of a different kind. She complained to Alice of a "difficulty" with a young stu-dent who threatened to bite her. The incident had so "affected" her that, she admitted, she "let him go unpunished." When she consulted with the Cleavelands about this educational problem, they helped her solve it, with a little help from the college. Parker wrote to the child's father about the bad behavior and, Hannah reported, the boy "has behaved very well ever since." These efforts to intervene in Hannah's teaching difficulties can be seen as paternalism in action—a strong male force stepping in to assist a weak female dependent. Yet Hannah's past romantic disappointment in the college world was well known in the Cleaveland family. Her present contentment was essential to Cleaveland family success. One neighbor wondered "how Mrs. Cleaveland would get along" if Hannah decided to abandon teaching, leave Brunswick, and leave all of the domestic work in the home to Martha. If the Cleaveland home descended into disorder,

Bowdoin College might also feel it. In light of her essential contribution to his household, Parker's action was simply yet another debt paid to the college family, and to Hannah.[60]

Hannah eventually did leave Brunswick and the Cleavelands, called away to assist another sister. Just as they invited John back for visits, Martha and Parker continually invited Hannah, offering her the chance at more teaching jobs and continued training in Brunswick parlors. Her domestic assistance was also still very much needed, although the Cleaveland daughters were now the prime assistants to Martha. Hannah turned the Cleavelands down, writing that she had, in effect, graduated from Bowdoin and its "little world." She had received all she could. "If I expected to follow school keeping all my life," she said, "I should certainly give B-k the preference, but as I do not, I think I may as well make a beginning of something else first as last." While feeling "much obliged to all" in Brunswick, Hannah plainly felt it was time to strike out on her own. Her brother John had left Brunswick to marry a wealthy wife and open a successful medical practice in a nearby Maine town. Hannah herself was now "in contemplation" of "some other means or rather plans of procuring a support." Under the tutelage of the college families, she knew she could successfully navigate the marriage market, as well as teach school. Thanks to both Parker and Martha, she had learned how to maintain order in the face of a disorderly environment. Always assured of the friendship and assistance of the Cleavelands, she now had the confidence to direct her own future enterprise. When she did eventually return to Brunswick on a visit—happily married, managing a home that included an assortment of stepchildren and her own children, and easily teaching them all—Hannah showed that she had become another successful graduate of the Bowdoin College family.[61]

Having been admitted into the many opportunities and advantages offered in the college world, John, Hannah, and many other young people showed that they were ready to explore the world outside of it. All struck out enthusiastically to seek their future, confident in the powers ascribed to their masculine or feminine identities. They were also confident in knowing that they had the guiding support of many "friends." Far from being a restful haven, an idyllic retreat, or an isolated academic grove, the "little worlds" at these new colleges were disciplined spaces that produced a class of young men and women determined to develop the new nation according to a developing moral and intellectual order. For the young men and women who came to these new college communities to pursue higher education, college families promised success through the endless refinement of one's gender and class. For their teachers it was impossible to tell just how far this training might take these young leaders, nor what use they would make of it. Establishing and inculcating some proven principles of success was the best they could do, whether they involved chemistry, economy, or prudence. What their students ultimately did with these varied principles was a problem for them to solve.

When a professor's son at Washington College graduated, married, and moved to Alabama, his thoughts constantly drifted to the society he had left behind in Lexington, Virginia. His wife, a "college lady" educated at the female academy in Lexington, shared in his homesickness. Their misery deepened when they discovered that the skills they had learned in Lexington did not translate well to life on the isolated Alabama frontier. Consulting with her husband "to learn" about gardening and managing an agrarian household, his wife reported to his sisters back in Lexington that "he does not know any better than I do; so we have to guess at it." Her husband portrayed his wife as a more-skilled theorist than himself. She worked hard all day at her "wonderful notion of gardening & raising chickens." This ignorant state made them feel "right awkward at times," but they treated their lack of skills philosophically—and with a sense of humor.

With all the principals they had learned in the college world, they soon realized that they were useless on the Alabama frontier. They began casting around for "something else to do." As their elders hoped, they relied on their classical training to guide their future toward a virtuous end. Planning on opening a school together, the couple realized they were in dire need of the tools of their true vocation. They needed books, not hoes. They requested their many "friends" in Lexington send them advice, as well as all the classical texts taught at Washington College and the Ann Smith Academy. Then they would begin to bring the principals of the college world to Alabama.

Along with many other graduates of college communities, this couple expanded the college world by building a new educational institution along the expanding American frontier. These new institutions often included separate male and female departments, reflecting the gendered ordering of their previous college communities and promoting the college-family ideal of a broad, educated, ever expanding family. Settling the republic—from Maine to Virginia to Alabama—with a blend of material and ideal assistance from the college world, young graduates clung to the classical knowledge acquired in their "little worlds," but increasingly, with prudence, they also began experimenting with all kinds of new "notions."[62]

Building the College World

"An Elegant Sufficiency"

JOHN AND MARIANNA WADDEL were seven-year-old twins when their father Moses, an academy teacher and Presbyterian minister, accepted the post of president of Franklin College in Athens, Georgia. In 1819, the whole family left their home in South Carolina and rode west to help expand the college world. John recalled their first impression of Athens, and it was not positive: "a straggling little hamlet stretching along the public highway, with no prospect of revival or enlargement." Their primary "object of interest" was their new home, a "huge pile of brick and mortar" called Franklin College.[1]

Franklin College was an early manifestation of today's University of Georgia. Its collegiate beginnings dated from a 1785 act of Georgian legislators who donated land to the trustees for the founding of a "public seat of learning." To the Waddel twins, the college possessed a "grand and solemn appearance" that provided a great contrast to the nearby log cabins and "grog shops" of early Athens. To many settlers in the region, this contrast between "grand" and "grog" went unnoticed. The main problem that the Waddels confronted in 1819 was that few Athenians took notice of the educational structure in their midst.

No one in Athens seemed to care that there was a college in town. A former president of the college complained that the "great concern" among "the people" was "to raise cotton, buy slaves &c." Frustrated in his attempts to attract any friends or funding for Franklin College, he concluded there was "little thought" among most Georgian settlers for "virtue and knowledge." Most settlers were focused on "constantly moving off" to the west, ignoring Athens and its "public seat of learning" in order to pursue their individual interests elsewhere.[2]

Along with college families across the republic, the Waddels tried to correct this growing national habit of bypassing what they viewed as the true definition of virtue: self-sacrifice for the common good. In the new college world, college families designed their communities, their buildings, and their very selves with this educational goal in mind. They needed to attract the interest of Americans distracted by the opportunities the new country presented. Once they recaptured the interest of striving settlers heading south and west, the Waddels hoped, their "business of instruction" would direct these individuals toward more-virtuous goals than cultivating cotton, slave trading, and creating private fortunes.

With the country rapidly expanding by territory and population, the old Revolutionary definition of virtue had seen many "innovations," and college families hoped to refocus what they saw as a dilapidated, divided society on the "true" meaning of this foundational ideal. The Waddels arrived in Athens at a time when Americans were busy rearranging their society based on a new set of highly gendered values. In the fields of commerce and politics, for example, within market exchanges and legislative halls the new "virtues" of aggression, competition, and personal ambition were specifically assigned to men and celebrated as the sure route to success. In these male-dominated professions, earlier standards of virtue that called for self-sacrifice and the common good had been devalued and virtually abandoned. Seeing themselves as guardians of the youthful male mind, college families objected to the characterization of aggressive competition among men as a virtue, and they focused their greatest efforts and strongest criticism on the very areas where these new values were promoted and celebrated.

By the 1820s, college families had set their sights on local, male-dominated gathering places such as public taverns, post offices, and even the public street. They viewed such places as full of corruption, confusion, and disorder—all of them in need of the influence of "true" virtue. College families hoped to inculcate their own ideals into their communities and regions, thereby reminding inhabitants of the necessity of classical virtue. They hoped to offer their world as a blueprint for how the wider world should look, demonstrating to their fellow Americans an odd, yet fascinating model of virtue in action. As they moved around their communities, on and off campus, college families were determined to show how classical virtue could be made to fit easily into American society. It all depended on the design.[3]

In contrast to the competition and personal ambition that characterized the masculinized worlds of commerce and politics, there were still areas where the values of restraint, selfless giving, and self-control endured, and these were increasingly to be found in the realms of religion, the family, and education. But even in the country's churches, private homes, and schoolrooms, the classical definition of virtue was viewed as a weakened ideal in desperate need of protection, or one dependent on some institution for its very survival. As advocates of what they viewed as the true, fundamental definition of virtue, college families wished to reinsert this ideal throughout American society; they saw the attempt in the broader culture to devalue classical virtue and relegate it to separate institutional spaces as a design flaw that needed correction.[4]

When the Waddel family arrived in Athens in 1819, their college campus possessed the three main structures found at every early American college in this period: a brick college building containing student's rooms, recitation rooms, and living quarters for faculty; a president's house chronically in need of repairs; and a chapel—in this case, an "old dilapidated framed building" that had been serving as the town's only "house for public worship." After making some "needed renovations," the Waddels took up residence in the president's house and assessed their situation. The college had only seven students. Moreover, legislative support was fading, most of the campus was surrounded by a "dense forest," and according to one trustee, the institution's reputation was "languishing." It was under such dire circumstances that the Waddels, a few trustees who lived nearby, and a sparse group of "friends of education" began their renovation project.[5]

Within their mental toolboxes, college families possessed a set of ideals that dictated their design blueprint. Disciples of the Scottish philosophers of the late eighteenth and nineteenth centuries, who posited that all humans possessed a moral sense (or "common sense") that provided them with a reliable standard for ethical behavior, college families believed that with divine help and the right environment humans could trust themselves to choose good actions over evil. Cautious environmentalists, most college families would always posit human nature as essentially depraved, but they promoted a world of discovery and experimentation bounded by certain limits. It was their sense of order that established these limits.[6]

As Moses Waddel observed, the "two great departments of the human subject," the "intellectual and the moral," had to be established before Franklin College could make the "correct" impression on observers and attract the right kind of interest. Visitors to college communities expected to see this moral and intellectual order on display and were quick to point out any evidence of disorder. A visitor in the 1820s to Bowdoin College in Brunswick, Maine, was shocked to discover the wild disorder of the town itself, especially its growing commercial district. Many buildings had been built "beyond the direct line" of the street and thus lacked "elegance." The college structures, however, offered a regulated order that made a deep impression. With its brick buildings set at perfect right angles and faculty houses mandated by trustees to "be at least two stories, and on a line twenty feet from the road," the whole assembly emanated a "great exactness and symmetry." To observers, these colleges were the symbols of civilization, especially with the wilderness still lurking around most of these early sites. The erection of Bowdoin's buildings had transformed the nearby forest from a "swamp of spruce, fir, and pine" into "a tapestry of a drawing room." The nearby blueberry bushes, once a gathering place for local Penobscot Indians, had been trimmed into an "academic grove" for students and local townspeople alike. According to this visitor, Greek, Latin, and other civilized languages were drowning out "aboriginal" speech. Likewise, a Union College student praised the construction of his college: "Where once echo'd savage shrieks and yells, the sov'reign voice of elocution swells." Visiting the new "literary villages" was a popular pastime for early republican travelers, and many were "impressed" with the order of these new college buildings, in contrast to the disorder of their neighboring villages. As was the case for Bowdoin College, one visitor to Union College noted that the buildings were built "in a line" on a hill overlooking (and contrasting with) the wild, canal-town atmosphere of Schenectady.[7]

Providing a contrast to the wild disorder of the forest and the new disorder of commerce and politics, these new institutions and their communities modeled singular spaces, designed and built around "moral and intellectual" construction principles. With their right angles representing principled control, the groves of the academy provided a place in which everyone could think and converse in a new, civilized language, purified of all threatening, passionate influences.

For college-world builders, morality was superior to the intellect. A system of "moral" principles based on Christian tenets had to be set in place well before any intellectual activity was allowed. President Waddel ensured, therefore, that the college chapel on campus was ready for services as soon as his family arrived. Only after establishing this "moral department" did Waddel begin renovating the college's "intellectual department." A two-story brick building called "Apparatus Hall" soon appeared next to the college chapel. Originally meant to house the "philosophical apparatus"—a collection of scientific instruments purchased by a professor on a buying trip to Europe—the structure also included an experimental "chemical furnace," shelf space for over one thousand books, and an upstairs room for faculty meetings, student literary-society events, and weekly prayer meetings. Like all college buildings at the time, these two buildings—the chapel and Apparatus Hall—were not restricted to college students. The public was invited in to inspect the work being done at Athens.[8]

A spirit of necessity influenced the invitation to public scrutiny. The social and economic survival of educational institutions depended on the "liberality" of collective and individual gifts from the wider world. College families solicited donations from state legislatures and individual citizens. They envisioned an entire community of "friends" working in harmony to maintain the fledgling colleges. Closer to home, in their separate college towns the efforts of "town and gown" were needed to attract students, retain them, and help train them in the ways of virtue.

New colleges, therefore, could not afford to be closed to any group or individual. In their early years they were literally open to the public, their campuses lacking any walls or high fences. In fact, college-owned land was often viewed as common land and early trustees and faculty would regularly observe the townspeople herding animals across their campuses, harvesting wood from the college-owned forests, burying their dead on campus lands, and squatting on college-owned tracts of land outside of the towns. College festivities, like commencement and exhibitions, were always open to the public, and college families assiduously transacted their "business of instruction" before the eyes of all. At Franklin College, the trustees had convened in an Athens tavern for their first meeting, to negotiate the purchase of land and donations from locals, as was also the case for the trustees of Dickinson College in Carlisle, Pennsylvania. Arriving in Carlisle for that first trustee meeting in 1785, Benjamin Rush and John Dickinson had turned down repeated invitations to stay in private homes, preferring to take rooms in the town's "large & excellent" tavern where all the college business would take place. College hiring was also done publicly, where everyone could see, hear, and, if necessary, dispute the decisions of the trustees. When Moses Waddel and his trustees hired a local merchant to provide food for students in a common dining hall in 1822, they "concluded the Negociations" on the new contract "under the Oak" near the college chapel—close by the construction site for a new dormitory and in full view of curious workers, enslaved and free, and a street full of onlookers.[9]

Just as had been the case with Bowdoin College, visitors streamed into Athens to visit Franklin College. Rather than bypassing Athens on their way west, after 1820, many settler families now stopped to see what little John Waddel characterized as the "new order of things" that was arising in this frontier town. His father's diary records increasing numbers of parents—with children in tow—arriving by the new stagecoach line from Augusta. Many visitors were from the Carolinas, friends and relations of the Waddels. Others arrived from points farther north after the trustees hired a local academy teacher from Vermont, Alonzo Church, to serve as the new institution's mathematics professor.

Visiting families called at the president's house on campus and asked for tours of the college's buildings. They met the faculty, "tea'd" and "suppered" with faculty wives and children, chatted with students, viewed the scientific equipment in Apparatus Hall, watched the exhibitions at the newly founded Athens Female Academy, and visited the chapel to observe students practicing their oratory skills, to be used when they became republican leaders of the future. Many also met with the local trustees, deciding to purchase or lease college-owned land near Athens so that they could build a house, settle in the midst of such a curious "moral and intellectual" community, and claim a place in the "new order." If they returned to a home in the East, many made their impressions known. By the 1820s, Philadelphia and Boston newspapers, as well as new publications from settling regions like Ohio, all reported that Franklin College, once in a "state of non-existence," was now fulfilling the trustees' early "pledge of prosperity."[10]

The Waddels and the rest of the faculty families could now regularly be seen touring the campus, the college lands, and the streets and parlors of Athens accompanied by the college's trustees. By 1820, there was a recognized "college set" in Athens, and this new elevated class of college families began cultivating a group of ideal workers to do the dirty heavy-lifting as their construction projects increased and intensified. Relying on wealthy trustees to work with him on establishing the new moral and intellectual order at Athens, President Waddel also relied on them to provide most of

Franklin College. All of Moses Waddel's construction projects in Athens, Georgia, are on public display in this popular 1854 periodical. After Waddel's retirement in 1829, Alonzo Church, the new college president, continued the strategy of using campus structures to attract middle-class interest.

Courtesy of Hargrett Rare Book and Manuscript Library, University of Georgia Libraries.

the actual laborers. A class of hired "college servants" grew alongside the new college buildings at Athens, a distinct set of enslaved workers owned by the trustees but employed by President Waddel and his faculty.

One of Moses Waddel's first hires for Franklin College, Dick Carey, was one such slave. The first person that visitors saw as they crossed the unfenced and open campus, Dick Carey was literally responsible for the regulation of college activities. One of his duties was to stand in front of the president's house and ring the college bell, "suspended between two huge oak trees," to signal the start of classes. Besides bell ringing, Carey guarded the buildings. Barring pesky stray animals from campus, he was also known to drive off with "stones" persons (black and white) he judged to be interlopers on campus. The Waddel family also used Carey as their "factotum," and he was often seen leaving the president's house, atop the family's wagon, off to collect purchased goods from the local shops and markets in downtown Athens.[11]

Dick Carey was owned by a local widow, originally from Virginia, who received a hundred dollars a year from Franklin College for her slave's labor. His "training" by this Virginian "lady" was celebrated by white Athenians. One alumnus reminisced about the "aristocratic" Carey, noting how the slave seemed to be an ideal servant for the improving college: Carey was "well dressed"—a "tall, fine looking old negro" who wore his "white hair very long" and "deported himself as if he considered his office in the college second only" to that of the college president. Carey's refined appearance and manners reflected the new environment—even if he did occasionally throw stones at white people.[12]

Such descriptions of Dick Carey and other such "college servants" reveal their special role in the moral and intellectual order promoted by the college world. Whether slave or free, "college servants" worked as a class of subordinates deep within the inner precincts of the educational structures created by the college. Their employers expected them to exert model behavior, as well as be influenced by it. In the 1820s many college families did not consider slaves like Dick Carey to be permanent members of the republic. Such slaves were meant to be Christianized and refined before their return to their original homeland, Africa, where they were expected to cultivate civilization according to the moral and intellectual precepts they had learned in America.

Ardent "colonizationists," college families promoted this idea of racial improvement enthusiastically. Like their colleagues across the republic, the Waddels disliked slavery and advocated for the emancipation and removal of black men and women from the republic. The college world supported the new African colony of Liberia with cash, words, and deeds. As recorded in the movement's official organ, the *African Repository,* college families across the new nation donated cash to this movement, their names and colleges prominently listed in the periodical's subscription columns. On one fundraising and lecturing trip in 1837, a colonization agent collected almost five hundred dollars from Franklin College families and students. College families also wrote articles and letters to the *Repository.* Before the Nat Turner Rebellion that sparked official bans on slave education, many Southern faculty families educated their slaves to prepare them for their trip "home." They favored slaves like Dick Carey, "pure-blooded" and "well-trained," as ideal types to bring the "voice of peace, Christianity, and Civilization" to the "savage shores" of Africa.[13]

Unlike the town's other students, these black "students" were never expected to learn how to teach themselves self-control, self-direction, or self-assertion. It was expected that their future would be based on learning and following directions from whites. If they were sent to Liberia, they would always be supervised by the American Colonization Society and its own Board of Trustees. If they were chosen to stay and work in the college world, they were expected to help build and maintain a world that was exclusively designed for the cultivation of the white mind only.

The private opinions of enslaved Athenians, and their consistent attempts to circumvent this white guidance and supervision, reflect a corresponding world of opposition to this exclusive, white-only blueprint. Except for those few chosen "college servants," slaves were officially banned from the campuses in Southern college communities like Athens. Unofficially, however, they were on campus all the time, constantly participating in the exchange of goods and ideas. Slaves mingled with students, took part in the flourishing black market, and participated in social interactions on a spectrum that ranged from collective fun to racist violence. College families tried to regulate this culture of exchange, fining students "for purchasing anything from a negro in College," while Waddel himself fined students for "chasing Negroes in and about the College thereby making much noise and disturbance." The interaction of students with slave women presented enough of a problem that Waddel felt the need to record how the local trustees took matters into their own hands, carrying out a "correction" of "negro girls'" after their "misbehavior at the bridge"—a site along the river near campus where students flocked to swim. There was no mention of any student "correction." While violence against slaves by masters was part of the everyday slave system, any student carrying out violence against a slave was considered an aggressive act that "disturbed" the president and his faculty and required redress. When one student struck a college servant named Simon, Waddel convened the faculty to decide on the matter, citing the student for the violent action and later, in the chapel, announcing new regulations against abusing college servants. Waddel's son, James, stopped a group of students from attacking one slave in the woods. He was disgusted by their passionate behavior, but he also complained that the presence of slaves on campus was the root cause for such student passion; it would be better for all, he believed, if the slaves were relocated to Africa.[14]

Forced to help construct the new order, college servants learned to use college families' favorite call to virtue to their advantage. In the name of education and moral improvement, they learned, rules could be bent to their advantage but still in accord with their subordinate position. Barred by her mistress from initially attending the college chapel with all the "learned folks" to listen to Moses Waddel's sermons, one trustee's slave, named Rachel, won her argument for attendance by claiming her right to hear moral lessons like everybody else. She was soon exhibiting a detailed knowledge of theology that shocked her owners. The information she had picked up at the weekly sermons, Rachel asserted, had "done her good." Dick Carey, on the other hand, was able to exploit his duties in regulating the college to his benefit by relying on his privileged status to be able to throw stones at white Athenians and by refusing to "take orders" from anyone but the man who had hired him—the college president. Both Rachel and Dick Carey easily identified and took advantage of whatever benefits they could from the world they were forced to serve and maintain.[15]

The public display of such "model" servants proved as essential to the "new order of things" as the visitations of curious, white, middling-class settler families to the college's buildings. These new structures, inhabited by such friendly, elevated families and staffed by such "refined" servants, were meant to make a strong impression on all those "fleeting people" now stopping by to see the construction projects and improvement programs of the emerging college world.

Like all "friends of education" of the time, the Franklin College supporters began submitting promotional "pieces" about their institution to newspapers and periodicals. As one "gentleman of respectability" from Athens observed, student numbers had quickly expanded from seven to seventy and students were doing well under the "new order" that had been initiated by the Waddel family. Students were "as studious and orderly as any equal number perhaps ever known to be collected together at such a place." There were "no irregulars" among the students of Franklin College, Moses Waddel reported in his own "piece." He would not allow students to "study only a few of the Sciences, and then go away." None were allowed to study in his "intellectual department" without attending to his "moral department." All admitted to the college at Athens would, as in all colleges, study Greek, Latin, and higher mathematics, and they would also attend the president's lectures on moral philosophy. Young men needed to spend time in both departments so that their minds and bodies would be regulated to the new order of the college world. This demand for regularity was, on one hand, an invocation to the favored classical tradition of the college families, but it was also part of their move to protect their new "business of instruction." To differentiate their new collegiate institutions from the growing masses of academies, institutes, and seminaries in the republic, college families demanded that their students follow a "regular collegiate course" that ended with a public commencement ceremony in which graduates publicly received their diplomas. As college families intoned from Maine to Georgia, "no irregulars" would be allowed to emerge from their new world. That would be bad for the future moral and intellectual success of their graduates—and bad for the promotion of their new order.[16]

In 1826 a Franklin College junior began "neglecting" his college studies, announcing to friends and teachers that he planned to study law. Junius Hillyer's family was thrilled with his new direction; the college families at Athens were not. In the previous year the faculty had fined Junius for fighting with students, misbehaving at the Female Academy, and skipping classes. Moses Waddel himself had admonished him for coming unprepared to his moral philosophy classes. The young man's behavior proved to Waddel and his colleagues that Junius was still part of the "lawless race of boys" rather than a man who should study law. In addition, Junius's impulsive, and publicly discussed, decision to skip the classical curriculum threatened the entire purpose of the college world. President Waddel moved quickly, summoning Junius to his study for a "long and friendly talk." The young man heard that he was establishing "a precedent so dangerous that it could not be permitted with propriety." Junius argued with the president that an exception should be made for his irregular behavior. His premature actions had been forced upon him by worldly demands and family duty. Studying law was "absolutely necessary," Junius argued, because his widowed mother's property was threatened by a lawsuit. She might need his legal assistance in the near future. Moses Waddel was impressed with this position—and sympathetic. He refused, however, to allow Junius to be "irregular" at Athens. The president and the student worked out a deal that ensured the security of both their worlds. With much "fear" Waddel allowed his lawless student to study law while finishing his course at Athens. Various trustees, lawyers, and judges could assist him in this endeavor.

In the interest of the college, however, Junius "agreed to forfeit a place of honor at Commencement." He would receive his diploma, but not publicly. Once the "matter was settled," Junius remembered, Moses Waddel's fear quickly turned to concerned "interest." He made Junius a surprising offer of assistance, informing him that he could procure law books at a 25 percent discount from a Philadelphia book publisher. Like Junius, Moses Waddel had been dealing with the disordered world too. He was proud to boast of how he had wrested a generous donation for the college from several competitive, profit-driven booksellers, and now he was eager to share this gift with a needy student, anxious to exhibit a model of generosity and self-sacrifice to a young man still in need of regular training.[17]

This collective imperative for such moral and intellectual order became part of the professional qualifications demanded from college instructors themselves. It was especially important for the leaders of these new institutions. When he was offered the presidency of Dickinson College, one professor declined it, not thinking himself the "right man for the office." His "intellectual capacity" could "fill the post creditably," but his "moral fitness" was lacking. Known for a somewhat fiery temper, he thought himself "too impulsive, too unsteady, to be taken as a model for young men." Since the "young men of a college will make its president their model, if he is a man of any mark at all," he did not feel qualified and he turned down the offer.[18]

With their "college at Athens" undergoing such promising external transformations, Athenian college families began focusing on its interior workings. Their "brick-and-mortar" structures were sound by the mid-1820s, but they still had to work on stabilizing the moral and intellectual order within their community. They began by cultivating the assistance of local "friends" who could help bolster their "new order."

Staunch Presbyterians themselves, the Waddels worked on alliances with other Protestant sects. When a Northern Methodist couple arrived in town to take over the teaching duties at the Athens Female Academy, Waddel invited Mr. Stanley, a minister, to preach in the college chapel. He was alarmed, however, to hear a sermon that "made human nature more innocent than I think the Scripture warrants." As a college president and Presbyterian minister, he worried about the influence of "error" on the impressionable young minds under his public charge. The Presbyterian Waddels and the Methodist couple argued over theological differences, yet they did so through "interesting conversations" at the president's house rather than in public. The two families were linked to each another through the educational network forming in town, and both, for personal and professional purposes, needed Franklin College and the Female Academy to succeed. In spite of their theological differences, they strove to model a sectarian alliance in the name of their "new order."[19]

Maintaining this sectarian alliance was a daily chore. After hearing that some townspeople had publicly criticized the Presbyterians for trying to "dominate" Franklin College, Moses Waddel made a point of chatting and socializing with a variety of Protestant ministers and visiting missionaries on the streets of Athens and at the college. Like most college presidents in the 1820s, he was a corresponding member of the American Board of Commissioners of Foreign Missions, an organization that had been founded in the community surrounding Williams College in western Massachusetts. The ABCFM envisioned a nation that worked along broadly defined Christian principles, and its members condemned sectarian tension and advocated for ecumenical alliances over missions. As a member, Waddel sent notices of his "improving work" in Athens to the organization's publication, gaining national exposure for his institution. He also invited local leading men of various Protestant faiths near Athens to join his Georgia Education Society, a charitable organization that helped poor ministerial candidates (of all Protestant sects) attend Franklin College. In addition, he and fellow college families at Athens busied themselves collecting money and coordinating supplies for Protestant missionaries who worked with nearby Cherokees, and they always assisted Christianized Cherokees who came to visit Athens and the college. By 1826, however, the president had to inform visiting Indian missionary Jeremiah Evarts that the college world supported his work but that the "people of Georgia will do nothing for missions," since they were "agitated" against the Creeks and Cherokees. Waddel warned Evarts over breakfast that his fellow Georgians were beginning to call "en masse to defend state rights" against Indian rights, but, he said, Franklin College would continue to maintain ties with the cause of Indian missions in the name of sectarian cooperation.[20]

Moses Waddel was not alone in supporting cooperative activities. His wife Eliza was well acquainted with the workings of the new college world, having been raised and trained in the circle of families that supported Hampden-Sydney College in Virginia (she had first met her husband, a Hampden-Sydney alumnus, at a college event). Upon her arrival in Athens, Eliza had lent her expertise to the founding of the "Female Mite

Society of Athens and Vicinity," which included Presbyterian, Methodist, and Baptist women who collected funds for a Baptist charity. As the president's wife, she also hosted social activities in the Waddel parlor to further enhance the college's social ties with Athenian families. These activities had given Athens its first social scene. This scene, however, was not merely for social enjoyment; it also served to further the ongoing intellectual and moral construction of the college and town. When, early on in the Waddel administration, a Baptist woman in town was heard to loudly criticize one of President Waddel's sermons, Eliza began calling on the woman socially, accompanied by other socially prominent ladies who had an interest in the success of Franklin College. Whether the female dissenter was flattered or intimidated by this socializing is unknown, but her criticisms ended, at least publicly.[21]

Professors' children were also key components in the movement to attract alliances to the college world. The Waddels' children were no exception. A Greek testament placed in his hands at age eight, John Waddel was sent to the local grammar school with other young boys to prepare himself for college. In a few years he and his schoolmates would move across the campus to Franklin College. The Waddels' teenaged sons, William and Isaac, were enrolled immediately at the college, and daughters Sarah and Marianna (John's twin) were enrolled at the Female Academy, in spite of their parents' misgivings about its Methodist teachers. The Waddels also recalled their eldest son, James, from Princeton so that he could finish his senior year at Athens and assist his father as a tutor after graduation. James would eventually become a professor of Greek and Latin at Franklin College. With his marriage to a Methodist trustee's daughter, James and his new wife would literally embody the sectarian alliance that his parents had worked toward. In these early college communities, faculty children mingled with members from various Protestant sects—the sons and daughters of their emerging community's professional class. In the case of the Presbyterian Waddel children, attending Methodist camp meetings, accompanying their father on preaching trips to rural Baptist congregations, and, for the twins John and Marianna, operating an ecumenical Sunday School library out of the family parlor, were all ways to demonstrate how divergent religious beliefs could be harnessed to one ideal: maintaining their new world dedicated to knowledge and true virtue.[22]

Along with their buildings, faculty families used themselves to showcase their vision of an ideal American society—a society ordered along the moral and intellectual lines of the families' classical version of virtue. Like most college families, the Waddels and their colleagues were regular visitors to the main streets of Athens and constantly talked to local Athenians. Waddel's diary chronicles his daily visits to the construction site of a new college dormitory on campus, where he observed the progress and "talked much" with masons and carpenters before he strolled into town. He and Eliza visited merchants together, observing and discussing with fellow citizens the merits of all the new "sundries" brought by wagon from Augusta. The men of college families could be seen at the post office, listening to and discussing with fellow male Athenians the posted election returns or presidential proclamations. At the post office Moses Waddel bought paper and pens, the tools of his trade, and exchanged gossip. He and his colleagues were also regular visitors to the front piazza of the town's general store, where men gathered to discuss the "affairs of the nation, state, town and college or talk politics, religion, philosophy and farming."[23]

Family members' inserting themselves into the town's various public spaces was a highly conscious act meant to model their design of moral and intellectual order. A Williams College professor reported to a brother that he daily went "out into the village" to mingle with the locals. One day he was pleased to be "hailed" by a circle of local men "lounging about the store" who wanted his opinion about a local political candidate. "So," wrote the professor, "as I felt rather political—that is lazy—I took a seat in the middle" of the group and tried to secure "a vote or two" for the man in question, who, he pointed out to the men, possessed the true definition of virtue—selflessness and the desire to serve the "common good." His companions disagreed with him, condemning the candidate as too wealthy to be selfless. What ensued then, the professor reported, was a debate over "the merits of our public men in general." Eager to engage in the many definitions of "merit" with fellow voters, the professor was careful to position himself physically "in the middle" of the circle of men, where they could all hear and see him even if they did not agree with him. Consciously placing his world's definition of virtue squarely in the midst of the towns' political and commercial culture, the professor hoped to insert his distinct definition of virtue into the middle of what he considered was a society in need of renovation and redesign.[24]

When college citizens went out "into society," they were always conscious of walking a fine line between influencing it and it influencing them. The troubled relationship between colleges and local taverns demonstrates the problems involved in the attempts by college families to renovate social spaces along their virtuous design.

One Saturday morning Moses Waddel sat in his office in Franklin College writing letters and keeping an eye on students playing ball on the campus. He soon observed with his "spy glass" that two students were stealthily making their way to a local "public-house" on the edge of campus. Waddel followed the boys, "met them" at the tavern door, and confronted them about their violation of college rules. He was not surprised by the incident. Earlier that year he had stood with a friend watching the tavern sign being "put up," and he later warned trustees about the possibility for future "trouble." No one reacted to Waddel's comments then, or stopped the tavern owner from setting up close to campus. Apparently, to Athenians, the tavern owner was free to pursue his self-interest wherever he chose—without the restraint of having to consider how his activities would influence the common good. In their relations to their surrounding towns, college families constantly objected to such prioritizing of self-interest over the collective good. The place of the tavern in the college world was one of eternal contention between students, their instructors, and townspeople.[25]

In the "catalogue of crimes" in the college world, "tavern-haunting was one of the principal," noted Nathaniel Hawthorne, a Bowdoin graduate of 1825 and a notorious tavern-haunter himself. Written soon after his graduation from Bowdoin College, Nathaniel Hawthorne's novel *Fanshawe* and its portrayal of a college tavern represented the general student position on the issue. For Hawthorne, a public house offered a "scene of comfort" toward which students were "driven" by "undefined apprehensions" about their futures. They turned to the "artificial excitement" of spirits, hoping to replenish a "wit and whim" that was dulled by the routine of college studies—that demand for moral and intellectual order they were forced to obey. For Hawthorne, the tavern was a private site where students should be able to replenish their spirits in peace. More importantly, he and his fellow students defined drinking as a private choice that should not be influenced by others, namely, their instructors with their ubiquitous "spy-glasses."

For students, such a space offered a different set of instructors that offered an alternative vision of society than the one promoted by college families. Hawthorne's fictional students bestowed a "professorship of Poetry" on a local tavern keeper to honor his storytelling talents, but the publican declined, arguing that such an academic post was less important and less powerful than his position as publican. He was a "public man," he told the students, working for people who were "loath to spare me from my present office" for poetry. He had a duty to protect the people's right to find comfort and diversion in his tavern.[26]

College professors also claimed the title of "public men," swearing oaths of "office" to uphold the national and state constitutions and, according to a Dickinson College faculty oath, to perform the "duties" of instructor "with fidelity and to the best of his abilities." They viewed their positions at colleges as part of a powerful public trust that demanded the moral and intellectual monitoring of students. Their duties called them to monitor even that private world of students.[27]

As all of Hawthorne's professors at Bowdoin College would have pointed out, the individual choices of students, made without consultation or guidance from "wiser heads," inevitably led to public disorder. The public always demanded that professors sort out this disorder. Like Moses Waddel in his interaction with the lawless Junius Hillyer, college families were always engaged when their students insisted on following their own sense of order. If faculty tried to avoid the issue or claim ignorance of their students' behavior, the public let them know loud and clear. Complaining that college students were "running our street at improper hours after some very indecent girls," an anonymous writer informed the Dickinson College faculty that the students had learned all this bad behavior at a "general loafing place" near a tailor's shop on the main street, and the writer hoped that the faculty would "find them out" and reestablish the much-vaunted "moral and intellectual" order at Carlisle. After similar student "sprees," townspeople might search out faculty members, not the offending students, for compensation for any damage to private property or reputations. In spite of his "new order" at Athens, President Waddel frequently had to deal with "very angry" Athenians who came to his door demanding retribution after the drunken rampages of the growing numbers of young "gentlemen" enrolled at the college. College families continuously fought to counter public accusations that their virtuous world was actually a center of vice. They connected much of the violent behavior, vandalism, gambling, and illicit sexual activity of their students to the growing disorder caused by public drinking.[28]

It is no wonder that many faculty families became ardent promoters of temperance. Two years after Hawthorne graduated from Bowdoin College, a group of drunken students burned a tar barrel, set off gunpowder underneath an instructor's chair during class, and in the general melee that followed, stole the college bell from the chapel and threw it into the nearby Kennebec River. When notices about the "Bowdoin Riot" spread, Bowdoin's professors convened a meeting and quickly published their own notice announcing the actions they had taken as a result of the riot: there has been student expulsions and the students themselves had made the decision to form a temperance society.[29]

Temperance activities became a common component of the "new order of things" in college communities. College buildings became popular venues for temperance lecturers, with "reformed drunkards" eagerly imparting their personal knowledge about "demon rum" to large fee-paying audiences. Some college families even attempted to direct their town's rowdy heavy-drinking element to adopt their "new order." Inspired by the example of temperance lectures that warned young men of "spontaneous combustion" if their blood became too full of alcohol, the faculty families at Bowdoin College inaugurated a community experiment. They invited a notorious Brunswick "sot" into a science hall on campus, drew his blood, and ignited it. As the blood "burned with a hard gem-like flame before a cheering gallery," the world of the tavern and the consequences of the private choices made there were placed into clear contrast with the "moral and intellectual" structure offered by the college world. Bowdoin college families certainly captured the public's interest with this stunt. The ghoulish spectacle entertained the audience, but it also prompted many to observe how an individual choice could ultimately end up being placed under the collective scrutiny and judgment of those who practiced and promoted more-virtuous lives.[30]

In college towns professors were often "the most conspicuous in the Temperance cause." Some families, mostly from the New England colleges, became extreme "cold water" practitioners, publicly swearing off all stimulants and adopting harsh regimens of food and exercise in order to reach moral and intellectual perfection. The women of one Bowdoin College family went to such extreme lengths in following the Graham regimen of whole-wheat bread and water that they were deemed "wraiths" by one of their colleagues, Martha Cleaveland. While her family advocated temperance, Martha was unimpressed with such models of extreme behavior. In a letter to her daughter she imagined the deplorable state of her colleagues' table on the upcoming Thanksgiving Day holiday, and hoped that they would not be hosting any hungry students on that day. Such personal

extremism, she implied, was not conducive to the prosperity and reputation of the college. The majority of her colleagues would have agreed with
her. Extremism and radicalism were never part of the "new order." It was
no surprise to Martha and the rest of the Bowdoin family, therefore, when
their Grahamite colleagues began criticizing Colonization Society policies
and soon moved on to calling for the abolition of slavery.[31]

College families began embracing temperance as part of the new order
for their communities and for themselves. "You will modestly maintain
your character as a temperance boy," ordered Union College president
Eliphalet Nott to a grandson away at school. As part of the Union College
family, young Clarkson Potter was not only duty bound to represent temperance, but to actively promote it at his school. "Make as many other temperance boys as you can," his grandfather urged. As hard as they might try
to be role models, however, some members of college families fell under the
influence. When a Dickinson College professor stumbled into a colleague's
home for evening tea "so intoxicated that he could not lift a tea cup," the
other families consulted with each other about the problem. Personally,
they cared about the man and sympathized with his private problems. Pro-
fessionally, they saw him as a "victim of rum" and saw his "condition" as
one more problem to overcome in their promotion of moral and intellectual order. As one professor noted in his diary: "It is too astounding—I can
hardly believe it. . . . I fear-fear-fear for the future." The drunken professor had once been an ideal representative of their "new order." He was a
personal friend to many, a popular teacher among students, and a talented
writer. Could such irregularity be made regular again? If they could figure
out what made their colleague drink, they might then know how to make
him stop. In this way, they figured, they might claim an advantage in their
constant struggle with local tavern owners, "rum-sellers," and other rep-
resentatives of worldly temptations. Their collective attempt at regulating
their colleague was intimately tied to their collective need to regulate (and
restrain) the growing numbers of saloons and hotels in Carlisle that sold
liquor and promoted this vice among Dickinson's students.[32]

For the good part of a year, Dickinson college families allowed such an
irregularity into the very center of their "new order," for the purposes of
study. As a group, they monitored the afflicted professor's every movement
and listened closely to his conversations to ascertain any moral and intellectual errors. Faculty children also shared in the project, accompanying
the professor on long walks or on horseback-riding trips into the "pure

country air" around Carlisle, undertaken to purify the man's mind and body. To keep him away from saloons and other temptations, the professor was required to take his meals with a college family living on campus. He even was allowed to continue teaching, under supervision. Family members engaged the errant professor in "long and friendly" talks, trying to find a reason for his irregular actions and thoughts. After one such conversation, one professor marveled at how a man just like himself was now "utterly broken up—just like a baby." The fragility of their moral and intellectual order was always apparent to the families. After one local trustee spied the professor staggering in the street and another found him passed out in a stable, the families ended their study. His individual actions were threatening their collective order. For the "interest of the college," they sent him to an asylum, where they continued to study him by writing and visiting their "irregular" colleague. They never solved the mystery of his drinking. As a former colleague observed, his loss was a "tragic loss" for Dickinson College.[33]

Some college communities were more successful than others in attracting local assistance to bolster their "new order." After a series of regular bouts of riotous students destroyed enough private property, local town families became "interested" in helping college families with their temperance cause. College families always applauded such local support as proof that their new order was working. The growing "bad conduct" among Moses Waddel's students finally prompted Athenians to vote to tax merchants who sold "spirits" in the vicinity of their enlightened village. Along with this public control, Waddel and his faculty announced in the local newspaper that a stricter set of college fines against drinking would be imposed and that the Franklin College Temperance Society would begin discussions on the issue. After a particularly destructive round of "licentiousness" at Brunswick in 1836, Bowdoin College families determined to make a public example of one "headquarters of the evil" that served students near their campus. "We have assailed & procured an indictment of the owner before the Grand Jury," reported a professor, in the hope that public censure would shut the tavern down. Whatever happens, he supposed, "good will come of it" because public opinion had now become "enlightened" about the problem of student drinking. By the 1830s, the temperance cause was "quite common" among Washington College families in Lexington, Virginia. With the help of town families, the college had successfully banned "grog shops" from town, while "distilleries have gradually disappeared from its vicinity." According to one proud graduate, Washington professors had been very prominent at a recent meeting in the new university town of Charlottesville "for the purpose of promoting the cause of Temperance." No one at Washington College was surprised to hear of the student disorders then rocking Jefferson's "academical village." As they would have argued, Jefferson's design of the university was flawed, since the campus was bereft of a chapel (and thus a moral department). When asked about the prospects of sending a young man to Charlottesville for higher education, a Washington College friend offered the typical college family assessment of Jefferson's institution. It was the "worst place" a young man "could be sent" because it "has always been tinctured with the immoral, irreligious opinions of its founder, who, though a great statesman, was fearfully in error regarding these highest of all subjects." While Jefferson himself would have a "dreadful account to settle with his maker for the destruction of his own Soul," he would also have to account for how his flawed construction project of a university influenced the young men "committed to his charge." To such Lexington friends the persistent discipline problems in Charlottesville simply emphasized the fact that it was Washington College, the college that Washington had once patronized, that exemplified true virtue. As a proud alumnus reported, Lexington as a town was "remarkable for its morality, order, and intelligence," and the college at its center was responsible for this reputation.[34]

The stabilization of this moral and intellectual order was an ongoing problem. College families always acknowledged that strong forces hindered their goal of infusing virtue throughout society. It was the eternal problem of the self—and its interest. Attending a temperance lecture at the Williams College chapel, one professor was happy to see many town families in attendance. He was equally enthusiastic about the lecturer's tactic of condemning the selling of spirits as well as the drinking of them. The man was a "rouser," he reported to his brother, who made the "practice of vending and distilling ardent spirits" seem "criminal and detestable." If anyone "continues to do these things" after attending the lecture, the professor decided, he would be made by Williamstown citizens to feel he was sinning "against his conscience, if he has any." Sure enough, the local newspaper announced that students had founded a temperance society. Even better, according to the professor, the "merchants" of Williamstown had promptly "cut off their plugs and washed up their measures," swearing not to pursue their fortunes via "spirits." Williams College families and the lecturer they had invited into their chapel had successfully convinced the community to accept their notion that all should direct self-interest toward the common good. Long experienced with the economic needs of townspeople and the convivial desires of students, however, the professor was not optimistic about this continued state of collective harmony. The draw of self-interest always threatened their carefully constructed "moral and intellectual" structures. As he observed, "Lucre is a strong reasoner and can not always be expected to yield so easily." He hoped that the same lecturer would appear again soon to reinforce the "new order" promoted at Williams. It was only with repeated calls to virtue that the college families could counter the persuasive power of "lucre" and the individual pursuit of self-interest.[35]

College families were not only determined to renovate public spaces, they also used those structures considered most "private" to the wider world—their homes and their very selves—to model how self-interest, the element that always threatened their design, could be made to work for the common good. Just as they considered themselves models of virtue, they expected their families and homes to be models as well.

Eliphalet Nott, the president of Union College, described the basics of this model home to his brother. The Nott family, the families of his professors, and their servants all lived in the wings of two college buildings on campus, with their students lodged, two by two, in rooms between them. Everyone ate together in a basement dining room. With "every minute of every day supervised," reported Nott, life moved in a regular, orderly fashion with few "disorders." Visitors left Union College "astonished at the order, punctuality, and diligence which prevails." Just as had happened with Moses Waddel's Franklin College, Union College began to attract large numbers of students and greater financial support from "friends." The "moral and intellectual" order flourishing in Schenectady, New York, was always on display for visitors to see.[36]

Although as president Nott was duty bound to be confident about his "moral and intellectual" order at Union, most of his fellow college families there found it difficult to live according to this order. Their private living spaces in the college buildings appeared less than respectable to most onlookers. While all early American colleges began with small buildings where students and teachers lived together, living patterns varied as the colleges expanded. But at Union College, and at Dickinson, some college families continued to live in the wings of the colleges' buildings until the early twentieth century. Many at Franklin College and at Washington also lived on campus. When given the opportunity, some families opted for a little breathing space between themselves and the students, building homes adjacent to campus, as Parker Cleaveland had done at Bowdoin College, often on land they initially bought or rented from the college's trustees.

These college living spaces were truly common spaces—maintained by college treasuries that were chronically short of funds or empty, and supervised by trustees who often did not live in the community and so were neglectful about upkeep. A Dickinson College professor was appalled to find that the "rooms in the western end of the college" assigned to his family were "very much out of repair." There were not a "sufficient number of rooms." There were "no closets for clothing," no pantry, nor any of the other "ordinary accommodations" to be expected by a "private family." To add to the problem, he had learned from his wife that there was a "general impression in the town, that a family could not be made comfortable" in a college building. His duty was to prove that they could live a respectable private life in a common building. After consulting with the local trustees, the professor had renovations carried out by local laborers "under my direction," adding a closet for clothes, partitions to create more sleeping rooms, and "papering and other things which (though of a little different character) were not less necessary for living comfortably and respectably." To command respect and attention in their communities college families felt they needed to inhabit structures that reflected the genteel world of a "private family," yet they also viewed their homes as common spaces for educational activity. Their homes were important teaching tools with which families hoped to demonstrate lessons on how to be "private families" working for the common good. As college families, they knew their behavior would be on public display, and they acted accordingly. Another Dickinson College professor described to his brother-in-law how he had improved his "modest home" on campus: "We cut a door through the parlor into the garden; and put a little porch and arbor there for summer evenings." There was also a "pretty portico at the front door." Open parlors and porches, as well as the Greek Revival fashion for "porticos" and "piazzas," were characteristic of college homes, where family interactions guided by virtuous ideals were meant to be on public display.[37]

Early college home renovations always involved the tearing down or breaking through of walls. Finding a wall between his home's study and his classroom, a college professor living in one of the dormitories with his family requested that a door be cut through to allow easier passage between the two spaces. The renovation would not only facilitate easier interaction between students and professors, he argued, but it would balance the whole building. His new door would exactly match the door of another professor across the hall. Close friends, the two professors hoped this new design would allow them to divide up their student policing duties and provide them with more time for conversation. Their harmonious relationship (and their double open-door policy) would, they hoped, also impress upon their students that they were concerned, watchful counselors ready to discuss problems or solve disputes rather than monitors ready to discipline. Such "natural" behavior of collegiality and friendship, however, was as much a studied part of the moral and intellectual environment of this college world as a door cut into the wall.[38]

Alpheus Packard, Bowdoin's professor of rhetoric, and William Smyth, his mathematical colleague, designed a house on campus especially for their two families. As one of Smyth's sons remembered: "Professor Packard and my Father built a double house together and occupied it, he with his large family on one side and we on the other, until separated by death, a period of about forty years for my Father and over sixty for Prof. Packard." Both clans lived such a communal existence that Smyth's son, who spent time in German universities after graduating from Bowdoin, remembered the Packards as family, not neighbors: "I have never seen anywhere else, either in America or Germany, such close ties of friendship in a community and such united common life." There may have been "brick-and-mortar" walls separating the Smyths and the Packards at Bowdoin College, but a specifically ordered sense of undivided space unified them.[39]

There was no chance of finding seclusion or privacy for college families. Even a professor's study, a space one might assume was reserved for focused, isolated, quiet thought, was actually a space for collective exchange, edification, and conversation. After he moved to his new president's house, Moses Waddel happily recorded in his diary the day that he "entered my new study." His study hours, however, were not spent in silent contemplation. As John Waddel remembered, his father's study was "at all times open to those seeking assistance, and he would lay aside the most interesting and important business to answer the inquiries of a student." Moses Waddel recorded that trustees, townspeople, and family regularly dropped by to "spend time in my study" to discuss "students & religion," land deeds, or "horse-swapping." Many called to "look at my diploma" from Hampden-

Sydney College, hung prominently on the wall for all to see. They might also peruse wall maps of "Floriday" or Alabama that former students sent to their old president—images that illustrated the growing influence of Franklin College in these new territories. Professor Parker Cleaveland's study in his home at Bowdoin College served as the "eating room, and to some extent, the sitting room" of his family. Cleaveland did not seem to mind the "noise and talk" swirling around him. As one student marveled, the professor would "turn, with singular facility, from his desk to the company, and back again to his desk," studying and conversing with guests and family at the same time.[40]

It was left to the "college ladies" to organize these homes according to the "new order"—a challenging task that included caring for one's own children as well as the interminable waves of others: student boarders, various "sort of cousins" who were sent to live with faculty families to "get an education," and a fluctuating array of servants or slaves. Maintaining even the appearance of respectable gentility proved challenging in the crowded and often chaotic world of the college home. Parker Cleaveland's daughter reported to a sister that there had "been nigh well a *second* flood" at home, with "every *chick* & child" making "such a *hurly-burly*" after classes ended that their mother Martha never found enough time to finish a letter, never mind the sewing. The college home was a busy place, and honing collective effort, especially among "college ladies," was a necessary skill for survival.[41]

College families regularly faced public criticism that their homes were "extravagant enough" and full of selfish luxury. The "prosperous state" of their educational enterprise led to the material prosperity of their own homes—and the public noticed. "You ought to come down and see how nicely Eveline is fixed," gossiped one Lexington woman to a friend. She reported that Eveline had married a Washington College trustee and was living among its white-columned buildings on College Hill. Eveline's house was the "nicest fixed of any on the hill." This was quite a social achievement, the gossip explained, as "you know they are very stylish up there." One visitor to a professor's home at Williams College watched some local boys enter its lush gardens to pick flowers. She heard them say that if their families had a yard "so gaily decked with flowers they would feel set up."[42]

In an effort to counter charges of luxury, materialism, and selfishness, college families steadfastly displayed their moral and intellectual order. Ornamented with "useful" objects and offered regularly as venues for instruction, their homes were consciously planned to provide a contrast to more worldly homes, which were condemned by college families as private, exclusive retreats that cultivated selfish pleasures and frivolous idleness.

When the science professor at Williams College, Albert Hopkins, began work on creating a study in his new home next to campus, "making his large room in his house" into a "Library and Cabinet," his wife Louisa expanded on his design. She insisted on adding a "conservatory" to the home that would contain a piano and favorite plants for study. She also designed space to contain "her shells, her minerals, her pictures" and "her German, French, Italian, Spanish, Latin, Hebrew and Greek library." Williams College students, local academy girls, and public visitors all appeared at the front door of this home, invited in to view the couple's cabinets of curiosities or to tour the botanical garden they had planned together in their back yard. Cabinet, conservatory, garden, and the Hopkins themselves were all on public display, equally representative of a college mission that promoted the use of space for the "good of all."[43]

Faculty homes were also classrooms where people could enter and learn how to live according to the "new order." Professorial women taught their housemaids how to read in their kitchens and tutored students in Greek and manners in their dining rooms. Students and local townspeople learned how to make proper, punctual calls and act like "gentlemen and ladies" in faculty parlors—or they were not admitted again. In Athens, Moses Waddel endeavored to educate the children of his slaves "as he did his own"—by "catechetical instruction" in the family parlor on Saturday nights. As Waddel noted in his diary, his kitchen became the scene of further educational activity when their enslaved coachman Ben gave his own commentary on Waddel's sermons. Some Athenians did not appreciate this Waddel family practice. As one neighbor complained, this educational activity was "calculated to ruin all the negroes in the neighborhood." Evidently, some in Athens saw slave education (and their eventual relocation to Africa) as a college-family practice that threatened, rather than secured, social order.[44]

College families refused to regard their homes as spaces devoted to personal enjoyment. All items in the home had to serve an educational and collective purpose. Pens, paper, books, bookshelves, "spectacles," musical instruments, luxury items bought for college festivities, desks, and even a "chair for writing" that one Athenian citizen had presented to Moses Waddel—all were considered essential accoutrements for a life dedicated to cultivating moral and intellectual order.[45]

For professors the natural world was also an ideal classroom—often for the edification of college-family members themselves. At Dickinson College, Augusta McClintock proclaimed her husband to be a true "Professor of Cabbages" who took "great pleasure" in his gardening "the more he learns about it" from a local farmer. One winter, when Isaac Jackson, a mathematics professor, captured an owl in his chicken coop at Union College, he determined to keep it as an ideal natural-history exhibit for students and the public. Unfortunately, he was unable to see his educational plan through because the bird, "poor fellow," perished in the heat of Jackson's study.[46]

As the ideal of private family life grew popular in literary and religious writings, college families found themselves in conflict with many of the actual families who provided them with their students. These families insisted on prioritizing their individual family interests over any notion of common good. In the 1830s, Dickinson College faculty families struggled with local town families who embraced quite a different set of family values than those promoted by the college circle. In a petition to the faculty, local parents "felt and acknowledged" the "benefits" of Dickinson College but objected to the college family's "new order." They requested that students who lived "in their father's families" be exempt from mandatory attendance at morning prayers because the college demand had sowed nothing but "trouble and inconvenience" throughout the private homes of Carlisle. Their homes had been "broken in upon" by a college order that demanded that their children be "dragged from their beds, half clothed and half frozen" to report to the chapel "in no condition of body or frame of mind for prayer." Viewed from the perspective of the town families, the collective exercise of religion in the college chapel, a practice viewed by college families as an essential component of their moral and intellectual world, made prayer "burdensome and repulsive" to students "forced" to leave their warm beds in town and walk to campus. Prayer should be a private, individualized affair, the town parents lectured the Dickinson faculty, a "family habit" performed at the private "family altar." They characterized the college as merely a "surrogate" family—and only for students "lodging in the College who are deprived of their own family associations." Seeking to foreclose any faculty counterarguments, the parents announced that it would be "vain to attempt to reason them out of a feeling that nature has so deeply planted in their bosoms." According to these parents, the "new order" implemented by the college families in Carlisle was subordinate to the "natural" ties of "family association." In college families' attempts to implement their own version of virtue, they thus found themselves constantly at odds with tavern owners, students, and parents who believed their individualized sense of order was more important than the college world's promotion of the "good of all."[47]

It was not an easy life, living in a college household. This semi-public, semi-private world perplexed those who did not live within it. Many viewed the lives of college families with curiosity, suspicion, and even sympathy. One professor's wife received nothing but pity from her mother-in-law about the "open" state of her home, especially during the busy commencement season: "I hope you will not be as much troubled for help as you have sometimes been. I wish you could for once keep closed doors." This world that promoted a new order proved to be an unstable environment for many of its promoters. One professor complained that "being constantly exposed to the observation of a hundred people who are ready to talk about everything you do and say" was "very unpleasant."[48]

In spite of the unstable internal environment they were trying to inhabit, college families succeeded in creating external structures in their communities that made quite an impression. As Franklin College flourished under Moses Waddel and its network of ever expanding "friends," a whole new generation of Southern middle-class strivers discovered the benefits of pursuing a "collegiate course" of moral and intellectual order within Athenian college buildings. One young lady from Augusta attended the college's commencement ceremonies in 1826 and reported to her brother that she "had no idea our native state could boast of so delightful a spot, in the interior, as Athens." On the evening before commencement the new buildings were "illuminated" with candles in every window—a "very brilliant scene." The next day, the young woman wrote, she listened to student orations in the chapel, impressed at such a large crowd "collected in so small a place." Athenians themselves were "agreeable acquaintances" who kept her "visiting from the time I arrived until I left there." As their world and its new order expanded throughout the 1820s and 1830s, college families noted their success by the number of new students, new buildings, and new friends. They also noted with dismay that divisive passions and the power of self-interest in their communities also expanded. To them, the growing strength of their communities actually hid a myriad of internal weaknesses and building flaws that needed another round of renovation.[49]

Passing by the construction site of his new dormitory one day, President Waddel observed the raising of "heavy timbers" to support its roof. He also watched as a stagecoach "full of boys" arrived in time for the new term, and realized that more boys would mean more disciplinary problems. "Brick and mortar" structures, no matter how "grand and solemn" they appeared, proved unable to stabilize a moral and intellectual order all by themselves. Worrying over the increasing "bad conduct" of his students, Waddel also noted the behavior of Athenians themselves. His trustees were not always focused on his college's needs. Some of them had become involved in political intrigues; others were distracted by speculation on the new cotton factories to be built in town. In local newspapers, anonymous broadsides, and satirical "quizzes" that circulated around the town, Franklin College was criticized for various reasons. The local Baptists, a Protestant sect that was growing in numbers, were less interested in alliance. They were particularly hostile to the college, decrying it as a power base for Presbyterians and a vice-ridden playground for wealthy young men. As was the case at Dickinson College, Moses Waddel, as president of Franklin College, also received a fair share of anonymous notes from townspeople. One note in 1829 "from a friend to justice" demanded, like all the others, that he control student behavior and manage the college better.[50]

How was it, college families continually wondered in letters and diaries, that the external improvement and expansion of their educational enterprises always led to a weakening of their colleges' internal order? Success always seemed to stimulate the corrupting power of self-interest, "filthy lucre," and divisive partisanship. Just as with the success of Franklin College, prosperity at Bowdoin College attracted new "manufactories" to town, more population growth, and an increase in property values. Even as Professor Alpheus Packard marveled at Brunswick's growth and noted that he himself had invested in a local factory, he worried that this "prosperous state" would lead to a loss in true virtue—to himself and to the college. "Worldly prosperity" he observed, "always brings the symptoms of moral disease—nay the disease itself." Continued success demanded renewed calls for self-sacrificial acts of virtue and actions for "the good of all."[51]

Sitting in his study, Moses Waddel mused over ways to strengthen the moral and intellectual order in Athens and to stabilize order at home. One evening, he had to "rebuke" his teenaged son for bad behavior. Another evening, another son had flown into such a "passion" that he and his wife were forced to have a "serious" conversation the next morning about the state of the child's soul. Initially pleased that his son had married a trustee's daughter and taken up a teaching job at a nearby academy, Waddel now worried about the young man's tendency to fall into debt because of his love of luxury items. The father and son had many heated talks about this problem. Even his daughters, Sarah and Marianna, needed to be reminded of virtue. Noticing that there were "few females" at his college prayer meetings, Waddel lectured his daughters and their friends about being "bad women," then spoke to one of his trustees about assisting with the problem of "disaffected females" among the college ladies. Another round of renovations seemed in order, but this time the college families at Athens needed to focus on repairing the internal faults and fissures within their own world.[52]

The ideal college-world solution to this internal problem was to make it external, placing all private grievances, social tensions, and the problem of self-interest in public view. When Waddel's daughters returned from an evening prayer meeting at the Female Academy and reported that a few college students had started to attend, Moses Waddel moved quickly to encourage this new interest among the young gentlemen and ladies of Athens. College families also began monitoring the numbers of students who appeared at Waddel's Sunday sermons, as well as the behavior of students on campus or Athenians in town, hoping to identify anyone in need of extra tutoring when it came to understanding the morals involved in helping to maintain their new order.

By the 1830s, college families had added a new task to their job description. Always on the lookout for potential "friends" among whom they could cultivate virtue, they also began to evaluate the state of virtue within their model communities. They were always attentive to any students or townspeople who expressed an "interest" in moral subjects. One professor's son at Washington College described the "interesting state" of the townspeople of Lexington. They suddenly began flocking to the college for Bible classes and Sabbath services, "intent on acquiring reformation." The "inattentive & careless" college students often lounging around the college buildings were now "frequently seen with their Bibles" in town and on campus, "studying either the verses from the day or the lesson for Sunday." At Lexington there was "decided improvement" in the air and a "close engagedness" by many on moral questions that "betokened the precursor of a revival." Religious revivals, which made their way around the college world on a regular basis after 1800, were welcomed by college families, who viewed them as important stabilizers of their new order.[53]

Anything might start a town revival, college families discovered, but the sudden death of a student or professor through illness or accident was a sure spark among students. Such a "dreadful accident" occurred at Williams College in 1843. Two students, both minister's sons, were playing with a gun in a dormitory stairwell when the weapon was accidentally discharged, fatally wounding one of them. As one professor's wife informed her mother-in-law, it was a tragedy on many levels: "The poor young man was sixteen years old, had no religion, retained his reason for a few moments only, during which he said he was going to hell, lived several hours longer in a state of unconsciousness, & then died." Tragically, the father did not arrive in time to speak to his son. The professor's wife noted that there was a "great sensation produced in college by this terrible event; but whether it will be productive of any permanent good is doubtful." Her husband and his colleagues had moved quickly, giving the students a "solemn sermon" a few days later that had "some reference" to the boy's death. Discussions about the event continued and another professor reported "some favorable appearances in college to hope for a revival here." The professor's wife reported that her husband "has had visits from several students to talk on the subject of religion, who date their impressions from that event." She decided that the tragedy "seems to have done some good" for all of Williams College. If encouraged by attentive elders, the moral state of one student could be carefully cultivated into a collective conversation that would force everyone to think about others and how to work to improve the "good of all."[54]

News of any college revival spread quickly through the college world. These collective events encouraged many to wonder about the influence of their communities on each other—and on the world at large. Hearing about a revival, a Bowdoin trustee's wife was "much rejoiced at the state of things at college" and requested "more particular information" from the wife of the college president. Living in a town far north of Brunswick, she watched her community attentively to see if Bowdoin's awakening signaled "a better state of things" for her own home town. She was disappointed to report, however, that "as yet nothing very important has occurred." A college revival was deemed an "important" event because it had the potential to influence the commercial or political world. Whenever Franklin College experienced revivals in the late 1820s, observers noted, a "simultaneous influence has been communicated to almost every part of the state." Junius Hillyer, Waddel's lawless student, began questioning his moral state before graduation, much to the relief of his instructors, who worried about his future regularity. In his reminiscences, Junius provides a glimpse into the atmosphere of a college town under revival. The everyday regulated workings of Athens paused during revival. Time stopped while "everybody talked about religion, everybody prayed and exhorted. The college bell did not ring. All business in the town was suspended, and the exercises of the College were closed." Rather than reflecting a "state of prosperity," college communities cultivated a "state of religious feeling," where social tensions eased, the pursuit to make money stopped, and collective harmony flourished. During a college revival, during the quiet and pause of everyday life, everyone could clearly hear the reminders about the need for virtue. Many would respond to it—for a while.[55]

Although everyone was expected to work out his or her own moral relationship with God, a community effort was part of this process in the college world. The new order demanded that individual choices about morality be celebrated as public achievements of the college world. Junius Hillyer became "concerned about religion." As a "sinner," he believed, the "time had come" when he needed to "settle" his "religious convictions and "take my position for life either with the people of God or with the people of the world." He started to undertake this decision by himself, organizing time for "private prayer," but soon discovered others were also wrestling with the problem of salvation. In fact, he observed, "without any apparent concert, simultaneously," many Athenians of various sects became "powerfully exercised about religion," and he soon realized he was part of a wider moral event. Conversations about morality were held in the "College, the town, at private houses, and in the churches." Moses Waddel and his carefully cultivated ecumenical fleet of Presbyterian, Methodist, and, finally, Baptist ministers "took an active part in these meetings" and "gave themselves wholly to prayer, preaching, exhortation, and visiting privately those who were concerned." Junius took advantage of all of these conversations, eventually choosing to join the Baptist church.[56]

Seasons of revival were highly instructive for college families, who utilized the events to seek out unforeseen flaws in their ordered design. After listening to his students publicly confess to illegal activities carried out under the very noses of their instructors, one Williams College professor was stunned to hear that students who possessed "irreproachable character and high standing in the community" had been so "dreadfully wicked." He took this important lesson about the "wickedness of the human heart" into a faculty meeting, where he and his colleagues discussed possible revisions to the way that they supervised students and a rewrite of the college rule book issued to all freshmen, to reflect fresh warnings about the penalties, moral and intellectual, for the breaking of the college's rules.[57]

Revivals made a deep impression on some students, and no impression on others. A Williams College student described to his parents how he "went to watch" a prayer meeting with a friend. They were amused at the spectacle, until he was left alone by his roommate, after which he "thought a little about the subject of religion." He decided it was a "serious matter" that needed to be considered before he graduated. Some students watched with a skeptical eye as other students who they "absolutely detested" suddenly wanted to become their friends, as well as servants of God. One pious student feared for his friend who had made the decision to choose the world—and hell. Experiences varied, but most students and townspeople agreed that a revival certainly created a renewed sense of order in the town and in the college.[58]

A post-revival college town seemed "very much changed." "You would hardly know Lexington," one trustee's daughter informed a cousin, "it has altered so much." The recent revival had, she thought, re-regulated the college's direction, and it now "promises to be a delightful place after while." A South Carolinian visiting post-revival Athens also noted the "delightful" aspect of Waddel's "college village" with its blend of moral and intellectual order on visual display. He saw this order in the college chapel, where he heard the "oration of the students" constantly invoking "reverence" for biblical authority. He heard it in the speeches of two invited alumni—a judge and a senator who spoke in a "perspicuous and nervous style," a contrast to the empty, dry speeches he had heard from other public men. It was also on display among the young people of Athens, as on the evening of commencement when he was amazed to see a "crowded church" and a "deserted ball room."[59]

Attending the same commencement festivities, a young woman from Augusta took a dimmer view of the recent renovations in Athens. The "public ball," she complained to her brother, was "miserable beyond description" because of its lack of ladies. Athenians had informed her that the ball had once been "very crowded," but now, she scoffed, "the young girls think it absolutely wicked to be found at such a place." She objected to this extreme social practice and found it both annoying and intriguing. "With moderation," she mused, "what can be more innocent than a little dancing?"[60]

Whether they agreed with the new order or not, visitors were always impressed with the "miniature world" in action in college towns. Because of the collective efforts of families like the Waddels, the new colleges had themselves become "objects of interest," offering a peculiar environment stubbornly dedicated to unifying divisiveness and calling for collective, rather than individual, endeavor in the name of a distinct definition of virtue. The Waddels and their colleagues across the republic helped ensure that their world made a "grand and solemn" impression on a "fleeting" people. Some of these people, and their children, sought to spend at least some time in this college world, interested in pondering the problem of virtuous design before moving on to design their own future.

Working in the College World

"Ease and Alternate Labor"

BY THE LATE 1830s, Louisa Payson was a busy young woman, her life full of the reading, writing, debating, and teaching that characterized the work of the growing college world. Her father, Edward Payson, had been a famous revivalist preacher in Portland, Maine. As a trustee of Bowdoin College, he had assisted in its early promotion and trained many of its graduates in divinity. He had also trained his eldest daughter in the classical languages and subjects of the college world. By the age of sixteen, after her father's sudden death, Louisa had published a popular novel, *The Pastor's Daughter,* based on this education by her father. Having found "remunerative" success, Louisa, the eldest of five, supported her family with her writing, submitting stories and book reviews to various periodicals. By the 1830s she was also a seasoned instructor, having taught at female academies in New York City and then Portland, which also added to the family finances.[1]

Louisa Payson was a well-read, precocious young woman who excelled at reading, writing, and philosophical debate. She longed to labor permanently in the world of ideas, preferring to mingle with people who enjoyed what she called "the active spark of mind upon mind" by discussing "subjects I love most to talk about"—"books, authors, the laws of mind and spirit." When she read favorite writers like Goethe, Lessing, Coleridge, and Wordsworth, she felt "admiration, reverence, and affection" for these "men of genius." She also felt a puzzling "painful excitement" that she identified as a yearning to cultivate such genius in her own mind. As she noted in her literary journal, "Next to possessing genius myself would be the pleasure of living with one who possessed it." By the late 1830s, as she entered her thirties, Louisa determined to pursue genius at all costs.[2]

This determination did not seem natural or healthy in a woman. Watching the trees outside her window one day, Louisa wondered if she could ever emulate their "eloquent" yet "silent" image, the paradoxical ideal of womanhood that was modeled by her mother and the many respectable married ladies the family knew in Portland. In her opinion, these women spent most of their mental energy learning how to "wave and bloom for others." Even though since the death of her father much of her labor had been for the benefit of her family, she could not imagine herself leading that life forever. Additionally, since her "bump of combativeness" during debate was legendary among her friends, living in silence would be impossible. Louisa often pined to live in "the light of another world" in which she could explore intellectual ideas without such feelings of unease.[3]

When Louisa met Albert Hopkins of Williams College, of Williamstown, Massachusetts, in a Boston parlor in the summer of 1840, she was shocked to find a man who had not only read her book but encouraged her to produce more. As they chatted, the science professor let her know that he admired her attempt to explore her mental powers through literary means. At Williams he had been investigating his own powers though scientific experimentation. They came to an understanding, and Albert wrote to his mother that he had discovered an additional college lady for Williams, a woman "whom I love so much and who I think is so worthy of my warmest affections." Albert was quick to note, however, that "my dear L" was also a published author. As he justified his choice of a wife to his mother, he was also preparing to justify it to his colleagues at Williamstown. Louisa's ability to produce intellectual work would be as valued in the college world as her personality. Indeed, the word had spread about Albert's matrimonial plan. He had heard already that "everybody" at Williams was "enquiring" whether he had read her book. He had, and he urged his mother to find a copy. All of the college families at Williamstown were "eager to see it for the purpose of finding something about her character."[4]

As for Louisa's character, Albert believed that she had the "aptitude" and "the education" to "fill an important niche in connection with an institution like ours." As he later remembered, Louisa was a "lady of refinement and cultivated taste" who had great "expectations on coming to Williamstown." She "expected much" from the "society of literary persons connected with the college" and hoped, "by associating with students, to do something for them." With her religious, educational, and literary pedigree, Louisa Payson promised to be an ideal addition to the growing Williams College family. Her combination of affection and intellectual production would contribute much to their world's new kind of labor—"college work."[5]

The early republic was emerging from an agrarian labor system in which the image of the independent yeoman farmer and his industrious helpmeet had set the cultural standard for measuring the value of labor. The new "brain-workers" of the college world were professional pioneers who explored a different way to measure the new kinds of work and the new workers who were appearing in the early American economy. Professors and their families were the first class of worker to live on the proceeds of moral and intellectual activity. They were determined to survive in genteel fashion while pursuing genius. In their estimation, this made them a little different, and a bit more elevated, than the striving middle-class families who increasingly sent their children into the college world for instruction in attaining virtuous success.[6]

The possibility of cultivating genius was a popular topic of discussion among college families because if a college family should produce such a genius—like Parker Cleaveland and his mineralogical talents—then the entire college world would benefit as there would be economic rewards for all. In their collective attempts to harness mental power in the service of such prosperity, college families discovered an exciting world of pleasure in their work. They would also discover a world of pain and unease.

Historians have traced how the expanding cash nexus of market capitalism forged a social ideal that privileged the production of white male "breadwinners" over the productive capacities of women in middle-class families. Women's housework was unwaged and therefore invisible to the emerging market forces. A "cult of domesticity" increasingly turned the "business of housekeeping" into a form of leisure. For men in the college world, like Professor Albert Hopkins, much of their everyday work was just as invisible to the market—and to their own eyes. Establishing a solidly middle-class masculine identity through "college work" proved a worrisome, unnatural, even unmanning experience. If men relied only on their mental powers, what would happen to the strength of their bodies? Professors' diaries are full of this chief worry—a yearning for a reconnection with nature and muscular power. Their need to see and evaluate the products of their "college work" shaped their professional lives and the very institutions they were building. For college ladies, like Louisa Payson, engaging in "college work" demanded that the female mind figure out how to blend the traditional "business of housekeeping" with the new "business of instruction." This was a lot of work to perform. Perhaps too much. College ladies had the assurance, however, that their new world had urgent need of both their minds and their bodies.[7]

By the early nineteenth century, manual labor was defined as profitable work performed in fields or workshops by virtuous yeomen. The power of muscle to effect change provided the standard for the value of production. With the rise of a new political and economic order after the Revolution, Americans also saw the emergence of a less-muscular power that could also yield profits. Creating medical cures, structuring legal arguments, amassing commercial acumen, the management of workers (free or unfree), and literary publication could also be profitable. Yet, could any of these innovations be defined as the true, virtuous work of the yeoman? The value of the profits achieved through moral and intellectual labor, in a college community especially, remained a mystery to be solved by the new republic.[8]

What did this new college world produce? Ideas, students, books, civil society, a new class of leisured aristocrats? In the early nineteenth century, Americans eagerly assigned value to all kinds of new commodities, but evaluating the products of the college world proved just as frustrating to the new "brain-workers" laboring within it as those puzzled observers working outside of it.

Academic labor had always been a target of intense curiosity—and skepticism. In 1803, a *Port-Folio* satirist took his readers on a guided tour of a "great college of arts and sciences" that he called "Abracadabra Square." He pointed out its professors—"philosophical adventurers" pursuing impossible projects, like digging to the center of the earth or traveling as ambassadors to Plato's *Republic* or Moore's *Utopia*. Readers were guided past madmen who stared at the sun "through telescopes." They passed "rows of rebus-makers" and "conundrum parties" laboring to find the exact definition of the soul or making puns "upon every word of the Old and New Testament." The "tour" ended at a ceremony in which "a very showy gingerbread medal" was presented to the graduates of this odd world. Such was the value placed on scholarly activity in 1803. As more young men streamed through the expanding college world in later years, paying tuition and receiving diplomas, the exact profit to be made on their higher education continued to mystify Americans. This mystery, however, never stopped socially enterprising, economically striving families from sending their children to college, eager to cash in on college families' promises of virtuous prosperity and patronage.[9]

To many, college families did not teach the next generation of leaders how to cultivate the "common good." Rather, critics argued that there was absolutely nothing virtuous about the college world. The Revolutionary War veteran and "Labourer" William Manning famously condemned the new "orders" of men coming out of Harvard, who "associate together and look down with too much contempt on those that labour." Why is it, Manning wondered, that these "few are always crying up the advantage of costly colleges, national academies & grammar schools" that barred many young men, and produced a "numerous and needless set of youth" who were being taught how "to live without labor"? For many observers, the college world merely produced a new class of aristocrats who disdained the virtue of "bodily labors" and expected to live off the efforts of the truly virtuous: yeoman farmers and artisans. For many critics of colleges, a classical education produced more vice than virtue for the republic.[10]

The virtuous yeoman farmer, tilling his own field and profiting directly from his own manual labor, remained the template for ideal masculinity in the early republic. This iconic yeoman always had an accompanying wife who represented ideal femininity for the new republic, a woman who shrewdly kept the home free from debt and dependency. If this was the standard of gendered production that created success and security for the future, many asked, what was the worth of a professor who actively tried to work without "bodily labors"? Was his wife—managing a home and family based on the speculation of genius—truly a model for American women to emulate? Or were they "new creatures" entirely, as college families argued—an ideal new class whose productive powers needed to be measured along a different scale of value. Only when the emerging market world began placing a correct value on the college world and its workers, asserted college families, would the republic ever realize the worth of true virtue—a commodity that was, indeed, priceless.

As a published writer, Louisa Payson knew her precise value in the market world, and she was uneasy with this knowledge. The commercial market eagerly demanded the fiction of women writers, and Louisa supplied periodicals with stories and book reviews. In her home in Portland she often felt the "pressure of obligation to write something," and it made her "morbid and anxious." Everyone in her family, supported by her writing, had an opinion about what might gain her more money. Her mother wanted her to produce "children's books." Her sister thought a "book of Natural Philosophy for schools" would be more lucrative. Louisa herself wanted to write about German metaphysics. Stopping in her magazine writing one day to translate some German, she pondered the worth of her labor. To her, the translation was priceless, a piece that opened a door to a whole new transcendent world of thought. When she estimated it at market value, however, her conclusion was that it "looks so little." It would "get a few dollars," which would "buy bread and butter" for her family, and that would be "the end of it."[11]

While writing for the market was not satisfying, editing was even worse. Fascinated by Schleiermacher and his "evolution of the idea of God," because it "recalls some thoughts which I had on this subject," Louisa hoped to write about this connection. She was too "hurried," however, having promised to take over the editing of a friend's periodical in Boston for a few weeks. Instead of writing philosophy, Louisa spent "half my time looking over newspapers" and popular books, making "selections" for excerpts and reviews to fill up magazine columns. All of this paid labor turned out to be "most wearisome and profitless" to Louisa. She valued her German philosophy more, and concluded that she "would not edit a paper for the world" ever again, nor did she want to continue writing if the world continued to demand such trivial, superficial products from her.[12]

After mastering the classical languages, Louisa had moved quickly into the intellectual currents of the 1830s, learning "modern languages" like French and German and exploring the literature of European romanticism. In these new works she was "beginning to see dimly some new truths— such I believe them to be—in theology," and she wanted to explore them. The economic necessities of her family, however, kept her producing for a literary market that would have provided little cash for a scholarly discourse on German authors, especially one written by a woman.[13]

Like Louisa Payson, Margaret Junkin was also a young, busy writer struggling with the demands of the literary market. As the daughter of a president of Washington College, she also possessed classical knowledge. As one of the characters in her first, semi-autobiographical novel, *Silverwood*, noted, she hoped to "put into marketable form some of the results of former days of study." Junkin wanted to write poems based on her classical scholarship, but was disappointed that such "poetry would bring her no money." It was that "pretty flowery, ferny kind of literature" produced by

Margaret Junkin Preston. A college president's daughter and professor's wife, Preston was one of many "college ladies" deeply committed to the maintenance and promotion of the expanding college world.

Courtesy of Special Collections Department, Leyburn Library, Washington and Lee University; photograph by Michael Miley, ca. 1880s.

the "sisterhood of wood-nymphs" that made the real cash, she observed. Junkin disdained such work. There would be no hiding behind flowery pen names for most "college ladies." Both Payson and Junkin admired women who were like themselves, unafraid to exhibit their learning and to use their real names in their publications, as they were to do during most of their careers.[14]

Elizabeth Barrett Browning was a popular heroine in the college world among college ladies since she was a woman who demonstrated deep classical scholarship alongside what was viewed as a distinct "feminine" understanding. Like the world they were involved in building, college ladies believed that their minds were equal to those of their male counterparts in learning, but different in understanding and activity. When Margaret Junkin reviewed Browning's work, she praised "the learning, of which her pages furnish unmistakable proof." In her verses Browning had a "perfect naturalness of her ever-ready classic and scholarly illusions and illustrations" that "compel a respect which the masculine sex is slow to yield, except as a matter of chivalry, to one of the opposite sex." The fact that Browning disobeyed her father, eloped with her lover, and lived in exile in Italy was scandalous, but it also proved the lengths to which a true woman would go in the pursuit of genius. Browning was producing serious works of genius, so endangering her respectability was, for many of her female admirers, worth the effort. Much had to be sacrificed to pursue the "truth" demanded by the pursuit of genius. For Margaret Junkin, Browning's work was a contrast to the "everlasting twaddle" of the majority of women writers, who were just as intelligent and well read but, she suspected, hid their learning under the flowers and ferns of popular literature. Browning never hid her learning. In fact, it was so remarkable that men were unable to ignore it. Like Louisa Payson with her Schleiermacher, Margaret Junkin continued to write her classically themed poetry and stories, all the while calling out to literary women to demonstrate more seriousness in their roles as thinkers and writers.[15]

Louisa Payson referred to her periodical writing as "scattered knowledge" or "trash." She and her Portland friends often debated the practice of "writing, its pecuniary profitableness, subjects for it." When one friend jokingly "wished I would take some other topics besides German authors" to review, Louisa announced that the "alternative" would be "metaphysics." Her friend laughed and "retracted the wish." In spite of such friendly advice and family demands, Payson forged on, carving out valuable time to explore topics that gave her much pleasure but little commercial profit. She worried over her tendency for what she called "literary self-indulgence," and she constantly looked for a position where she could indulge her passion for scholarship through more selfless goals.[16]

In her journal, Louisa voiced a theme that regularly appeared in all of her writings, private and public: "I wish I knew what I was made for—I mean, in particular—what I can do, and what I ought to do. . . . I do want to be of some use in the world, but I am infinitely perplexed as to the how and the what." She desired to become an effective "instrument" that would "leave an impress on other minds." She wanted, as did so many other intellectual women of the era, a "vocation."[17]

Louisa struggled with the idea that she had no ideal place in which to exert her intellectual powers. Observing her brothers and the many Bowdoin students who visited her home in Portland, she wanted their wide range of professional choices. "How I envy the other sex!" she wrote in her journal. "They have certain fixed paths marked out for them—regular professions and trades—between which they may make a choice, and know what they have to do." She was often struck by the confidence, even arrogance, of some of these visiting students who had, in her opinion, such simple choices to make and such an easy path to follow. One young gentleman informed her that her preoccupation with metaphysics rather than marriage disturbed him. As she recalled later in her journal, he "tried last night to convince me that they are the result of physical derangement" and not the "expression of a sane mind in a sound body." She "laughed at him" that evening, but brooded later, in her diary, over the "suspicion that he was right."[18]

Payson's more well-known contemporaries—Catherine Beecher, Margaret Fuller, and Elizabeth Peabody—had all followed her route through the classical curriculum and into the wider literary world of "modern" foreign languages and philosophy. As women with intellectual aspirations, they had all pursued their studies with the same blend of enthusiasm and "despondency," and had all experienced the same brand of criticism from men who doubted their intellectual abilities and their sanity. All had pioneered ways to seek out ideal positions in society from which to exert their intellectual powers. Fuller eventually left the country to find her future as a journalist in Europe; Beecher turned to teaching, academy-building, and teacher recruitment; and Peabody promoted a range of radical transcendental causes and educational theories. Louisa Payson followed another common route for intellectual women of the nineteenth century: committing, through marriage, to a life of moral and intellectual labor in the college world.[19]

Engaged to a professor and anticipating her new life at Williams College, Louisa found herself "forming new purposes and plans for the future." Her brothers would soon head to Bowdoin for their education, since the sons of a former trustee traditionally received their education free. Louisa had educated her younger sister, who was now working in a Virginia academy and assisting the family. She at last felt free to leave home. She also felt free to draw up an intellectual plan "of more vigorous effort and more persevering self-culture than any previous season of my life." Her reading list of German and philosophical works grew. Working through the *Aeneid* again with a Portland girlfriend, she brushed up on her Latin. Upon arriving at Williams, Louisa expected to undertake work that would allow her to use her knowledge of such classical texts. Familiar with the Bowdoin College families, she knew she would not only be a wife, but a member of a community in need of her help, both mental and manual. She had to be prepared. "In the universe everything may be had for a price," this busy writer who longed to be a scholar reminded herself. "But nothing can be had without price." The price of "self-culture" was "unremitted toil, labor, and self-denial." Was she "willing to pay it"? She resolved that she was and dedicated herself to seeking the "Spirit of all Truth"—an apt subject for someone in pursuit of genius.[20]

Visiting friends in Boston before her marriage, Louisa took in a series of lectures by a young Harvard graduate named Ralph Waldo Emerson who was exploring the idea of genius, like herself. The intellectual goal that a genius pursued, Emerson explained, was "Truth." This goal was not the "truth of facts, of figures, dates, measures—which is a poor, low, sensual truth." Louisa would have recognized this low version of "truth" as the one she encountered whenever she engaged with the demands and remuneration of the literary market. According to Emerson, a genius pursues "ideal truth." This form of truth could be found anywhere—"in a temple, a song, an argument, a steamboat," or a "Copernican system of astronomy." The key to its possession was that the genius-scholar had to look deeply into a subject and find the true meaning behind it. Louisa hoped to explore such "ideal truth" at Williams College. There was "no halfness about genius," warned Emerson, and anyone pursuing it might be considered "mad" for trying to transcend common sense and "utter things for their own worthiness because they must be said." Louisa would have agreed with this point. Her family and friends regularly laughed at her senseless pursuit of unprofitable metaphysics when there was a fortune to be made on other topics for the literary market. While "common sense stops at a fact," Emerson observed, a genius will move "behind it" to a deeper understanding. The "work of genius" was a "species of worship of the supreme Being," and he believed there was a "perfect analogy" between "virtue and genius"—a partnership of "ethical" and "intellectual creation." Attending this lecture before her marriage, Louisa added Emerson's ideas to her own, pondering about the kind of partnership she was about to make—with Albert, with Williams College, and with "ideal truth."[21]

While nineteenth-century women intent on pursuing a life of the mind were just beginning to imagine a place for themselves as intellectuals, academic men faced the task of figuring out how to be "breadwinning" intellectuals. Could a man actually achieve the emotional and economic success of that iconic yeoman with only the power of his mind? Albert Hopkins would have disputed Louisa's breezy estimation of the ease with which college graduates discovered their "vocation." They certainly received encouragement from their families in choosing a profession, yet this support was often a form of pressure that made many young men doubt their capacity to work—and be men.

The postgraduate journeys of Albert Hopkins and his two brothers provide a glimpse into the route that many college graduates took as they sought to become professionals—men who relied upon their brain power rather than manual labor to earn a living. Many of the first generation of American professors had been raised as the sons of farmers, artisans, or shopkeepers. Albert and his two brothers were no exception. They had spent their youth working on their father's farm in Stockbridge, Massachusetts. Their mother's hopes had centered on the boys acquiring a college education and leaving the farm for a profession. In their letters home as young men, it was "Ma" Hopkins who was always urging them toward professional occupations, while their father lobbied them to stay and support the farm. In the 1820s and 1830s there was an overwhelming choice of occupations and professions for young men to pursue, whether they possessed a college degree or not. The Hopkins boys seem to have tried them all.[22]

After interrupting his education a number of times to raise funds for his tuition by teaching school in Virginia, Albert Hopkins's eldest brother Mark finally graduated from Williams College in 1824. When an assistant teaching position opened up at Williams the following year, Mark accepted an offer from the trustees to return as a tutor, but he continued to seek a future away from Williams College. Having decided to become a doctor, he attended medical lectures in New York City and Pittsfield, Massachusetts. While in New York, he taught at a female academy with fellow

Williams College graduates and mingled with other college men in one of the city's literary clubs. His new club friends urged him to publish some essays on the subject he most loved—metaphysics. He knew, however, that there was no lucrative future in philosophizing, and so continued with his medical studies. After receiving his medical degree in 1829, Mark practiced as a doctor in New York City, but was soon unhappy with his profession. Moreover, he was not able to survive economically in New York, send money home to help out his parents, and help fund the travels of his two brothers as they each sought their future. He also still yearned to explore metaphysics. Returning to Massachusetts to try opening a practice closer to home, he also began studying theology.[23]

Second brother Harry never finished college, an eye ailment forcing him to leave Williams College early. Harry remained on the farm, his aging parents increasingly dependent upon his labor. During winters, he searched for a future off the farm. Artistically gifted, he tried studying art in New York. He also worked at mining in Pennsylvania and even tried being an overseer on a Southern plantation. Much to his chagrin, these occupations never panned out and dwindling finances always forced him back to Stockbridge, where he resumed helping his father in the fields. Still, whenever there was cash available from his brothers, he would regularly follow their mother's advice and make another attempt to escape the life of a farmer.

Albert Hopkins, the youngest brother, graduated from Williams in 1826. His postgraduate meanderings involved studying engineering at Albany, teaching school, working on mechanical inventions with Harry that they both hoped might yield lucrative patents, and helping his old science professor at Williams carry out a state geological survey. Albert was notorious in his family for his many "schemes," and most of these plans involved constant travel far away from western Massachusetts. He talked of practicing law in Cincinnati, teaching school "at the West," or traveling to Greece as a missionary. As he informed Harry, he did not believe in "staying in the chimney corner" any more than Harry did. He told Harry, "When a man once starts he may as well go somewhere as to make a fool of it," adding, "You know I've a disposition to see the world." This did not sound like a good future plan to "Ma" Hopkins. With Mark settled as a doctor, and Harry settled, however reluctantly, on the farm, "Ma" Hopkins continued to worry about the odd wanderlust of her youngest son.[24]

Even a sudden religious conversion at the hands of a Finneyite minis-

ter on a trip through upstate New York did not settle Albert. He began a
term of itinerant preaching, his Congregationalist family surprised at his
enthusiasm for highly emotional preaching. His brothers were shocked at
the change in his personality after his conversion. Mark, studying to be a
minister himself, marveled to Harry: "He confesses that his salvation is all
of God—and can scarcely speak of God's mercy, without tears. Is he mis-
taken or not?"[25]

A letter from the trustees of Williams College in 1827 finally solved the
family problem of Albert's future. In need of another teaching assistant,
the trustees turned as usual to their roster of recent graduates. Albert's
continuing friendship with his science professor, his interest in engineering, and his conversion (with its confirmation of "moral regularity") all
contributed to this offer of a tutorship. To Albert, the job offer was more
of a scare than a success. As he told his brother Mark, who had worked as
a tutor in the past, he was worried. As a tutor, the other professors would
expect him to be "superior to his class in everything which regards knowledge." He was unsure that he had that much authority—or that he even
wanted it. If he accepted the position, he felt it would be a test of both
his intellectual and masculine identity: he wanted to be "lookd up to" and
"respected" by students and professors, "not merely as a Tutor but as a
Man." Albert linked his recent call to God and his call back to Williams
College as part of some divine plan, but he did not obey either of these
providential orders easily. Indeed, his teary religious conversion, and now
his prospect of a job at Williams, seemed to unman him in such a way that
he would spend much of his professional future exploring his manhood
and creating new standards by which to test it.[26] Evidently, Albert was a
successful tutor in the eyes of the William College families. When his old
science professor retired in 1829, the trustees offered him a professorship
in mathematics and natural philosophy. He had worked successfully as a
teaching assistant, both supervising students and living alongside them in
their dormitory. He had proved to himself that he was capable of the job.
Albert accepted the post, since no other "scheme" had panned out and
his regular salary would support him, help with the family farm, and also
allow him to reciprocate in the family strategy of financially supporting
brotherly endeavors to explore various professions.

In 1830 the Williams trustees invited brother Mark back to the college
as well, to be its professor of moral philosophy. Mark now abandoned medicine for metaphysics. While he had already tried out one profession and

knew it was not his "vocation," he was just as uneasy as Albert had been about a return to Williams. Albert's professional time at Williams College in his salaried position had involved much work, but none of the labor felt profitable to him. Mark would grow to feel the same way as he entered into his teaching duties. Both men initially saw their positions at Williams as temporary, and were always on the lookout for a chance to leave and "see the world." Yet, in the end, the prospect of a regular salary and the intellectual status associated with college teaching proved too tempting. Still, even as Mark and Albert got more comfortable with the idea of being in the new "business of instruction," they soon discovered that there would be unforeseen costs involved—to themselves and to their family.

Since many members of the Hopkins family felt that higher education was the route to success, the move of both Mark and Albert to Williams College sparked letters from extended family members full of congratulation and envy. With Mark "teaching the young idea to shoot" and Albert "talking big of Triangles & conic vections," an uncle congratulated their mother on having raised and given direction to such successful offspring. Harry, however, was never praised as a success in family letters. In fact, he was often portrayed as a boy rather than a man, the brother bereft of higher knowledge and responsibility. According to their uncle, Harry was a "real professional farmer" who spent his time "fiddling some & laughing some." In reality, Harry was the one who actually performed most of the labor on the farm owned by his aging parents.[27]

Harry certainly resented this relegation to eternal boyhood, but he was never above using it to tweak his rising, professionalizing brothers. Agreeing that farmers were a "shiftless set," Harry nevertheless loved to remind his brothers that agricultural labor was still needed. It was farmers, after all, who supplied the new lazy professional classes with nourishment. "Rich men must be fed," he taunted his brothers, because "it takes all kinds to make a world." He also constantly described the dire economic state of the family farm, reminding his brothers of their wealthier status and of their obligations to their parents. As a "shiftless" famer, Harry instructed them, he would never be able to carry on the "family name" like they would. His letters praised the brothers as "rich men" who did not have to work—an observation that Mark and Albert vehemently disputed. They did labor at Williams College—and both argued constantly with Harry that they worked hard. They just could not figure out how to explain this new "college work"—to Harry or to themselves.[28]

Albert and Mark were not unusual in this inability to describe their work. In their attempts to evaluate their productivity, new professors measured their effort by the traditional standards of manual labor: muscular force. Measured in this way, their "college work" felt unsatisfying and worrisome. Mark tried to explain to Harry his frustrations with his new job lecturing to students on moral philosophy and rhetoric while supervising their lives. He "had to work in a rather different style" than when he was "lazying away" with Harry on the farm. He tried to explain how he felt about his new work culture: "There is a great deal of difference between being busy and working—the most of my life I have only been busy." At Williams, teaching metaphysics, Mark hoped to finally carry out some real work. He looked forward to reading and writing about his favorite topics, making a strong impression on the world of metaphysics with the power of his thoughts. Unfortunately, his new job kept his body "a good deal confined" in his office and his classroom. He had little time to do any deep reading, much less writing. He also felt increasingly weak and overwhelmed at the end of the day.[29]

Albert was afflicted with the same problems. He assured Harry that his "labours this term" in his science classes "will be pretty arduous." Along with his teaching, however, he had added new "schemes." He reported that he was drafting some articles about electricity and magnetism, new scientific topics that fascinated him. The articles, however, turned out to be "meager things." Why? Because he was always being interrupted by having to hear student "recitations in Astronomy and fluxions," plan a new class about optics, and deal with various discipline problems in the dormitory where he lived alongside students. They "all kept at me," he complained to Harry. He could never write anything about these new subjects with any sense of satisfying completion.[30]

The diaries of early professors in the college world are filled with the number of study-hours logged, the number of books read, the number of lectures worked on, and the class-hours taught, as well as complaints about the hours spent "wasted" or "distracted" by reading newspapers and novels, shopping, dealing with creditors, negotiating household disputes, socializing, and "tea-ing" with other college families.

Professor Isaac Jackson, Albert Hopkins's mathematical colleague at Union College in nearby Schenectady, New York, shared his same career path. A Union graduate in 1826, he had moved, via trustee invitation, into a Union tutorship and then full professorship of mathematics and natural philosophy. Isaac also shared the Hopkins's work woes. Along with his teaching, student supervision, and daily chores like fetching barrels of pork from town or "hanging the doorbell" on his house on campus, he attempted to work on a treatise about optics, a topic that had sparked his passion. His diary is full of disappointment over his productive capabilities in regard to this textbook. He recorded every hour in his diary, trying to figure out exactly what he had done all day and why he could not find time to work on "Optics." Most of his entries involved complaints like "In no good humor all day—this evening in a positively bad one—why? Because I see no end to the engrossement of my time by paltry little matters."[31]

Professors were obsessed with this self-accounting and self-evaluation, constantly searching for ways to organize their day into blocks of satisfying labor—work that did not just produce "meager things." This obsession with time replicated the strategies of many middle-class diarists eager to keep a record of their daily thoughts, activities, and expenditures. Yet professors kept diaries to evaluate the productivity of their own peculiar, new "college work," searching constantly for any moments that might reveal the mental power, or "will" as some called it, to transcend the real world of "paltry little matters" and perform, to their minds, satisfying labor. They imagined such satisfying labor as involving deep, sustained, uninterrupted thought—the pursuit of genius. In their diaries professors searched constantly throughout their daily activities for signs of success and failure. Did their minds or activities hold any evidence of the power of genius? The success of their college families, their own personal families, and their own sense of manhood depended on a positive answer to that question.

Professor John McClintock, the son of a Philadelphia shopkeeper and a new professor of Greek and Latin at Dickinson College, recorded his constant search in his 1841 diary for time to work on a classical textbook and literary articles for the *Methodist Quarterly*. His ability to work on these texts—to make an impact on society with his thoughts—suffered because of the "constant occupation of my time." Like his fellow Dickinson College peers, he spent much of his time at the end of the school year in the "preparation of exams, examinations," and helping to evaluate seniors ready to graduate. He was also busy as the college secretary, "arranging the business of the year, writing up Journal of the Trustees &c." All of these activities, he admitted, formed a "part of my reason for not writing."[32]

Yet there was also a more worrisome reason for his inability to write. Perhaps it was not "college work" that distracted him from his writing, but a weakness in his mind. Perhaps he did not have the "inclination" or enough mental force to pursue genius. If he did, he worried in his diary, the "*will* could soon have found the *way*" to transcend "college work" and focus on pursuing genius. This "will" was a matter of concern for many professors who felt, and taught, that refining and directing one's mental power was the key to economic and emotional success. If they could not figure out a way to avoid distraction and incline their "will" toward pursuing genius, they would fail their new college world as workers and, according to McClintock, they would fail as men. "Wonder when I shall have manliness enough to be above these fluctuations of spirit," he confided in his diary, depressed once again at the end of the day to discover that he had let the world distract him from the world of ideas.[33]

Harry Hopkins was never impressed with these problems over "college work." He countered his brothers' complaints with descriptions of the farm work he performed: "getting in corn" in a rainstorm, spending the whole day cider pressing, driving sheep to market, or stopping the haying to pull oxen out of the mud. He felt "*dead* with hard work"—a feeling, he believed, his brothers never felt at Williams. Writing after a particularly "back-aching evening," Harry thought his brothers needed some "deep & sage remarks" on the "condition & destiny of man as arising from occupations." After an entire day of herding his sheep to market and selling them at a disappointingly low price, he concluded that "a farmer is a mere crowbar in the hands of professional men, a mere fulcrum on which they & the merchants raise their edifices of ease & luxury."[34]

Harry's observations contained uncomfortable truths about their new life and work for his brothers, and they immediately answered him, employing the usual nineteenth-century response to uncomfortable change: romantic imagery. Mark and Albert were fond of portraying their brother as Pan-like, a free creature of nature who had luckily escaped the restraints they felt. Unencumbered by new professional demands and still working in the earth, Harry was, in their minds, the real success story in the family. They may have possessed regular salaries, but Harry had the more regular life.

To Mark and Albert, Harry actually represented the true man. As the last brother left in nature, Harry was always viewed as the most adept "ladies man" of the trio. Known to fiddle, sing, and flirt with ease at country dances, he made impressive conquests in love. He taunted his brothers that their long terms of teaching kept them away from the "young ladies" in Stockbridge, who made "constant inquiry after the Profrs." If something "decisive" was not done with these young ladies, Harry suggested, he would assume the "frigid zone has descended below your heart & left no heat in anything but your legs." In a joking letter of response, Mark tended to agree with his brother. Their chosen paths at Williams, and the college world's demand for moral and intellectual regularity, had certainly transformed their virility. As a science professor, Albert "holds a straightforward staunch course, studies philosophy and mathematics and minds nothing about the ladies." As a moral philosopher, Mark sent Harry a quote by Edmund Burke that characterized his situation as a professor: "To love, and to be wise at the same time, says Burke, is not given to mortals." Mark explained to Harry: "As my station requires me to be constantly wise, I do not know when I can find time for the other."[35]

Albert was fond of imagining Harry "walking round there in 'the land of your Beulah' amidst the singing of the birds and the cooing of the turtle." In contrast to the masculine force and fertility of Harry's world of work, Albert's life at Williams seemed full of bodily and mental weakness. "This is the seed time of the year," Albert joked to Harry in April as he watched the "breaking up of winter." "Sow good seed." Sitting in his office at Williams, Albert worried about the power of his own seed—and the weakening of his body. His letters home were always full of pining for his youthful days in the fields alongside neighboring farmers, "wielding the scythe and the cradle." In contrast to his "college work" at Williams, farming at Stockbridge seemed easier to comprehend and discuss. After a full year of "college work," Albert wrote to Harry that he could "boast of but few acts of prowess this season." By the early 1830s, Albert had begun digging a vegetable garden on campus, anxious to feel the earth and to feel like he was really working.[36]

With the numbers of college-educated men increasing throughout the 1830s and 1840s, the nation was full of critics who condemned the college world's weakening influence on the nation's youth. Although the Hopkins men were Whigs, Harry Hopkins easily wielded the class rhetoric of the Jacksonian Democrats to tweak his brothers about their new life of "ease and luxury." In contrast to his virtuous farming self, he always portrayed Mark and Albert as "rich men" living off farmers. They knew lots of definitions up there at Williams College, Harry joked in his letters, but none of that "college set" knew the meaning of real work. At Williams, in 1832, Mark watched as another such skeptic, an "old long bearded Slouchhatted fellow that lives on some of the hills," strolled by campus with some fellow farmers. The men all stopped to watch Albert, who was "digging away with his coat and hat off and his sleeves rolled up" in his new vegetable garden, surprised at this show of physical exertion by a professor. As Mark listened nearby, the men commented aloud to each other that Albert "acts like a man . . . a rugged man." They watched approvingly as he sweated, one of them hoping that "heaven will bless him with a crop." With the comment "There's an example for you," the farmers sauntered off, leaving the Hopkins brothers to ponder again the connection between manual labor, masculinity and the true measure of virtue. By the 1830s, the men of the college world had a new task to add to their list of duties. They had to prove their worth to the hard-working republic while trying to address their own private worries about productivity.[37]

To Albert and Mark, the mental and physical feelings they felt after a workday at Williams were different from those felt by their "rugged" brother Harry in the fields. After moving to Williams to teach, Albert always complained about "sore eyes," and Mark's chronic complaints of nerve weakness or "highpo" worried his family. As Mark informed Harry, "The only thing that wears on you is what applies directly to the bone and muscle." What wore on Mark was something more mysterious: "If I had at all times health and firm nerves, I should not care, but at times it is irksome." The new "college work" led to an odd weakening of many college-family members in body and mind. This new affliction of the college world commonly began with eye pain and headaches and a general weakness that spread throughout the body, targeting muscles and "nerves." The brain was the last to go. Insanity was the last stage of this mysterious disorder, a fearful problem for those who toiled in a new world that depended on mental agility. College families tended to call this weakened state "the blues" or "neuralgia." Its victims complained of feeling "confined," trapped, or overwhelmed. Others were anxious, confused, and unable to define what was wrong with them. Because they felt unnatural, college families often opted to seek out a natural cure.[38]

Professor James Waddel of Franklin College in Athens, Georgia, dutifully recorded his daily round of work: classes in Latin and Greek, family tensions, student-discipline decisions, and household-debt negotiations. Along with this full calendar, he tried to read literature, hoping to write a work himself, or at least produce reviews for a periodical. He never got around to writing, and was often "troubled with much neuralgia." One morning during the usual opening prayers and announcements that started the college day, he suddenly left the campus to "retire to the Forest." He was "feeling very much out of order all day." His escape was a typical attempt by male faculty to connect with natural forces—forces from which they felt increasingly alienated as they carried out their "college work."[39]

In one letter to his mother, Mark Hopkins sounded happier than his students about an upcoming vacation: "I shall be glad when the term closes, for if I go on in this way there is no knowing what would happen." He described himself as so weak that a "wind" might blow him away. It was no surprise that the college town that was satirized in the 1803 *Port-Folio* article was situated next to a hospital for invalids (or *malades imaginaire*). The tour guide in the article pointed out the "gentlemen" there, who reclined on beds with their legs "converted into glass bottles," as they had experienced "general vitrification." Men like the Hopkins brothers and their colleagues, who moved within their lifetimes from relying on manual labor to depending on mental labor, worried that the overuse of their brains, like the overuse of muscles, would "rust" them out. College families studied the problems involved in mental work, searching constantly for ways to find a sense of balance, regain the sensation of muscular effort, and make "college work" feel more natural and productive.[40]

Down in Georgia, James Waddel regularly tried to cure his "neuralgia" by devoting part of his time to planting trees and creating a series of walkways on the campus at Franklin College. While it was slaves who commonly performed the heavy manual labor on Southern campuses, Waddel did such work himself whenever he felt depressed or "melancholy." On a day when he had worked alongside Alfred, a hired college slave, Waddel observed in his diary that he had "worked like a trooper" and that after a day of such work he could "feel it now." One wondered what Alfred felt, laboring the whole day alongside his white employer in the garden.[41]

In his need to "feel" the impact of a day of manual labor, James Waddel reveals what many men in the college world feared—that their new world was sapping their "rugged" masculine strength. Adding manual labor back into their daily round of "college work" seemed to be a rational, virtuous course to pursue. Their efforts at self-regulation via manual labor (tree planting, vegetable raising, garden cultivation) literally cultivated their world. When Isaac Jackson complained to his college president about his growing weakness, Eliphalet Nott told him to spend a few hours gardening each day so that the manual labor might balance out his mental exertion.

Jackson began digging a vegetable garden, and by the 1830s he was busy laboring at a form of "college work" he felt to be more satisfying and natural. He had rapidly transformed his private garden into a large botanical garden for Union, a site where manual labor could be paired with scientific projects that required a strong mental focus. Within his garden Jackson used and felt his muscles, explored and taught various subjects, supervised student assistants whose constitutions would also benefit from manual labor, and profited in many ways through his pursuit of horticultural science. That Union College possessed a botanical garden—and the genius who created it—was a benefit duly noted by the Union College family. They advertised the many benefits of the garden in their college catalogue. Students began coming to Schenectady because of the garden and Jackson. Jackson sent various plant specimens from his garden to other colleges, Albert Hopkins being one recipient and "friend to Union" among many. Jackson's status and salary rose after he figured out how to combine mental and manual labor to promote a new, more profitable way to perform "college work." Feeling more balanced, Jackson eventually published his textbook on optics as well, bringing even more acclaim to himself and Union College.[42]

The gardening activities at Union were part of a wider movement influencing the college world. By the 1830s, college families modeled this balanced regimen of mental and manual labor as one benefit of their world. The president of Andover Theological Academy, outside Boston, had begun this educational experiment by organizing the days of his divinity students into study hours and labor hours. He hoped Andover would produce ministers as strong in muscle as they were in faith, which would prepare them for mission fields anywhere in the world. Various forms of this "manual-labor movement" were added to the moral and intellectual order of the college world. New colleges, such as Lafayette in Pennsylvania and Oberlin in Ohio, were founded with this new idea as central to their order. At these new experimental colleges, at least for a time, there would be no studying without laboring. With students encouraged to plant campus trees, grow their own vegetables, hew wood, draw water, and take care of their own domestic concerns while also studying, college families could now easily answer their critics by pointing out how their world strengthened both the minds and the bodies of their students. They could also cut operating costs for their institutions, since students now carried out some of the labor that servants (or hired slaves in the South) often performed.[43]

The benefits and "virtues" of this new educational system filled the pages of the educational periodicals and the letters of college families. Agnes Branch, a college lady at Hampden-Sydney, informed the Baxter daughters at Washington College of the transformation taking place on her campus in 1842. "You can't think how the improving system is progressing on the hill, in yards & gardening I mean." Students and professors had "cut walks" around campus and "planted flowers & shrubs along the borders." Seeing the men and boys working to refine the campus as well as their minds, she saw nothing but "great improvement."[44]

At Williams College in the 1830s Albert Hopkins seized upon this new "scheme," which promised the benefits of "opportunity, utility, masculinity, and social harmony" for himself, his brother, and their community at Williamstown. Founding a Horticultural and Landscape Gardening Association at Williams, he rallied students to participate in digging, planting, and hoeing projects around campus. The new association encouraged "scientific curiosity," developed "muscle and the cure of dyspepsia," encouraged "model behavior," provided free labor for the cultivation of the college grounds, and, most important to the recently converted Albert Hopkins, drew students closer to nature and therefore God.[45]

Students were enthusiastic about any opportunity that promised escape from the dull rounds of classical and mathematical recitations. Most were thrilled to hear "Professor Al" tell them to put down their books and follow him out to the forest because "nature is to be studied rather than books." One student happily recalled the botanizing trips Albert led to the nearby Berkshires in order "to enliven the monotony of our pursuits." During these trips Hopkins urged students to speak about their spiritual state at local churches, his old "scheme" of itinerant preaching now linked with his new one of investigating nature. Once pining for escape, Albert began focusing his restlessness and unease on cultivating the "common good" at Williams with this experimental blend of manual and mental labor. "In quest of birds and other objects in aid of their investigations of Natural history," he traveled with his students to Nova Scotia. Upon their return, they placed their objects in his new Lyceum of Natural History, with students assigned the tasks of collecting, cataloguing, and studying the items. After securing four thousand dollars from the college trustees, he traveled even farther, sailing to Europe to purchase a "valuable set of Apparatus" for his science classes, which he hoped would encourage students to work with him in his campus laboratory and workshop.[46]

Busy with all of this new and improved "college work," Albert began to notice a change in his body and mind in his travels around Europe as a representative of Williams College. As he read letters from his brother and other colleagues full of college news, Albert realized that the college world, once so restraining, had become a source of familiarity and security to him. Mark's letters, full of "recitations—giving out appointments—books, shop, and various other things which you mention form a kind of 'tout ensemble'" that "has become pretty well beat into the constitution of my habits." In Paris, Albert began to plan one more scheme. As he observed to Mark, the "old systems are going to crumble gradually"—but they would crumble. Their college needed to be ready to model new systems, new standards of production, so as to promote new kinds of success. He now had greater plans for Williams College than merely landscaping. Influenced by the scientific buildings he had toured in Europe, Albert planned to build "an Observatory" in the center of the campus where he would teach his new passion, astronomy. The new building would also help him promote the college world's distinct, orderly "scheme" for the world, in which collective harmony and virtuous self-interest would bring about success. When Albert returned home, the men and boys of Williams College would research, plan, build, and use his observatory in a collective manner. It became the ultimate symbol of Albert's success at balancing his desire to exert both manual and mental power. He ordered Mark to consult with some local men and "see about the stone."[47]

Just before Albert's departure for Europe, the sudden death of Harry, who was taken ill on a trip to New Orleans in search of yet another business opportunity, had shocked and sobered the Hopkins brothers. Any nostalgic pining for the farming life had ended with Harry's tragic early death. So, too, did the brothers' uncomfortable debates over the virtues of manual labor versus the "ease" of life at Williams. By the 1830s, new professors like Albert Hopkins or Isaac Jackson were slowly learning how to assess their personal and professional worth based on the expansion and prosperity of their colleges—and their college world. As they worked to cultivate this world, they also learned to cultivate themselves as new professionals and new men, making this strategy their "fixed path" toward success.

Soon after Albert's return to Williamstown, a reporter for a local newspaper wrote that the "walls of an Observatory (the first, we believe, in this country) 50 feet in length, of a chaste style of architecture, have just risen" at William College. One year later, the observatory was a "beautiful building, every way fitted for the purposes for which it is designed." On open-ing day in 1838, Albert gave a speech and presented the structure as *his* gift to Williams, since he had ended up building it "more than three fourths at his own expense." The last fourth had been donated by "friends of the College"—trustees and the circles of families he had personally solicited on "begging tours" throughout New York and New England. According to one report, the building was a "standing monument to his industry and devotion to his profession," a demonstration of the combined power of manual and mental exertion.[48]

With the construction of his observatory completed, Albert Hopkins felt settled enough in his position at Williams that he purchased a house and land adjacent to campus. Mark and Albert urged their parents to retire, suggesting that they lease the family farm to others and join them on College Hill. "Your sons are at least supporting themselves," Albert announced to his aging father. Their parents "need not trouble" themselves about the future of their boys anymore. Like all of their male colleagues, the Hopkins boys had become Williams men, their identities and productivity fused with their success at cultivating their college and the world that supported it.[49]

It was on one of Albert's "begging tours" for his observatory that he met Louisa Payson and took steps to connect her to Williams College—and himself. After meeting "the remarkable Miss P," as Mark called Louisa, Albert was ready to exercise his newly constructed manhood and add another family to the college world. Like the classical curriculum itself, marriage in the college world was viewed as a traditional institution that not only supported, but stabilized fledgling institutions like Williams College. In the college world, professors were expected to marry and multiply. More workers for the college world, trained from birth in the "business of instruction," were always needed and welcomed.

For young professors, marriage yielded a range of substantial economic and emotional benefits, since marriage brought a lifelong partner in "college work." The newly appointed science professor at Dickinson College, Spencer Baird, was, like Albert Hopkins, a graduate and tutor who had quickly been elected by the trustees to become a professor. With a starting salary of four hundred dollars, Baird taught "Natural History & some of the Mathematics." A few years later, he decided to marry Mary Churchill, a young woman who had been raised in University of Vermont circles but who now lived near the college in Carlisle, Pennsylvania.[50]

Before proposing, Spencer first consulted Dickinson's president on his decision. President Robert Emory was enthusiastic about the plan. First, he informed Spencer, marriage often led to the prospect of more money for young professors, especially those with new families. Hoping to keep Spencer and his potential genius at Dickinson, Emory "most emphatically" assured him that he would receive a raise if he married. President Emory then pointed out the other reason why a professor needed a wife: he would experience an increase of productivity. Within the married state Spencer would "study much better, doing more work in the same time, and that it would be best on every account." If he chose the right partner, familiar with "college work," Spencer would find time to refine his mental powers and pursue genius. Raised as a "college lady," Mary Churchill would know exactly how to facilitate this mental production in her household. After acquiring the "consent of the college," Spencer approached Mary's parents, who also consented. The couple were married by their colleague, Professor John McClintock, and Dickinson College added another working family to its community.[51]

At Williamstown, Mark Hopkins discovered the same benefits when he chose to marry. In 1832, the moral philosophy professor married Mary Hubbell, a local trustee's daughter who he met at one of his religious lectures in town. A year later, he received his license to preach in the Congregational church, adding a divinity degree to his medical degree. In 1836, with his trustee father-in-law championing his cause, Mark was elected president of Williams College. Williams students, past and present, also pushed his case with trustees. With Mark's popular lectures (to students and to town families) and with Albert's science teaching and manual-labor activities with students, the Hopkins men became closely tied to the rising fortunes of the college.

After marriage and his ascension to the presidency, Mark rarely mentioned "nerve" problems. He was too busy being the college president—and Mary's husband. His "college work" increased and he was busier than ever. Yet he now seemed to handle this workload with ease and enjoyment. Throughout the 1830s and 1840s, his sermons, articles, and commencement speeches proliferated, as did his family, numbering ten children by the 1850s. Mark could certainly confirm what his presidential colleague at Dickinson had promised: marriage did indeed increase production. This productive capacity also allowed Mark, like Albert, to begin measuring the value of his "college work" by the success and expansion of his institution.

The self-worth of a professor also had much to do with the activities of his wife. As the daughter of a trustee, "Mrs. President Hopkins" was well acquainted with her duties as a member of a college family at Williams. Mary was also well educated, having received her training in a local academy. Before he died, Harry had sent a teasing note to her wondering if she had begun her "reign" over Mark's life, "governing her husband," who was a man so weak that he "has only to look at you & your wishes are gratified." He predicted Mary would dominate his "philosopher" brother.[52]

Mary set out in her response to correct the "ignorance" of such an "old Bachelor" as Harry. Being a good wife had nothing to do with "governing" the husband. It was all about "managing" the home. The college world demanded that she cultivate genius, not dominate it or indulge it. As Mary lectured to Harry, a good wife "manages her husband well" and knows how to "conceal—(where she cannot mend) the faults of her husband." As a trustee's daughter, Mary was well aware of "college work" and her contribution to it. She laid out her duty to Harry: "Men in publick life are strangers to quiet—their minds are constantly agitated by the business and turmoil." They were known to "forget the lesser duties of the social circle." Mary fully intended to remind Mark of these "duties" and help him with his "many cares" when they were "too much for him to support." In these "cares" of college work, Mary observed, "I intend to share them with him as much as possible." Like all college homes, the presidential home on campus would never be a retreat where Mark could shelter or hide. Mary would manage it as an ideal work place, not a haven from work. The key for college ladies like Mary was figuring out how to create such a stimulating, yet organized environment.[53]

Albert followed his brother into marriage. Louisa Payson and Albert married in 1841 in her home in Portland. A month after their marriage, Albert noted in his diary that he had taken an afternoon off from his college "duties" for a "sweet season of prayer with my wife, consecrating home." They were happy, Albert and Louisa, but they were not living in their own home yet. Louisa steadfastly refused to "go a-housekeeping" until she felt ready, and the newlyweds lived with Mary and Mark in the presidential home. It took a lot of combined effort, mental and manual, to manage a home organized around the cultivation of genius, and Louisa desired to study the problem for a while before devising her own strategy for success.[54]

Knowing how to create a household that could cultivate genius was the key skill honed by college ladies. Because of her mother's incapacitating blindness, Margaret Junkin had learned this skill at a young age. She had managed her father's home at Washington College, learning to juggle her need for mental labor with a house full of younger siblings, boarding students, slaves, and visitors. She nevertheless found time to produce books, poems, periodical articles, and reviews based on her classical learning. How did such "college ladies" do it?

As Junkin often explored in her writing, it was possible to create a material world that allowed time for the study of ideals—or "Ideal Truth." It just took time to figure out, experiment with, and then adopt the right system. The wider world, however, refused to believe that a home could survive respectably on the power of genius, much less agree that a "literary woman" could be a good housekeeper. In one of her stories for publication, Junkin argued that a woman could "reconcile" what she called the "Real and the Ideal," combining an intellectual life with domestic duties. According to one skeptical male character in her story, the home of an intellectual woman would only produce "manuscripts instead of mutton-chops." He had no desire to live in a home full of "proof-sheets when there ought to be puddings." Junkin's heroine, Dora, successfully fights this prejudice by refusing to view housework and intellectual activity as two antithetical kinds of labor. Both can be accomplished well, and Dora proves it. She divides her morning chores between translating a German play and mixing muffins for breakfast. She does all of this in a quiet, hidden style that, for Junkin, showed the natural way an intelligent woman kept house. Being organized was the key. "She is so systematic!" Dora's younger sister exclaims to the male skeptic in the story, arguing that it was purely for want of systematic thought and action that more homes did not "reconcile the Real and the Ideal" and cultivate genius. The male skeptic eventually concedes the debate to the more reasonable Dora and then proposes marriage, now willing to live within her system.[55]

As Margaret Junkin well knew, it took a group of Junkin women and family slaves to bring about the successful management of the presidential household at Lexington. No woman, however "systematic," could maintain a household by herself without assistance. Additionally, part of this system involved the cooperation, encouragement, and understanding of men. Her romantic tale, produced for a popular periodical, was more than just a call for the public to accept this shocking new kind of woman and new kind of work. She invited readers into a home that ran effortlessly in spite of the fact that a "woman of intellect" was at its center. While many of her readers might have been surprised at this tale, none of this was shocking in her world at Washington College. In fact, it was essential to the success of the college world, and Junkin was trying to promote the benefits of her peculiar kind of household to the wider world. Using Dora's story, Margaret Junkin offered a blueprint for the ideal worker and the ideal work culture—one that promoted a new system of combined mental and manual labor that men and women could both perform together with success.[56]

College couples tried to perfect this system in their households, valuing the intellectual labor of wives while also viewing their domestic labors as essential. In fact, in the academic household the work of men could not be performed effectively without the assistance of women. In a joking letter to his brother-in-law in 1841, Professor John McClintock described the "heads" of his household on the Dickinson College campus. The first head he counted was his own—"large as ever." Referring here to his tendency toward self-importance, McClintock was engaging in an ongoing joke between him, his wife, and her family. His "self-pride" was a personal fault he always admitted to and tried to correct—with little success. With this large head constantly engaged in teaching, reading, and writing, he felt he was "adding to its [mental] furniture everyday." The second head in his household belonged to his wife Augusta; it was a head "closely connected with the first." Augusta's head worked "harmoniously and happily with the first." While he believed his head was made for inward, solitary, slow-moving concentration, McClintock described Augusta's head as full of the material for quicker, more active thought process. According to McClintock, his head might have potential for deep thought, but it was Augusta's head that held the material that spurred his thoughts into motion. Within her head was to be found "a good share of energy and activity—fruitful in expediments, firm in recollection, keen in judgment." From Augusta's head "emanates all orders for the refection of our inward man." He went on, "It alone, can declare whether the morrow's breakfast will, or will not, be enlivened with coffee and buckwheat cakes." Without Augusta's capacity for action, his head would not function. While he often portrayed himself comically as a patriarch in charge of a house full of dependent women, children, and servants, he knew very well that he could never perform his "college work" without the assistance and harmonious help of the "other head" of his household—Augusta. They were, indeed, highly dependent on each other.[57]

Struggling with their own work problems, professors were quick to recognize and appreciate the labor their wives performed. Spencer Baird bragged to a Yale colleague that his new wife Mary was a "first-rate" partner. Not only was she "well educated and acquainted with several tongues," but she accepted with ease the zoology professor's habit of cluttering her parlor with stuffed birds and fossils. She also fearlessly managed his collection of live snakes, coolly pulling escapees out from behind the parlor stove and returning them to their respective barrels—much to the horror of visiting women from the town. Mary also handled Spencer's correspondence. She did not passively record her husband's "great thoughts." Like many professors' wives, Mary read and edited his writings, criticizing him when he shied away from controversial scientific debates with colleagues. As part of her "college work" she read science journals along with literary periodicals and poetry. She, of course, had to be well read when they socialized with fellow faculty families. She also acted as his agent, using her University of Vermont family contacts to seek out possibilities for more-lucrative posts than their present one at a little college in Pennsylvania. While Spencer praised Mary's intellectual talents, he equally praised her skills at managing their home. Mary "regulates her family well," he observed, keeping him, their home, and their little daughter well organized and happy. He was especially pleased to note that Mary "does not grudge the money I spend on books," revealing her as a true member of the college world.[58]

Much of this cooperation and understanding between husbands and wives was due to the economic instability that still plagued the college world and its households. Managing a college home based on the speculative powers of genius never yielded economic stability. College-family fortunes were in as much flux as professors' thoughts. As a professor's wife, Harriet Beecher Stowe famously complained to a friend that her husband Calvin, a Bowdoin professor of Greek and Latin, was "rich in Greek and Hebrew and Latin and Arabic, and alas, rich in nothing else." Augusta McClintock echoed her sentiments. She discovered at Dickinson College that her husband John had the same earnings power as Calvin Stowe—very little: "I do not like to say any thing about money though we want it badly—as we are in debt here. . . . We have not bought any thing but bare necessities and hardly that."[59]

Happily for a professor's wife, there were always other faculty wives who understood their special domestic problem—economic dependence on the power of genius. Many times college ladies confirmed each other's gentility by shoring up their material environment with gifts—or gifts of extra help. As a young wife newly arrived at Dickinson, Augusta reported to her mother that "the ladies made all my carpet." Starting a new household that was already full of hungry boarding students, she seemed relieved that they also "sent us eatables."[60]

Studying the "reconciliation" of the "business of housekeeping" with the "business of instruction," college ladies tended to describe themselves as incredibly busy. Efficiency, organization, quick thinking, and affectionate collectivity were the primary requirements for their job. Intellectual production was acceptable and even desirable, but only as a side occupation. While the college world encouraged "college ladies" in the exertion of their intellectual powers, it ranked feminine intellectual production as secondary in comparison with the products of masculine minds. Men commonly pursued genius and women cultivated a world that made it possible for them to do so. Following the classical tradition of genius as an exclusively male characteristic, college families expected "college ladies" to care first for the great thinkers in their midst (professors and students) before thinking and writing great thoughts themselves.[61]

While Augusta McClintock had to concern herself with "buckwheat cakes" first, she and her female colleagues did have more access than most middle-class women to the world of ideas. They also had more freedom to pursue this world. It was not a perfect situation, helping to build a world that focused much of its energy on prioritizing the productive capacity of the male mind. According to one of Margaret Junkin's poems, however, the collective environment of the college world, as well as its idealistic goals, gave some women the "room to chant out free the silent rhythms I hum within my heart." As Louisa Payson was to discover as she entered the Williams College family as a new wife, as long as the college and the college home was established and successful, a "college lady" could study and write and converse without the usual sense of unease or fear of criticism that many women intellectuals experienced in this era.[62]

Collective ideals helped college ladies carve out time for intellectual activity. Harriet Beecher Stowe relied on her new neighbors at Bowdoin College as well as her sister Catherine to take care of her home and children while she made use of Calvin's office on campus and began drafting

Uncle Tom's Cabin, a particularly lucrative work of genius. Harriet Smyth, the wife of Bowdoin's professor of mathematics, had little time to write, but she made sure she kept up on all the latest literature. As her son George recalled, his mother had "led a life of toil, with a large family to provide for and very meager means to do it with." With seven children and boarding students there was "no time for reading or recreation during the day," but Harriet carved out time in the evening, choosing books and directing her children to read as she worked on the family sewing. Harriet made sure they read a "useful and instructive work" of biography, history, or even an occasional novel. This activity served many purposes for Harriet. It answered her own desire to keep up on new literature, directed her children's literary taste, honed their elocution skills, and allowed her to carry out the "business of housekeeping" along with her sewing. Harriet and her family were never alone in this work. Frances Packard, the wife of Bowdoin's rhetoric professor, visited her neighbor regularly, bringing children, sewing, and sometimes her husband. Frances played the piano, taught songs to the children, and entertained the little group. The two families often socialized and worked together.[63]

College ladies found time for such intellectual activities because they defined it as part of their "college work." They made the hours spent reading, writing, and in conversation (or debate) with family and students a part of their daily tasks as "college ladies." Thus, publishing their thoughts based on all of this "college work" was one more way to contribute to the success of the college world.

According to Margaret Junkin, "college ladies" like herself possessed "intenser susceptibilities" that "lay them open to more decided impressions from their immediate surroundings." Their "surroundings" in the college world were suffused with classical and Christian texts, constant educational activity, and the challenges of establishing standards and systems that measured and evaluated their new world. When they wrote, they focused on these themes. When they published their writing, it was always as intellectually engaged, hard-working members of the college world.[64]

In the early years of her marriage, Louisa Payson published work that reflected her observations as a college lady. She completed a sequel to her popular *The Pastor's Daughter* called *The Pastor's Daughter at School.* In a series of fictional letters between a father and his daughter away at a female academy, Louisa explored the way a new educational environment, outside of the family parlor and far away from fatherly supervision, contributed to the spiritual and intellectual growth of a young mind. The work suggested ways to work toward a permanent state of salvation on one's own rather than with the help of a parent. In the circles of families and students at Williams, Louisa daily observed young men and women encountering various intellectual and moral questions that they had to solve for themselves. Bereft of parents, they did have the guidance and assistance of college families, if they chose to use it and "claim kin." Louisa wrote her book as one more helpful guide, one more textbook from the college world that tried to direct young minds as they contemplated plans for their futures.

Louisa's next research project drew on her deep knowledge of the Scriptures and biblical commentaries. She began promoting the idea that one of her favorite biblical books, Proverbs, could be used as the basis of an ethical system of thought and action. Reviewing her work in 1843, the editor of the *American Biblical Repository* placed "Mrs. Louisa Payson Hopkins" in the same category as her brother-in-law, President Mark Hopkins. She was a moral philosopher. Like many of the publications issuing from the college world, her work would "incite intellect and improve the soul." She had "elucidated one of the best systems of ethics ever penned," and he hoped her "reward" would be the "happy influence" that her system would have "over the rising generation." Other reviewers praised the "argumentation" in her writing. The literary market insisted on advertising her book for young people, but her ideas were "so cogent that it may be read with profit by adult skeptics." In fact, many reviewers urged adults to read Louisa's books. They would find her writing "not only interesting but instructive." She was a writer of "no ordinary capacity, research, and labor." There were no flowers or ferns hiding Louisa's thoughts, or her real name. Along with the similar works of her brother-in-law, President Mark Hopkins, Louisa's writing contributed moral and intellectual weight to the Hopkins "scheme" to establish a national reputation for Williams College.[65]

At Bowdoin College, Phebe Lord Upham matched Louisa's passion when it came to studying spiritual and ethical topics. Well versed in foreign languages, like Louisa, Phebe spent much of 1837 managing her college home at Bowdoin while "happily occupied in translating from the French some portions of Madame Guyon's letters." She was fond of imagining this devout Frenchwoman "speaking to me from her own inspired lips." Using his wife's translations, Thomas Upham, Bowdoin's moral philosophy professor, published various treatises and textbooks on spiritual topics as well. Phebe did not merely provide translations for her husband. She published her own translations of the letters, and then she published a study based on her findings. Interested in the new strains of perfectionism within Methodism, she carried out an investigation of "modern spiritualism," recording visits with mediums, describing her own visions, and analyzing the Bible as well as other devotional texts as part of her scholarship. She moved on to publishing Sunday School texts next, eager to impart to young minds all of the information she had learned in her spiritual research.

Like all "college ladies," Phebe Upham carried out her intellectual work while managing a busy college home and shaping society around Bowdoin College. While she carried out her research, she was "occupied, *first*, in the care of my family, which was considerable." She and Thomas were childless, so they "adopted six orphan children without father or mother." She also noted her "labor" in the Brunswick Sunday Schools, organized by members of college families to exert "special efforts to benefit the poor, neglected children of our vicinity." Because it was an essential part of everyday life in a college community, she never even noted her other chores: welcoming new colleagues, like Harriet and Calvin Stowe, to the Bowdoin circle with gifts and offers of assistance; translating and editing for her husband; and the usual feeding, boarding, and socializing with students and colleagues alike.[66]

With the feeding, boarding, and socializing of students in mind, Louisa and Albert began thinking of living in a home of their own near the Williams College campus in 1843. In this same year, Louisa produced her system of ethics, and she also produced a son. The birth of Edward Payson Hopkins had been difficult. Albert recorded in his diary that he "felt almost overwhelmed when the child was born," and as soon as he was "able to leave" Louisa, he had escaped to the woods, where he dedicated the child to God, "with deep feelings." They were both relieved and thrilled with their "little wonder," named after Louisa's famous minister father, yet the birth had come with a cost. After 1843 Louisa's health began to decline. While she began worrying constantly about being too tired or weak to perform household labor, her usual unease over intellectual labor disappeared completely after Eddy's birth. Louisa and Albert would only produce one child, a rare occurrence in a world where academic households regularly contained large families. She would continue, however, to produce a large number of books, articles, and poetry until the end of her life.[67]

In fact, the birth of her son actually spurred Louisa to focus more intently on her scholarship. College ladies like herself did not "sit still all day," she told her mother-in-law, "especially when I have so much to do & it does not hurt my eyes more to write than to sew." When she did tire, or if she was forced to deal with the growing mountains of sewing that her little family now produced, Louisa learned quickly to use the collective ideals of her world. She and Albert continued to live with Mark and his family, so there were always helpful hands around to assist her with chores. As for her intellectual pursuits, Louisa found a student to read to her in the evenings, "in return for which I am teaching him German." In fact, according to a Williams student of the 1850s, he studied astronomy with Professor Hopkins, and "Mrs. Albert Hopkins" conducted his German classes. Knowledgeable in the German language as well as German literature, Louisa was the only such authority at Williams. Instruction in this increasingly popular academic language became part of her college work, a task she undertook in exchange for assistance with her household labor.[68]

Louisa's metaphysical credentials also expanded at Williams. Her published explorations of biblical proverbs and parables attracted the attention of John Kitto, the editor of a biblical encyclopedia, who solicited entries from her on these subjects. Louisa's initials appear at the bottom of her entries alongside those of ministers, biblical scholars, and college presidents. To students interested in studying biblical scholarship or European philosophy, Louisa's language skills, her contacts with publishers, and her literary friendship with such men as Leonard Woods Jr., the new president of Bowdoin College who shared her love of German philosophy, made her a useful instructor to Williams students as well as an important contact.[69]

Seeing that she could actually continue her German studies while being "tied to a baby," Louisa began warming to the idea of managing her own home. For his part, Albert never expected Louisa to give up her intellectual work for the manual work involved in domestic chores and childcare. Professors enthusiastically supported their wives in intellectual activity because much of it benefited them. They acquired intellectual companionship, editing assistance with their own writing, and language translation services that facilitated their own scholarship. More importantly, their colleges benefited from the mental effort of both its male and female workers. Numerous publications by college-family members, male and female, flooded out of the college world, many proclaiming the name of the college as well as the author on the title page, written proof of their world's collective mission to insert its interpretation of true virtue into the wider world.[70]

Like most college couples, Louisa and Albert began working out a household labor system that benefited both of them. Now that she was assured of a partner who had "sympathy in my most cherished tastes and pursuits," Louisa would work on managing him and their home in such a way that genius could be pursued together. Their decision to move into their own house, however, was still only "partly voluntary" on her part. Louisa hesitated, worried about how the "bugbear of domestic cares" would distract her from her metaphysical studies. Albert argued that she needed to balance all of the intense mental work she regularly performed with some manual labor. Her eyes often hurt and her body was so weak that she had to retire to her room, where, she observed in her diary, the college world did not abandon her, but engaged with her. She was grateful to have a "chair to sit in, limbs free from palsy, books of all sorts to be read, and kind friends to read." Her condition of "delicate nerves," however, called for more balance. As Louisa informed her mother-in-law, Albert suggested that managing a home would give her "the amount of exercise I need." After many rounds of debate about this issue with her husband, Louisa decided to "yield to his arguments."[71]

They moved into a white frame house that Albert had built on land he had purchased near his observatory on campus. The new home was surrounded by a white picket fence as well as two acres of land on which they eventually created a "charming garden" and a "vine-covered arbor." There was also a "greenhouse" for plants that Albert often exchanged with a growing number of students and friends, especially one colleague known for his work with plants—Isaac Jackson at Union College. Inside, Louisa and Albert worked together building a mineralogical cabinet that contained a variety of rocks, minerals, and a "collection prepared expressly" for the "study of fossils." Albert built a study for himself and a "conservatory" for Louisa that housed her piano, her favorite flowers and plants, her bookshelves full of foreign literature, and a desk for her to perform some of her "college work."[72]

As Albert reported to his mother, Louisa had soon taken up her "duties as mistress of the house" and she was a "first rate cook." Cooking, however, was not a subject that Louisa needed to study for long. Albert was financially able (and eager) to provide her with as many assistants as she needed. Having linked his personal and professional success with that of a growing Williams College, Albert was wealthy enough to ensure that Louisa would be as free from "domestic cares" as she cared to be. "We have obtained a girl to take care of baby—we think her very good," Albert reported to his mother soon after they moved. Another girl "to do house work" was expected to appear at their door soon. In addition to domestic help, the Hopkins home became like all college homes—full of family, friends, students, and relations who added collective help. Louisa's widowed mother eventually joined the household and brought Elizabeth, a poor cousin, who remained in the household for years. In return for access to the moral and intellectual benefits of Williams College, Elizabeth provided domestic assistance and personal companionship to Louisa. The daughters of faculty families visited as well, taking over the care of Eddy in exchange for reading, drawing, and piano lessons from "Aunt Louisa" in her conservatory.[73]

Albert was proud to tell a friend that any "little changes about my house renders my presence necessary," and he was fond of calling himself a "bountiful provider," proudly bringing in so many goods and other "little things" to Louisa that she was unable to find places in their new house to store them. This marriage, child, and house finally settled Albert. He now felt himself a true breadwinner, always busy with "schemes" that cultivated the interests of Williams College and his own interest in the institution. He published articles on the religious history of revivals at Williams and began a "treatise on the Moon." The building of his observatory and his new passion for astronomy proved to be merely the first coordinates in the Hopkins "scheme" to plot out a successful future of profitable work for Williams College—and himself.[74]

Louisa continued on in her "college work," matching Albert's industry. A student remembered her as "heartily" involved in all of Albert's "plans for doing good" on campus and around town. She "accompanied him to his neighborhood meetings" arranged for the purpose of discussing intellectual and moral topics. She "threw open her house for such meetings," welcoming "all who came." When Albert's next "scheme" involved building a chapel in a poor, mixed-race district of Williamstown for the purposes of its "improvement," she was "in sympathy with him." It was observed that "they labored and they prayed together."[75]

In spite of her poor health, Louisa published novels, sequels to novels, periodical articles, and poems throughout the 1840s and 1850s. All of this work engaged her favorite scholarly topics: "books, authors, the laws of mind and spirit." In 1848, a *Ladies Repository* reviewer found something remarkable in one of Louisa's recent publications, written especially for invalids. The new book, *The Silent Comforter: A Companion for the Sick Room,* had been marketed as a typical gift book for invalids, but the reviewer found the material atypical. The collection of poems and essays (some by Louisa Hopkins, some collected), according to the reviewer, provided a true textbook about the problem of "neuralgia." The book explored "the management of the mind" and was not written to comfort invalids, as was the case for most authors writing in this genre, but to instruct them in "remedial influences put in operation" for the "renewal of strength and hope." Such a manual for how to improve the invalid through this type of "management," noted the reviewer, was much needed. It "is too little studied because too little appreciated." With weakness targeting both her body and her mind, Louisa had carved out some time in her "college work" to study her own situation carefully and publish some thoughts on it. She was lucky, as she constantly noted in her diary, that she had many helpful companions in her college world as she dealt with poor health. Her book, full of her own thoughts and encouragement, was written as a literary companion for women who did not have such a circle of friends offering assistance, encouragement, and intellectual stimulation.[76]

To some in the college world, Louisa Hopkins was overusing her mental powers. Her continued poor health spurred Williams families to try to help her find a sense of balance through their favored remedies of physical exercise or an escape to nature. During periods of vacation, the Hopkins clan visited the shore or went to establishments that advertised healing waters. There, they mingled with many other college families who came in search of the same improvements of bodily strength. Saratoga Springs, where Louisa could visit with old family friends from prominent ministerial circles, was a favorite destination. At other times she passed the season at the seaside resort of Nahant, Massachusetts, where she mingled with her old Boston and Cambridge colleagues. This seasonal visiting by the daughter of a famous minister and published religious author may not have helped Louisa's health, but it did help add many influential ministerial contacts to the ever expanding list of Williams College "friends."

At Williamstown, Albert took Louisa out for regular rides in their carriage, carrying her "into the woods in his arms" so they could look for botanical samples for their home collection. As a true breadwinner now, his salary slowly rising, Albert was able to purchase nearby forest land, where he planned a series of scenic walks and drives that featured views of

Mount Greylock, a common source of moral and intellectual inspiration for both of them and a common destination for their health forays into nature.[77]

After many years of carrying out her cherished intellectual and moral investigations, Louisa died suddenly in 1862. For Albert, Louisa would remain an ideal role model for the young Williamstown ladies who regularly accompanied him on his popular mountain hikes with students. Many remembered him constantly talking about Louisa. As he described her to one of his hiking companions, Louisa was a woman to be emulated because when her health was stronger she had "once looked upon Greylock, and also ascended it" with him. He was also careful to point out how she easily ascended the difficult, laborious world of thought as well, leaving behind an "enormous mass of manuscript, journals, extract books, translations, and work enough planned and begun for many lifetimes." Albert hoped to "prepare something from them" as a tribute to her pursuit of "Truth," but the science professor characteristically could never quite find the time to settle down "in the chimney corner" and write. His college duties and continual rounds of new "schemes" for the improvement of Williams College and the surrounding town kept him busy until his own death in 1872. His brother Mark, contemplating his own retirement from the presidency conducted his funeral.[78]

For professionalizing men in the college world, their experiences as new workers and new men led them to associate their personal and professional identities with the success of their fledgling institutions. Albert's early confusion over how to carry out the new "college work" prompted him to link his life with his work. His attempts at finding satisfying, profitable labor, his traveling, his teaching, his horticultural work, his observatory, his publications, and finally, his home with Louisa and their son—all helped him "settle" into his role as a professor and measure his worth according to a new standard of professional measurement. The growing success of Williams College and its growing number of graduates offered adequate "proof" to him that his labor was profitable and effective and that his manhood was secure.[79]

College ladies like Louisa also represented a new kind of professional worker—and a new kind of woman. But this new role did not seem to worry them as much as it did the men of the college world. They embraced their new identities as "college ladies" because, although more demanding, their new position offered so many more opportunities to them than being simply a "wife" or "mother." In fact, Margaret Junkin identified their participation as a new form of "wifehood" that demanded a more satisfying form of labor than the traditional role. In their attempt to "reconcile" the real and the ideal in their households, college ladies were expected to help establish a fledgling academic culture and cultivate it successfully with careful management. Their lives in the new college world were full of the "disciplines" that commonly "clog and bind" women, according to Junkin, but the collective, intellectual ideals of their world could also free them to pursue subjects like "ideal truth" without the fear of criticism or ridicule.[80]

The intellectual world of "college ladies" was not perfect. Within it, the male mind was often viewed as the most powerful, the one most eligible to pursue genius. Yet for many college ladies, their dual burden of managing the "business of housekeeping" and the "business of instruction" provided them with a strong sense of power that allowed them to pursue genius without any sense of unease about themselves. Their freedom was conditional, however, and based on specific economic and emotional needs. If they managed their academic homes and husbands well, they could contribute whatever they wanted to the world of ideas and find encouragement, assistance, gratitude, and collegiality along the way.

The early college world had need of the collective labor of both men and women, and their contributions to "college work" helped stabilize new colleges and the households situated within them. For many who lived and worked in college households, this innovative system of collective mental and manual power helped expand the influence of the college world for "the good of all."

Leaving the College World

"Gentle Spirits Fly"

WHEN A YOUNG MAN with dark skin graduated from Bowdoin College in 1826, the event was a "perfect novelty." Newspapers and periodicals reported on it widely. A Portland, Maine, newspaper described the young student's commencement piece, "The Conditions and Prospects of Hayti," as "happily selected," an appropriate topic for a "person of African descent." Showing him their "favor" by "hearty applause," the commencement audience evidently approved of his oration too. This model of "African eloquence" graduated "with the kindest wishes of his Tutors and Classmates for his future happiness." For his postgraduate plans, John Russwurm, Bowdoin's first "colored graduate," intended to join the "great emigrations of free blacks to Hayti."[1]

This future goal made perfect sense to his audience, his fellow students, and his instructors. To the college world it was unthinkable that such a mind could expect to find success in the United States, no matter how classically trained in virtue. The collective activity of the college world actively supported the collective solution to the problem of such dark-skinned people as Russwurm in the American Republic—exclusion and emigration. Exploring how the college world treated minds that it judged to be different or "dark" reveals how this new world of educational enterprise promoted the construction and collective support of one class (a "corporate entity" destined for success and secured by a leadership class) and one race (the white race), as it excluded many others or placed them in a circumscribed condition meant to establish their collective stagnation.[2]

College families viewed their own minds as well as the young minds they were training as full of dynamic potential, strictly refined as masculine or feminine, and identified as "white." As they promised their students, their time spent in the college world under the refining influence and supportive guidance of its families would produce a moral and intellectual polish that led to power in the outside world. For themselves and their students college families became deeply involved in the refinement of gender and class position. This "college work" helped define for the nation the terms "lady," "gentlemen," and "educated society." College families also had a particular aesthetic obsession for celebrating the attractive, influential power of whiteness.[3]

The color white was a "most striking property," according to Parker Cleaveland, who noted in his celebrated mineralogy textbook that "snow white" was the primary—and "most brilliant"—of the eight "fundamental

John B. Russwurm. From Penn, *The Afro-American Press and Its Editors.* One of the first black graduates of the college world, Russwurm was both praised and excoriated for his attempt to connect Liberia to the expanding college world.

Courtesy of Manuscripts, Archives and Rare Books Division, Schomburg Center for Research in Black Culture, The New York Public Library, Astor, Lenox and Tilden Foundations.

colors" to be found in the natural world. College families endeavored to focus the world's attention on their model world of moral and intellectual order. Showcasing classically designed, brilliantly white structures on their campuses became one of their favorite strategies. At Washington College, George Baxter's daughters kept a recipe book that outlined a step-by-step process for maintaining the white brilliance of the many columned buildings that rose above Lexington. By directing slaves to combine burnt alum, loaf sugar, and rice flour, the Baxter women would create a "thick & well boiled paste" called "Brilliant stucco" to be used on a building's surface to "retain its brilliancy for many years." The white brilliance of Washington College's buildings provided an aesthetic and a political message that the college world hoped onlookers would perceive. The recipe noted that the "east end of the President's house in Washington" had received this same wash. For the Baxters and their fellow families, the buildings at Washington College needed to match the brilliance of those that were rising in Washington City. The educational community of Lexington prided itself on being a shining beacon of virtue to the rest of the republic. It had to compete with the brilliance of the political world, especially if, as college families argued, it was their world that retained the true, pure form of virtue.[4]

The Englishman James Buckingham and his wife were almost blinded by this white brilliance when they visited Athens, Georgia, in the 1830s. There, it was natural forms rather than buildings that seemed to glow. Attending a "brilliant party" at the president's home near campus, the Buckinghams mingled with Franklin College families as well as "all the principal families of Athens." Mr. Buckingham rhapsodized over the "white muslin" of the ladies' evening dresses and their decorative touches of "pearls and white ribbons," also praising the "fair complexions" of the "college ladies." The Buckinghams were excited to witness, along with a "large party" of assembled college families, the "night-blooming" whiteness of a Cereus plant in the college botanical garden. This "natural" display of whiteness enlightening the dark was highly interesting to this circle. Indeed, it was his conversation and polite interaction with white Athenians, among whom he sensed vast amounts of "enlightened" power, that prompted Buckingham to predict their success at transmitting "general intelligence" and "elegance of manners" to the rest of Georgia and the nation. There was much social power to be gained in showcasing the refinement of one's gender and class position and then adding white brilliance.[5]

College families made it part of the "business of instruction" to determine who could join them in their elevated society. As they built their college world, they worked hard at constructing inclusion and exclusion policies, relying on their learned knowledge to assist them in this project. Parker Cleaveland informed his young daughter Martha Ann that her studies in math and science were not "ornamental art" but professional training for her future role as a refiner of society. Her study of botany, zoology, and the new science her father had introduced to the college world, mineralogy, would assist her in determining "the class, genus & species" of everything (and every body) she encountered in future life. With trigonometry and geometry, she would gain "a true perspective" of "bodies under their proper angles" and become an expert at aligning herself properly in relation to others. If college ladies mastered these skills, they would be able to categorize with ease, ideally, as her father noted, without "book in hand."[6]

The college world made the science of categorization, with its rules for exclusion and inclusion, a naturalized social behavior. The educated, refined, white, and English Mr. Buckingham who came to Athens, Georgia, to lecture on his travels in the Middle East was eligible for inclusion. So was his wife. The couple received a similarly warm welcome from Dickinson College families when he lectured at Carlisle. The Buckinghams fit in naturally in the college world, and the families of the college world made sure they felt welcome.

For an educational enterprise determined to create the organizational categories that would last far into the future for an expanding nation, young male and female minds that could be taught to master the necessary analytical skills in a natural, sociable manner were indispensable. After marrying a Bowdoin student and setting up a home in Boston, Parker Cleaveland's daughter Martha Ann revealed her mastery of this organizational skill. She was a true college-family member. People like the Buckinghams would be welcomed in her world—and in her parlor. Others, she perceived, were not welcome because they were not a natural fit. Some were downright unnatural to her educated views. "Our black Chloe who is 'high strung' has taken it into her head that she will leave here," Martha Ann complained to her mother about her black maid. Martha hoped she could find "some white girl," for "I dislike black for help as much as Pa does." She told her sympathetic mother that she always avoided looking at Chloe's "white eyes & teeth if I can help it." This blend of darkness and whiteness in her home made her reel in disgust. She hoped, like many of her Northern colleagues, to avoid proximity to such darkness. In Northern college families black servants were viewed as second best. White servants were preferred, viewed as more refined and easier to train. In college families, whites—even poor, lower-class whites—had some potential for training. Blacks did not. The notion of dealing with black minds, black skin, and assisting black hands was merely tolerated in the early college communities, North and South.[7]

Martha Cleaveland's observations demonstrate another important organizational tenet of the college world. Any mixture of the brilliance of white with the darkness of blacks was a disturbing problem in need of a solution. College families at Franklin College placed their blooming cereus plant under glass, keeping that fascinating contrast of black and white exposed to collective scrutiny. At the Cleaveland home at Bowdoin College, the family initiated a set of exclusionary hiring practices that kept the family and its home completely and purely brilliant. College families based the management of their world on a very literal cultivation of enlightenment.

As one of the first "colored" graduates of this college world, John Brown Russwurm experienced this problematic form of cultivation at Bowdoin College; his education there taught him the power of inclusion and exclusion. The son of a Virginian planter and a slave woman, Russwurm was born in Jamaica but raised in North Yarmouth, Maine, where his father married into a shipping family. His white stepmother accepted this "black son" without question, raising him alongside her own children and continuing to mother him after her husband's early death. Russwurm attended a local Maine academy with his white half-siblings and then moved to Boston to teach at that city's African School. In a letter to an uncle, he described how he had "fixed" his "residence in Boston, relying upon my own exertions" to raise funds for college. Like so many of his white colleagues, he sought to prepare himself for admission to Bowdoin College both intellectually and financially. When he applied, Bowdoin College accepted him. Russwurm's family possessed the social power to help him attend these institutions. They evidently did not have the financial resources to help him through them, however. At Russwurm's commencement, a reporter noted that his "prudence and economy" had helped him "lay up a sufficient sum of money to defray the expense of his education." Like many poor college students, Russwurm had worked as a teacher to raise money for his college education. He may have also had access to funding from religious groups who expected the black men and women they supported to ultimately leave the republic. In the college world, young "colored" men like Russwurm were educated for the express purpose of creating a successful future in leadership outside America.[8]

Thus, Russwurm's commencement speech in 1826 made perfect sense to his audience. Bowdoin College had trained him in classical knowledge, virtue, and social leadership. Now he would oblige Bowdoin College (and any of his other financial patrons) by taking himself out of the country. Russwurm certainly had high expectations for his future as a leader, and he seemed in accord with this collective view that his future was outside of the republic. If he was not "particularly invited by the Haytian Govt" to take up a political post in that black republic, he informed an uncle, he would "study Medicine in Boston previous to an emigration to Hayti." In possession of a college degree, Russwurm foresaw a professional position as a political leader or a doctor in his future. The college families of Brunswick supported this professional vision enthusiastically. Russwurm assured his uncle that he had "secured many valuable friends" who took "a deep interest in my future welfare." As they did with white students, Bowdoin college families and friends helped Russwurm plan a successful future dedicated to virtue. Yet, as he noted to his uncle, he had won their assistance because of his "correct deportment." There had been specific conditions to their assistance—an enthusiasm for Hayti and his acceptance of the idea of the proper alignment, as Parker Cleaveland would have said, of black and white "bodies under proper angles." In 1826 Russwurm could claim the right to the privileges and benefits that came with his Bowdoin College education. Unlike his fellow white graduates, however, this "colored graduate" could only "claim kin" if he embraced exclusion, left the country, and claimed his "proper" place as an elevated mind among those of African descent.[9]

Preoccupied with the potential power of the mind, college families were fond of imagining such a "black genius" as Russwurm, under the guidance of his white tutors, creating a flourishing republic in a distant outpost—"Hayti" or some community on the west coast of Africa. When it came to their position on slaves or free blacks in America, college families held colonizationist views. Judging slaves and free blacks as unnatural elements in a society they idealized as white, college families fixated on the new colony of Liberia especially, founded by slaveholders and missionaries as a repository of freed American slaves, as the ideal solution to their problem with promoting pure white brilliance.

Helping to found the New York State Colonization Society in 1829, Eliphalet Nott lent the support of Union College families to this cause. His views reflected those of the majority of the college world on the subject. Moving to Liberia was the only means by which "our citizens of color" would ever find success, Nott informed the Society's members. In America black minds had been "degraded by slavery." When slaves were freed, Nott asserted, they were "further degraded by the mockery of nominal freedom." There was no hope for black improvement in America. The only solution was emigration. Africa was favorable because it was "their country. In color, in constitution, in habitude, they are suited to its climate." He did allow that black and white minds shared the same "faculties," but the "force of condition" had led to "degradation." Only in Africa would people of color "be blessed, and be a blessing."[10]

Like Nott, the majority of college families tended to "favor and facilitate" the colonization movement. College families from Brunswick, Maine, to Carlisle, Pennsylvania, to Athens, Georgia, organized and joined antislavery societies that promoted Liberia. They raised money for the colony; collected supplies for it (boxes of books were favored); wrote speeches, poems, and essays for the society's paper, the *African Repository;* celebrated the colonization ideal of a "dark" homeland; and educated specially chosen "ideal" slaves for emigration. The families at Washington College were very active in such educational activities. In the Presbyterian church in Lexington, Virginia, the college families of Washington College regularly held services in which groups of black emigrants were blessed and sent "home" to Liberia. After a speech by the college president and a prayer by the church pastor, there was always the collective singing of hymns. The president's daughter, Margaret Junkin, composed one of the songs, which began with the image of "elder sister" America greeting Liberia as a "beacon" that was "a stream of living light" far across the sea. Junkin was fond of calling Liberia the "true home" of the black men and women who surrounded her in Lexington. Calling her "children" home, Liberia did not have to receive them "poor and empty-handed," as Virginians once had when their black ancestors had been brought there as slaves, "with superstition branded, and want and woe and shame." In the view of the college world, black emigrants, educated by college families, would now be returned "back to their native sod" with an education in the model of white brilliance which, according to Junkin, comprised "our laws—our learning—Our freedom—and our God." The new black Liberians were to be the vessels of college-world virtue who would, one day, enlighten a darkened continent. At the end of the hymn, Junkin ordered them, with the powerful direction of a college lady: "Go, and may Heaven speed you." The emigrants really did not have a choice. According to Junkin, only "in that land of strangers" would they find "friends and Home."[11]

Liberia was not John Russwurm's first choice of a destination. He planned on Haiti, perhaps because it was not so dominated by white guidance and supervision as Liberia. Russwurm certainly had confidence in his own powers and felt he was of equal intelligence to whites. In his commencement address, he asserted publicly to his audience that "man alone, remains the same being," under the "torrid suns of Africa" or the "more congenial temperate zones." In contrast to Eliphalet Nott's assessment that the American environment had degraded slaves and free blacks, Russwurm did not consider his mind degraded in the least. His education had upgraded him considerably, and he felt considerably elevated.

The letters of white male college graduates are full of optimistic expectations about their future direction in life, and Russwurm's were no exception. In the economically unstable republic, assertions from young white men that they could "fix" their own "standing & destiny" sounded like arrogant bravado, and much of it was. Still, the young men were able to act on their assertions because they were often bolstered by an "anxious" assortment of "friends" who encouraged their adventures in achieving success, offering enough emotional and economic assistance to allow for such confidence.

As Russwurm quickly figured out, as shown by his "correct deportment," one of the prime benefits of the college world was access to an influential, expanding network of "friends." New graduates could, if they needed to, easily "claim kin" when arriving in a new city or new territory. College families were always helpful in connecting college graduates with alumni and trustees. There was always someone who would lend some money, provide advice, offer advanced training in divinity, medicine, or law, or provide a job lead—all in the name of "Old Bowdoin" or "Old Washington."

In discussing the possible future of some favorite Washington College graduates, the Baxter sisters were relieved that one of them, through the influence of the college's trustees, had found a local teaching job. Another graduate wanted "a school of a higher grade," because "the professors of College have given him a very high recommendation." Nancy Baxter assured her sister that the college family was active in job placement services—"a number of persons are looking out for a place for him." For most graduates with professional dreams, their first stop after graduation was academy teaching—a guaranteed posting that the college world could easily provide with its educational contacts.[12]

Some students stayed within the "business of instruction," moving to other academies or colleges for jobs based on their classical credentials (the diploma) and "high recommendation" from their college family. A Williams College graduate described a typical post-commencement scenario to a friend back at college. When he and another graduate ventured into western New York in search of their fortunes in law and medicine, they encountered many adventures but never failure. Just as Russwurm assumed, they discovered that their "classical education" was a handy commodity. Especially in developing regions, a college degree made you eligible for certain positions in society. "I am no longer a lawyer," the young man announced to his friend back at Williams, and "Mr. Palmer no longer a Doctor, or a poet." They had changed their professional plans because a more lucrative opportunity had appeared. They were "now nothing more nor less than pedagogues." Through the assistance of the Williams College trustees, the young men, fresh out of college, were now the "principals of a High School" in a New York frontier town. No longer able to "build our castles with cases won or cases cured," or "solace ourselves in the smiles of the sunset," their "present location" still proved very profitable. As they informed their friend, they were so settled and prosperous in their developing region that they were both looking for wives, a sure sign that both felt they were on the road to success.[13]

Many other students used their academy jobs after graduation as a springboard for making more friends and moving into other professions. One Union College student, Alexander Hamilton Rice, was so sure that a college "friend" would secure a place for him at a well-known academy after commencement that he dared his sweetheart to take a gamble on their future: "What say you to the consummation of our wishes on commencement night and keeping dark about it?" As an academy teacher, the young "gentlemen" teased, he would need the "services of a lady" and hoped to "employ you, ha ha ha ha." As co-teachers and lovers, he expected they would have "great times." The young couple did indeed find quick success. The young man's Union College contacts, his father's paper manufacturing network, and his new wife's political family connections facilitated his access into the world of commercial, educational, and political leadership. Alexander Hamilton Rice made his fortune in paper mills, sat on the Boston School Committee, and eventually became Boston's mayor and the governor of Massachusetts. From academy teacher to governor, Rice was a model for the elevating power of the college world and the potential to be found in the white masculine mind. As all of these young graduates pondered the direction of their success after commencement, a network of college "friends" nudged them forward, training them in how to exploit the various "advantages" and "privileges" they now possessed as classically educated gentlemen. They were elites and they had a right to use this status as a gateway to power.[14]

Except for the color of his skin, Russwurm saw himself as similar to his fellow white graduates. They all shared a Bowdoin College degree. Thus, he had proof, if he needed any, that he was as morally and intellectual ordered as his fellow graduates. All of them expected to become social, economic, and political leaders. So did Russwurm. He confidently asserted his elite expectations in his commencement speech when he noted that Haiti would soon equal the American republic in power. Its citizens simply needed some time to refine themselves and overcome the legacies of slavery and French violence. Envisioning himself as an elite leader of this developing black republic and an expert at refinement, Russwurm predicted nothing less than the expansion of political, economic, and social equality—for himself and for "Hayti."

Soon after graduation, however, Russwurm began hearing "unfavorable reports" from free black Bostonians who were returning from Haiti. These black families were full of warnings that the country was unstable and dangerous, and Russwurm began to revise his plan for success. Like many of his fellow graduates, he decided to move, and he chose New York City. If, as he had argued in his commencement speech, he was the "same being" in the tropics as in the more "congenial" regions, then he could use his classical degree and educational training just as well in New York as in Haiti.[15]

Indeed, Russwurm began his time in New York City by relying on his educational expertise, teaching at the only school that would employ him, the African Free School. A white minister and advocate of colonization visited the African School one day to observe "several hundred African youths" recite their lessons. He was pleased to "see our colored brethren ascend the hill of science" in preparation for their future move to Africa. When he thought of all of those young black girls and boys leaving the country, he easily asserted that their "genius" was in "every way equal to that of the whites." Their minds were simply "oppressed" by their unnatural presence in New York. The minister hoped Russwurm and his fellow teachers would "qualify many to carry the glad tidings of salvation to benighted Africa." When settled there in their success and stability, the settlers would attract more black people to their enterprise and thus "compensate the injured blacks for all their past sufferings."[16]

Russwurm's sudden change of mind—and the change in his life's direction—may have worried, and even irritated, his "friends." He had received no assistance from Bowdoin College after arriving in New York City. In Russwurm's mind, if Haiti didn't work out, he always thought he would become a doctor. But he was barred from medical lectures in New York because of his color, and he soon grew dissatisfied with teaching at the African School and with life as a "black gentleman" in New York. He was not welcome at the informal clubs and literary societies that had been formed by Bowdoin alumni. These were the very institutions young graduates found to be useful in their search for "friends." In contrast, Russwurm began to rely on a network of other friends—the free black community of New York.

He first taught in their school and soon began to write for one of their periodicals, joining the journalist Samuel Cornish as a co-editor of the first black-owned periodical, *Freedom's Journal.* Both men had been born in the West Indies and both were interested in reporting on the improvement of the condition of black men and women in the nation. The journal advocated the elevation of black Americans through the power of "virtue and knowledge" and championed all projects for self-improvement. It was openly opposed to colonization efforts as well as most emigration plans. The editors and their readers stood for emancipation, economic equality, and citizenship for black Americans.[17]

As one reader noted, the "coloured brethren" could not "reconcile" their minds to emigration and demanded a future vision of the republic that the "good men" who "are for sending us to Liberia" could not see, blinded as they were by their vision of white brilliance. To free black readers, the colonizationist minds—those of the college world—were the ones in need of enlightenment. They "have not duly considered the subject," and, more importantly, they did not possess the truly enlightened minds of "men of colour." If they did, they would "plainly" see that the "land which we have watered with our tears and our blood" is "our mother country." Black people were destined to find economic and emotional stability within the American republic because their hands had not only built it, but their minds had helped shaped its society, "where wisdom abounds, and the gospel is free." To the readers of *Freedom's Journal,* colonization was not the solution to a problem, colonization *was* the problem—a plot by slaveholders to empty the nation of virtuous black men and women.[18]

Attempting to carry out his professional plans in New York City, classical degree from Bowdoin College in hand, Russwurm came to the conclusion that it was a "waste of words to talk of enjoying citizenship." Finding success was "utterly impossible in the nature of things." His dark skin determined his future position in America. The "mere name of colour blocks up every avenue," he observed with frustration, and he returned to his old plan of leaving the country. He had "pondered much on this interesting subject," he informed his shocked *Freedom's Journal* readers, and had read "every article within our reach, both for and against" colonization. He had studied all of the "different plans in operation" for "our benefit." Haiti, his first choice, was now unstable. All other destinations were "limited" by the problem of white supervision and racial prejudice, or violent instability as in Canada or the western territories. Although Liberia was supervised by white "trustees," Russwurm had begun to favor the colony as his new home because he was attracted to its opportunities for leadership and development. Frustrated in the circumscribed racial order of New York City, he began to view Africa as a new world free of prejudice but in need of moral and intellectual order. In Liberia Russwurm could imagine himself as a leader exerting a refining power on society, an elite thinker who had the training needed to create and maintain a successful "new order."[19]

Russwurm knew that his changing "doctrines" about colonization would be unpopular with his "colored brethren." When the American Colonization Society appointed Russwurm the school superintendent of Liberia in 1829, the news provoked an angry furor in black communities from Boston to New York to Philadelphia. In the columns of *Freedom's Journal* he argued that his ideas were "conscientious ones, formed from no sordid motives," but were for the future "good of our brethren." He was moving to Liberia as an educational leader. According to college-world standards, he was bringing virtue to Africa and working for the "common good." Russwurm's intention to work for the improvement of the race in Africa, not America, enraged many readers. His decision to work for the

Colonization Society betrayed virtue as they saw it—the fight against white prejudice. As his reasons and justifications filled the *Freedom's Journal,* angry letters to the editor attacked his "personal character" and accused him of going to Liberia for the sake of profit and a regular salary. To his critics Russwurm's decision was based on self-interest, not self-sacrifice. Even as he left, editorials castigated Russwurm as an ambitious, elitist man who had emigrated in order to find profit, fame, and power. They were right.

For the free black community in Northern cities like New York who argued constantly with white America that they had the right to embrace and possess the national culture of expansion and opportunity, Russwurm's plan to take his college degree and gentleman status out of the country was a complete betrayal. To them, his reasoning was completely unbalanced and reflected the erroneous thinking of the college world that produced him. To Russwurm, like all college alumni carrying out the search for the best possible position in life, his decision seemed rational and self-evident. Russwurm lost many of his friends in the black community, but he found his old ones again when news about his Liberian plans reached Bowdoin College. As the newspapers noted, the new superintendent of schools in the colony of Liberia arrived "recommended" by Bowdoin College for his "intellectual qualifications" and "moral character." Any "statements" he made, the editor of the ACS periodical, the *African Repository,* assured his readers, could be regarded with "entire reliance" because of his training at Brunswick. Bowdoin College "friends" were happy to provide Russwurm with assistance and proof of his value as a leader—but only if he exercised his leadership outside of the republic. The Bowdoin graduate accepted this condition because he was confident that he would be able to "claim kin" from across the Atlantic and maintain important contacts and support.[20]

In his first letters from Liberia, Russwurm admitted that it had been difficult to describe the "sensations" he felt when he had landed at Liberia's capital, the port city of Monrovia. He was relieved to see "double the number of houses I expected" and colonists who "appear to be thriving" and "subsist chiefly by trading with the natives." As a Maine native from a shipping family, he knew the importance of a thriving shipping trade, especially in a seaport like Monrovia. The most striking image he reported was that of "coloured men exercising all the duties of offices of which you can scarcely believe." Echoing the thinking of Eliphalet Nott that Liberia was where black men could actually flourish, Russwurm noted "how pleasing" it was to watch this transformation. He was amazed to "behold men who formerly groaned under oppression, waking in all the dignity of human nature, feeling and acting like men who had some great interest at stake." Echoing Margaret Junkin, Russwurm was happy to be in the "land of my fathers," announcing his belief that the "descendents of Africa now in America must return and assist in the great work of evangelizing and civilizing the land." Having been present at one important commencement (at Bowdoin), he was now pleased to be present at another "commencement"—of the biblical prophecy of Ethiopia stretching forth her hand with influence and strength. In Liberia, Russwurm reported, "we have here a republic in miniature." In this, he was echoing the favored image college families used when referring to their own little republics of virtue. Excited by all the opportunities for leadership he saw during his first days in Liberia, Russwurm determined to take a leading role in this exciting new enterprise.[21]

Russwurm began his superintendence of schools immediately, assured by ACS officials when he took the job that they would "recommend" the establishment of a free school system and help fund it. He soon realized that he would have to actually build the schools first with charitable funds and then convince settlers to support them. Being from "the south of Maryland," most emigrants had "faint ideas" about supporting "free schools"; they were simply too poor. He also discovered a problem with the white trustees of the colony, who were not as virtuous in deed as they were in words. Visiting an academy of fifty students run by a black Presbyterian settler from Richmond, Russwurm found the young teacher "discouraged" because "he has not received that support which was first promised him." Recruited and educated by college families to be a teacher in Liberia, the young man did not have books or any teaching materials. His salary from ACS was also in arrears. A teacher himself, Russwurm knew "from experience" that "of all men who labour in behalf of the public," teachers received the lowest pay, and he commiserated with the young man. He made it his first mission in Liberia as the superintendent to improve the educational system and the treatment of teachers in the colony.[22]

Lacking the "means to build an academy and to establish more schools," and quickly abandoning the hope for money from ACS, Russwurm turned to his "friends" in the college world. In a letter to the *African Repository* he wondered if a "Ladies Society" in New England could raise money to support "two female teachers." He himself would become a teacher again, working to "qualify" young men and women in Liberia to teach in his schools. They would learn by watching him—and reading his books—"by observation and reading Mr. Bacon's publication which I have on the subject." Using his own books, the refined knowledge he had learned at Bowdoin, and donated goods, Liberia's new school superintendent hoped for "better things" in the future.[23]

A central component to the educational enterprise in Liberia was to be the transformation of "recaptured Africans"—men and women who had been rescued from slave ships and employed to "work in the settlement" by American emigrants. Some were skilled artisans and house servants; many others labored on the farms owned by black Americans. Russwurm reported that these Africans had excellent potential as students. They were "easily known" for "their copying as much as they can after the settlers." He saw a "great change" take place "in their condition" after they mingled with the American settlers. Such "transplantation," he thought, "has improved their natures much." This image of native Africans "advancing daily in the arts of civilization" after time spent living and working in the Liberian colony proved to American settlers like Russwurm that there was a refining atmosphere emanating from the colony. He noted disapprovingly that it was those natives who refused to live and work in Liberian homes and who continued to "adhere to their old customs" who did not improve.

While he was interested in natives who improved themselves under Liberian instruction, Russwurm was more interested in finding a virtuous community of Africans untouched by the moral and commercial contamination of the slave trade. Like college families who regularly romanticized their rural regions as repositories of virtue for the nation, Russwurm assumed these virtuous inhabitants would be living far from the city of Monrovia and he hoped to connect with them. He happily observed that "a road from a Liberian town to an interior village had just been completed," and he anticipated "much increase of trade with the interior, and a communication with nations whose manners and customs we are yet but partially acquainted." Using the benefits and privileges of educational and commercial power actively cultivated in Liberia, Russwurm hoped to add more virtuous citizens to his "republic in miniature." He assumed, like college families, that the people living in the interior would readily and eagerly accept the ideal model of society that he and his fellow Liberians offered.[24]

For college families, news about any educational "intelligence" was always welcomed and exchanged, by word of mouth, letter, and newspaper. Using his educational and editorial expertise, Russwurm eagerly began reporting on the activities taking place in Liberia, providing another source of Liberian news for readers beyond the Colonization Society's *African Repository*. By May 1830, Philadelphia, Boston, and New York newspapers were reporting that the first number of the *Liberia Herald*, a "small sheet of four pages," had arrived at their offices, and they began publishing extracts. Along with keeping the American public (and his college friends) informed about Liberian events, Russwurm wanted the *Liberian Herald* to "bring to light many facts" about a slave trade that America and Europe had officially abolished but that was "far from discontinued." As he sat in the ACS headquarters in Monrovia, he reported that European "slavers" within forty miles of the Liberian coast still "engaged in this nefarious traffick." He called for civilized governments to enforce the abolishment of the slave trade by stationing warships along the western coast of Africa and ending this system of "piracy."[25]

Long-established antislavery newspapers positively noticed Russwurm's attempts to call attention to the continuance of the slave trade, and they expected the new *Liberian Herald* to be "conducted with spirit and ability." The newly established abolitionist newspaper, *The Liberator,* however, only criticized Russwurm's advocacy of all things Liberian or African. Its writers disputed his assertion that Africa was the ideal environment for a "man of color, of republican principles." Attacking his work for the Colonization Society as the "faithful performance" of a good employee—or slave—one *Liberator* writer echoed the sentiments expressed by the angry readers of the *Freedom Journal* just a few years earlier. *The Liberator* condemned Russwurm as an example of a man who had been transformed from virtuous citizen to ambitious fortune hunter. His life was not dedicated to racial improvement or virtuous ideals as he argued; it was dedicated to profit. As one black Philadelphian observed, "Mr. Russwurm tells us he knows no other home for us than Africa." Would he have "gone to Africa even on a visit had he been in flourishing circumstances?" While Russwurm viewed his work in Liberia as extending the fields of opportunity for educated "colored" men like himself, abolitionists condemned it as hastening the destruction of Africa. They argued that any economic transactions in Liberia only increased "gold and silver" on that continent, encouraging natives to make "new wars to find enslaved prisoners to exchange for these metals." In contrast to its image as a black homeland or, as Margaret Junkin fondly called it, a "beacon," the Liberian Colony "planted in Africa a nursery" for more slavery.[26]

While *The Liberator* never forgot Russwurm and his allegiance to Liberia in their editorial columns, his siblings in Maine seemed eager to forget him. Writing to his half-brother Francis in 1834, Russwurm demanded to know why no one in Maine seemed to take an "interest in my welfare in this distant land." It had been so long since he had "heard from North Yarmouth" that he thought "half the town may be dead." Careful to answer "directly" any letters that his family sent, Russwurm never received any response. Why did they "forget" him? He hoped he was not "foolish enough to impute it to the *darkness of my complexion.*" He reminded them that "color is nothing in Africa," and he was excited to report on his new position in Liberia. More importantly, he needed to retain the ties with family and "friends" that traditionally helped college graduates. He was disappointed to hear that Francis had "relinquished" his "liberal course of education," and he was "anxious to know in what line of business you prepared to employ yourself." If it was "merchandise," he suggested, Liberia "offers greater inducements than any other at present." Monrovia's port was filled "with vessels of all nations," he boasted. Although some "engaged in the Slave Trade," he admitted, there was a "a respectable number in fair trade."[27]

After Russwurm married the daughter of the lieutenant governor of Monrovia, Sarah McGill, he assumed new duties in her family's shipping business along with his career as a school superintendent in the "business of instruction." The McGill family, mixed-race settlers from Baltimore, had political influence and also enjoyed an increasing economic presence through their shipping trade in the Atlantic. Russwurm's earlier attempt to initiate educational and commercial activity with "the interior" was "almost broken up," so he now planned to "embark on my own responsibility" on coastal shipping with his in-laws. Since Liberian merchants were still trying to figure out "what will sell best on the Coast," he planned to experiment, and he offered his American family the opportunity to share in this new opportunity. He sent samples of Liberian products back to the States with a Maine sea captain and hoped for "long letters" from North Yarmouth when the captain returned to Liberia. Desiring to be remembered "to all," he worked in one more connection to a "friend," asking his brother to remind a local editor that he had sent the man a *Liberian Herald* and thought the editor should "reciprocate" with a copy of his own paper, the traditional custom among American editors.[28]

Although Russwurm sought to maintain ties between Maine and Monrovia, his family did not respond to his invitations. "Why have you all been silent?" he wrote a year later. His economic situation was improving, he wrote, and trade had "grown more brisk." He now informed his family that along with wife and children he had decided to settle "in Africa" for good—but "not in Liberia." In his five years there, Russwurm had realized that his leadership skills were not as essential as he had once assumed. He had never seen "more fanaticism, bigotry, & ignorance" as at Monrovia among the black leaders. Corruption was rampant and white ACS agents were part of the problem. He hoped that his family had not "cast me off" because he was now in Africa, and he made one more attempt to forge some sort of familial connection with his siblings who remained silent: "My wife begs to be remembered—though a stranger to all."[29]

While his half-siblings would not communicate with Russwurm, his widowed stepmother did. The woman who had accepted her husband's illegitimate, mixed-race son as her own, and continued to mother him as a widow, apparently did not forget him. She kept in touch. He sent her news about his career—and money for her support. As one of his brothers reported to another Maine relative, Russwurm "has been very kind to my mother" and has "done all she could have expected had he been her own son." But for at least one brother, Russwurm's position as a Liberian leader was cause for amusement (and resentment) rather than family pride. "I sometimes joke Mother about her black son," he reported, and "tell her that I am jealous—that she thinks more of him than she does of her white sons." Whatever she felt about her other sons, Russwurm's stepmother was proud of him—and his professional career.[30]

If most of his family neglected him, Bowdoin College families did not. The *Liberian Herald* reported on and sent thanks for the numerous packages Russwurm received from the New England "ladies societies," filled with books, clothes, and other articles for his schools and his students. Now that Russwurm's "black genius" was in its proper and natural category, Bowdoin families, especially its network of college ladies skilled in fundraising, were ready to help him flourish.[31]

Russwurm's educational and editorial work soon incurred the wrath of the newly appointed colonial governor, whose character he had criticized in his paper. Liberian governors were not elected, but appointed by ACS, and many emigrants protested the appointment of yet another white governor. The governor dismissed Russwurm "without cause" and banned him from writing for the paper. Russwurm published his side of the scandal in 1835 in the *United States Gazette*, in which he worried that a "party" at Monrovia was trying to "injure" his reputation among a "rich circle of friends, scattered in various sections of the United States," who had known him "from my youth." He wanted to set the record straight. He had labored in Liberia for five years as a "public servant," and as a member of the college world had worked "against my commercial interests." There were now ten schools in Liberia that he oversaw, as well as the *Herald.* He had also been appointed the colonial secretary, a post he had lost upon his dismissal.[32]

Outraged by this undignified treatment, Russwurm was "bewildered" that the governor had acted with such arbitrary authority against him, comparing the white agent to "many a Southern man" in Russwurm's acquaintance who "before he has been aware, injured the feelings of his darker brother, awaking perhaps from a reverie, that he was in the wilds of Georgia, or his plantation, with his cartwhip in his hand." After traveling "4000 miles to be free," Russwurm felt he had been duped by white men who called themselves gentlemen. As a Bowdoin man, he knew what it meant to think and act like a gentleman. He soon decided it was time to leave Liberia.[33]

In his efforts to leave, Russwurm relied on Bowdoin College connections to find a new position for himself in Africa. Dr. James Hall, a Bowdoin Medical School graduate and a Methodist preacher, had become a missionary to Liberia, but he eventually left the colony, also irritated by the corruption he saw there. He then helped the State of Maryland buy property on the western coast of Africa from local natives (Maryland political leaders were hoping to found their own colony there for freed slaves). After governing this new colony for three years, Hall finally decided that his true "vocation" was in America. He thought "another could do better than" himself, a man who was more "fit" to be an African leader. So he turned to Bowdoin's other man in Africa, John Russwurm. Hall was "instrumental" in transferring Maryland's African colony, his "nursling & child," into Russwurm's care. The *African Repository* pointed out that Russwurm would be the "first governor of African descent" of a West African colony. James Hall was pleased to place Maryland Colony in the hands of a "man of mild and conciliatory manners" and "of great prudence and good judgment." Hall's fellow Methodists championed the move too, the *Christian Advocate* noting that, like Hall, Russwurm was "a man of good, sound classical education." In the late 1830s, Russwurm and his family moved to Cape Palmas, the capital of the newest American colony in Africa.[34]

Russwurm abandoned Liberia because its society had not reflected the virtue—or produced the virtuous leaders—that he had expected. With a population of fifteen hundred by the 1830s, the Liberian capital of Monrovia had become a world dedicated to cultivating political and economic power. The Monrovians were focused on commercial activities and political rallies. Citizens regularly celebrated their prosperity, and their Liberian pride, with "processions, addresses, prayer, and singing" in the city streets. Back in his New York City days Russwurm had criticized similar popular practices in the free black community there as leading to rowdy and irrational behavior. Out of all of this collective expression, however, there emerged a growing circle of Liberian leaders who protested against the power of the ACS and its white "trustees" and governors. Indeed, in 1847 black Liberian leaders declared their country's independence and, as new republicans, wrote their own constitution.[35]

Despite the country's new independence and the vibrant new black emigrant culture in Liberia, John Russwurm was disappointed by what he viewed as a lack of moral and intellectual order among the Liberian leaders. His plans for the Maryland Colony were different. He hoped to create a world of educational enterprise there, something that neighboring Liberia had neglected to do. Russwurm ensured that educational elites would be the guiding and defining force of his colony, implementing legislation as governor that banned anyone from a government post who "could not read or write." Literary knowledge should define both the rulers and the ruled. Like his colleagues in the college world, he would use educational structures to cultivate a culture of collective harmony. When tensions flared between settlers and local natives, Russwurm "effected a reconciliation" that was "quite satisfactory" to all parties. He built a "mission house and schoolroom" in the middle of the contested region that offered free education to the sons of both groups—settlers and natives. As a leader trying to model the virtue of "self-sacrifice," Russwurm built these structures at his own expense and then invited ministers and their families to live and teach in them.[36]

Accompanied by "an interpreter and assistants," Governor Russwurm continued to travel to interior regions, searching for minds "uncontaminated" by the slave trade. He wished to offer trade and educational opportunities to what he perceived as "pure" Africans. His approach was very systematic: "purchase a tract of country from the natives," draw up "treaties of alliances" with them that promised them trade and education, and then offer the land to missionaries who would build a school. By 1845, Russwurm had become a firm advocate of the missionaries, especially Methodists, who were early champions of his governorship. He eventually became a Methodist himself.[37]

Like many in the college world, the governor of Maryland Colony became highly skilled at using religious sectarian rivalry to further his own agenda for establishing a moral and intellectual order. Knowing Methodists were worried about the growing "Papist" presence in the Maryland colony of Cape Palmas, he offered them the "honor" of first bid on a property once owned by a Catholic mission. The Methodists bid too low, however, and the Catholics were successful at purchasing the land and building from Russwurm for six thousand dollars, where they eventually founded a school. The Methodists were now on alert for the next opportunity to build a mission in Russwurm's colony. As one observer warned readers, and potential fundraisers, in the *Christian Advocate:* "Let Protestants endeavor to excel in labors and sacrifices." Russwurm knew that encouraging more and more "labors and sacrifices" between competing religious groups would only increase the number of educational structures in his "miniature republic."[38]

When John Russwurm died suddenly in 1851, the *African Repository* memorialized their former employee as a "regular graduate" of Bowdoin College—a man of "honor, ability, and usefulness to the day of his death." He had been a controversial yet dynamic employee. He had made himself "eminent" by the power of his mind and manners, but most importantly he had fulfilled in the Maryland colony of Cape Palmas what he had proposed long ago in his commencement speech about black leadership. As a man of color, he had "vindicated" the "perfect fitness of his race for the most important political positions in Africa." Russwurm's widow received resolutions of praise from colonizationists in Maryland as well as money for a "marble monument" to be raised at Cape Palmas and Baltimore. For all of his labor, however, Russwurm's "miniature republic" at Maryland Colony faded quickly after his death. According to James Hall, the new, "unbalanced" governor of the colony instigated a war between the settlers and the local natives. The leaders of neighboring Liberia stepped in to end the conflict and eventually annexed the Maryland Colony in 1858. As for the free black community in America, they remembered John Russwurm as a voice against slavery. Irving Garland Penn began the first chapter of his 1891 work, *The Afro-American Press and Its Editors,* with the story of Russwurm, a talented journalist whose "editorial pen could battle with such force against" the "volcano of sin and oppression" of American slavery. Penn's praises end abruptly, as he describes Russwurm's career as having been "cut short" when his paper folded and he was "captured by the Colonization Society and sent to Africa." Penn then refers interested readers to colonizationist reports for further information on Russwurm. Penn's silence about Russwurm's African career was a strong comment about the painful memory of Russwurm's betrayal of free blacks in America, who felt he had chosen Liberian white patronage over the struggle for liberty and black self-determination.[39]

Although the free black community and members of his Maine family both refused to maintain their connection with him, Russwurm's family in Liberia flourished after his death, expanding their power through educational networks. Five years after her father's death, Angelina Russwurm participated in the annual exercises of the new Ladies Literary Institute in Monrovia, giving speeches and exhibiting her classical learning in front of a group of Monrovian families and friends. A reporter for the *African Repository* observed that the "young ladies of Monrovia seem to be ahead of the young gentlemen in efforts for self improvement." The Liberian ladies held the same assumptions about their mental powers as the college ladies from Bowdoin College or from Margaret Junkin's Washington College. They believed that the "mental and moral culture of females" would "sway a considerable influence" in Liberian society. Indeed, the school system that Russwurm initiated in Liberia had already expanded into a few primary schools and some academies, like the Ladies Literary Institute. In 1850, colonizationist philanthropists in Massachusetts and New York had sketched out a plan for a college to be established in Liberia and white trustees had initiated fundraising throughout the college world. By the 1860s, Liberia College, staffed with a black president and black professors but always supervised by white trustees in America, offered a classical curriculum meant to refine a set of young leaders for Liberia. College families had trained and supported Angelina's father and many of his Liberian contemporaries. In spite of a civil war that would put an end to the legal existence of slavery in America—and all popular interest in Liberian colonization—college families would continue to support (and oversee) the training of "Liberian ladies and gentlemen" for decades to come.[40]

College families prided themselves on their skill at identifying and cultivating a leadership class, designing a special environment for its training, and working collectively to promote its influence throughout the new nation. They also worked at cultivating a class of elevated servants for their ideal world. This was a challenging project because, for college families, ideal servants were defined as those who knew their inferior position in society, were content to remain in that position, and also worked hard at self-improvement and maintaining moral and intellectual regularity. As many college families observed time and again, such good help was hard to find, and to keep.

Owned by a trustee family in Athens, William and David Hull were enslaved carpenters all of their lives, working on the brilliant structures of Franklin College and surrounding Athens "for years." Observing William Hull working on campus one day, the mathematics professor Alonzo Church stopped him to ask why "Billy" was so slow in his work. Hull stopped and asked Church why he should rush. As he observed, he was not "working by the job, nor by the day; but by my life." Whether he finished his college chores early or late, he would still, as a slave, face a future of eternal rounds of work without profit. His quick answer apparently silenced all further inquiries from the professor, a transplanted Vermonter who certainly knew the difference between free and slave labor but who had to have a slave "enlighten" him on the subject. Professor Alonzo Church's students considered William Hull's brother David to be a "natural wit" and jokingly referred to him as "Doctor," as if he were part of the faculty. When some students spied him reshingling a roof on campus one day, they called out "'How d'ye do, doctor?' in quick succession without giving him time to answer. The slave stopped his work, stood up, waited until the boys stopped laughing, and then answered them clearly: "Gentlemen, I am *in statu quo.*" The boys responded again with laughter at a slave's use of Latin. David Hull's use of this classical and legal phrase—shouted from the top of a Franklin college structure—pointed out the essentially flawed relationship his family shared with a world that promised limitless improvement and success to some, eternal social and economic stagnation to others.[41]

Often talked about by colonizationist college families as temporary exiles who would return to Africa one day, slaves in Southern college

towns were truly dark fixtures on the college campus, essential to supporting its brilliance. The Hulls and their fellow college slaves were well aware
that their masters and employers (for many slave had both in a college
town) considered their work profitable, skilled enough to refine Athenian
structures and yield cash for white pockets. Yet their owners did not think
them "eligible" to profit from their own skills. They were not paid. They
were not freed. They were forced to remain "in statu quo," subjects of
intense study by their masters, as well as intense control. The Hull family
argument—that they were forced to work forever but could never progress
or succeed—revealed the state of unnatural restraint and stagnation that
college servants experienced in a world dedicated to cultivating success
within a specifically defined moral and intellectual order.

College slaves proved expert at learning this moral and intellectual order
and working it to their advantage. They knew, for example, that there was
only one key to their freedom in this "new order" promoted by the college
world—the approval or disapproval of a white man. Their thoughts and
actions fixed on this arbitrary situation, trying to find ways around it or
fight against it. Through his mistress, a Washington College slave named
Nelson sent his "complements" to his master, a college trustee working at
the state legislature in Richmond. Nelson added a wish that his master not
"make the laws too hard for the poor Black people." As a slave living in the
college world, Nelson certainly knew the law—and the lawmakers. He also
knew that laws could be debated and changed. A knowledge of the law, as
well as when to bend it, debate it, or follow it to the letter, was a characteristic of college slaves. Just as the black bell-ringer Dick Carey felt free to
throw stones at whites in the name of "protecting" the campus of Franklin
College in the 1820s, college slaves were happy to uphold laws that let them
display power over their rulers. When a "man-servant" refused to remove
his hat upon entering a college home, a professor's wife "asked him if he
hadn't been taught that it was proper to take his hat off." The slave freely
argued back, correcting the woman's knowledge of the law. As a slave, he
only took off his hat "to his Master"! Irritated at his "impudence," the
woman nevertheless could not argue against such an informed position. A
"dark" mind had won yet another point.[42]

Along with "ladies and gentlemen" on circulating display, college towns
were also known for an assertive, argumentative, "clever" class of servants. Notorious for their ability to think and act with a certain display
of freedom, servants who refused to be servile were a constant source of

complaint for college families. The English visitor James Buckingham observed that "in no place during our stay in the United States, did we hear so much of the immorality and depravity of the slave population" than in Athens, Georgia. As abolitionists, the Buckinghams regretted the presence of slaves in Athens, but they agreed with college families that their "college set" of slaves were indeed different. They seemed less restrained than those of other Southern cities. Another English visitor, Frederick Marryat, found the same evidence in another Southern college town. In Lexington, Kentucky, the Englishman noted that Sunday was the day when all the slaves took their masters' carriages and went "junketing in every direction." He was shocked at the confident behavior of the young black men who walked into a Lexington confectionary shop, casually conversing on various topics. They acted like Transylvania College students, treating each other to snacks with money from their own pockets. They calculated the change easily, knowing the worth of money. These men were not free, but they were surprisingly skilled, at least to Marryat, in behaving and speaking as if they were. Like the Hull brothers at Athens, they protested their restrained status in a town dedicated to improvement by exhibiting as many of their moral and intellectual powers as they could risk in public.[43]

In Northern communities, college families viewed their free servants, most commonly free blacks or Irish, similarly to enslaved servants, assuming there was little potential in such "dark" minds for improvement and advancement. Differences in "color" or religion made their minds dark, ineligible for advancement. A student at Williams College remembered James Melville as a "shrewd Irishman" who "abounded in mother wit" and was fond of chatting with students as he worked around campus. His Catholicism and his ethnicity, according to college families, excluded him from the benefits of a college world dedicated to the spread of "enlightened" Protestantism. Despite the fact that working for Williams College earned Melville a steady salary and the chance for intellectual engagement, "Jimmy" encountered a condescending attitude from students and professors that he resented—and protested with the power of his "wit." After a recent religious revival on campus, a newly converted student met "Jimmy" one day and attempted to proselytize, asking the Irishman his opinion about the afterlife. Melville retorted that he would probably end up in "the bad place." When the student, in classic Sunday School form, asked him to elaborate on what he might be doing there, Melville quipped: "Oh, just waiting on the students, same as here." A group of students nearby laughed and they all moved on. Like David Hull in Athens, James Melville used his "mother wit" to protest his situation. His comment implied that serving Williams students was, indeed, a kind of hell on earth.[44]

Melville fought the condescending inquiries of a college student with the ridiculous image that college families tended to idealize—that their servants would be happy to serve them and the college forever. For college families, any attempt by their servants to "move up" in the world, out of their servant class and away from college employment, was an occasion for collective warning, condemnation, and murmurings about the evils of self-interest and ambition. College families preferred that their servants know their place rather than know their own minds. Northern college families employed a stream of servants, like James Melville, who were poorer and racially or ethnically different from themselves. To be ideal servants, these individuals had to work on improving themselves along moral and intellectual terms, but to also remain content to keep this improving activity within their class. Like college slaves in the South, ideal college servants in the North did not transcend their class or their work.

At Union College, Maria Potter, the daughter of college president Eliphalet Nott, discovered that her Welsh housemaid, Maria James, loved to write poetry. In Potter's estimation, the girl possessed a form of genius that needed cultivation. Maria and her husband, Alonzo Potter, the professor of moral philosophy at Union, published a collection of the maid's poems in 1839. They were careful to point out, however, that they were not celebrating the girl's mental powers. They were merely promoting the correct way for elevated families like themselves to cultivate improvement in their servants. Had the Potters of Union College found Maria James "eaten up with the desire of praise," they would have "declined any agency in the publication of this volume." The cultivation of such ambition would make their maid "less simple and less happy," and that would threaten the workings of their academic home—and the workings Union College.[45]

Maria James was an ideal model servant. Taken into service as a young girl from a poor mining family, she had been educated in English by Union College families and "friends who had the discernment to appreciate and the kindness to counsel and encourage her." More importantly to the Potters, these instructors "wisely abstained from any appeals to her ambition." In his introduction to her poems, Alonzo Potter emphasized repeatedly how James composed her poetry "when she was hardest at work." For his housemaid, poetry was not a way to escape her job but a way to spend her time improving herself while performing her housework. According to the Potters, Maria James wrote poetry without abandoning her "diligent discharge of duty." This was an ideal servant for a college household, a worker who blended both manual and mental labor together for the good of the college. The Potters were thrilled to publish Maria's poetry, her "retiring and modest manners" reassuring proof to them that their maid would stay in "obscurity," working for their college world in her improved fashion.[46]

Although Alonzo Potter does not mention any of this in his introduction to the poetry volume, at one time, after receiving her education, Maria James did leave the college world. As many of her poems describe, she moved to New York City to explore the many options open to a young woman who was domestically skilled and, thanks to Union College, literate. She pursued life in the city, worked as a dressmaker, and made some money. Not enough, however, to satisfy her. Maria James eventually returned to domestic service in the college world. There, she became known for her remarkable talent at poetry, and managed by her own talents to have her employers publish her work at no cost to herself. For James, poetry was her first love but domestic skills proved to be the most reliable source of income and self-support. In the college world, she could find satisfaction from both the pen and the broom. As she noted in one of her poems, it was not Union College families but her broom that turned out to be the true "friend in need; / On this I lean,—on this depend." Her broom—and her skill with it—ensured her economic and social freedom. She described in her poem how her broom symbolized money for "silk or lace," but that it also served as a reminder of "prudence whispering" that money should be saved for a "rainy day." Like many college servants, Maria James learned how to make the moral and intellectual order in the college world work for her benefit. Acquiring both literary and domestic experience at Union, the young Welsh immigrant successfully navigated the job market in New York City. After this experience, she freely chose to return to Union College and take up service, and a literary life. The skills, mental and manual, that Maria learned at Union proved to be extremely valuable as the young girl determined her own future. Unwilling to stay in the place Union College first assigned her, Maria James used her broom, and then her poetry, to make up her own mind about the best place for her future success. Except for publishing her poetry and possessing the public authority to portray her as an ideal servant who knew her place, the Potters really had very little power to keep Maria James in that ideal place.[47]

Life was not easy for free servants in the college world, but many, like James Melville or Maria James, considered the economic and educational benefits they gained there to outweigh the pressure and prejudice they experienced at the hands of "elevated" employers attempting to keep them in their place. Like college slaves, college servants grew adept at understanding and using the much-vaunted "moral and intellectual order" to their advantage, consciously bringing up their grievances over their work culture or personal treatment before the entire college community. Like slaves, servants felt free to argue with college families. Unlike slaves, they could push their employers further on issues of self-improvement, working conditions, and the concept of self-determination.

The constant need for laboring hands in their homes and on their campuses compelled college families to argue back with their help rather than summarily dismiss them as "impudent" servants and find new ones. One local free black carpenter, Peter Coon, worked for Williams College and was a regular attendee at President Mark Hopkins's sermons in the campus chapel. He was known for his carpentry skills and his sharp, very public disagreements with the president's theological positions. According to one student, whenever Peter felt that the presidential reasoning got "too hot for him," the man would get up and leave, loudly walking out of the chapel in front of everyone. He also felt free to visit Hopkins the next day and "have the argument out with him." Peter Coon could be a difficult employee, but his skills were needed at a prospering college in need of new buildings. Mark Hopkins chose reasoning rather than dismissal in dealing with Peter Coon's disruptive behavior, condescending to argue with a man he considered of a lower class and race and forced to engage with the opinionated carpenter's moral and intellectual perspectives. At Bowdoin College, the Packard family was always at odds with their servant, Lydia. Neither Alpheus Packard, Bowdoin's rhetoric professor, nor his wife Frances, were ever able to "bring her to anything definite" about her working hours, duties, or term of contract. Lydia fought continually against any constraint by the Packards. She refused to be "this ones girl or that ones girl," but insisted on being treated like "a kind of visitor that will work all the time, and will stay as long as she likes her treatment." Lydia ended the argument by refusing to sign any contract. She had "made up" her own mind, declaring she would not "make any engagements and then she cannot break them." Even the professor of rhetoric could not argue her out of this position. The Packards kept her on, however, because of their need for helping hands in a college home that grew each year with little Packards and the usual assortment of boarding students and visitors. Like all servants, Lydia had no problem voicing her opinion in her employer's home, even criticizing the Packards on the education of their children. While watching the Packard's little daughter one day, Lydia commented that the girl, always called a "little lady" by her proud mother, was not ladylike at all. She observed that the child could not be trusted to behave herself but was only "good with tending." Irritated by a servant's criticism of her child's behavior, Frances mused to a friend that her training of Lydia had not gone according to plan. Instead of improving with age, the servant Lydia was "not as patient and good natured as when she was younger."[48]

From the ranks of their slaves and servants, college families often chose protégées who they intended to train as model servants. Under the careful tutelage of college families, those chosen were expected to become educated and to be efficient, dutiful, and, hopefully, permanent. Busy organizing and managing the college world, college ladies like Frances Packard favored the protégée approach, as they were always in search of extra hands (white preferable over black) that could take over the manual work so that they could carve out time for their intellectual work.[49]

Frances Packard was happy to report that she had finally found such a servant, who, with training, would help her maintain her college home— and perhaps one day replace the rebellious Lydia. Writing to her mother, Frances described how Rozilla, a young white girl, had sat by her, "reading," in the parlor. Whenever the busy professor's wife was "not interrupted," Frances informed her mother, "I attend to her instruction." As it turned out, Frances was always interrupted and Rozilla's reading lessons took place in between the many chores her employer/teacher assigned her. The girl was forced to put down her book to "tend baby," work in the kitchen, clean the house, and run errands all over Brunswick. With Rozilla handling the domestic workings of her home, Frances Packard found time to work on the "business of instruction"—reading new literature, writing letters full of college news to the wide Bowdoin network, teaching her children (whose instruction took priority over Rozilla's), and maintaining her world's "state of society" through constant rounds of visiting, in Brunswick and in the homes of powerful trustees in Boston. When Rozilla proved too busy with her chores to "tend baby," Frances took her young daughter along with her on these social calls, confident that in the homes of other "college ladies" she would find some other well-trained "girl" to watch her child. No wonder Lydia resisted being "this ones girl or that ones girl." The collectivity of "college ladies" facilitated their ability to perform the moral and intellectual labor of the college world, but it also demanded that their servants be available at all times to assist in any college home, and at any college lady's bidding.

The Packard household ran smoothly until Rozilla decided she had learned enough. With her refined housekeeping skills, her new talent in reading, and, possibly, Lydia's informed advice, Rozilla envisioned her future far from Brunswick and left the Packard home. Frances was not pleased and refused to believe that Rozilla had made up her own mind about her departure. For Frances, her servant girl had been tempted away by the higher wages in a nearby factory or some other non-service occupation. Whatever the reason, college families never viewed servants and slaves like Rozilla and her fellow domestics as brilliant enough make decisions on their own. College families viewed them as eternal students in need of direction, dark minds immune to brilliant enlightenment and part of a permanent class of workers dedicated to serving the college world. When "college servants" were legally enslaved, these collective visions of ideal servitude sharpened considerably.[50]

In the late 1850s, Sally McDowell shared with Frances Packard and other college ladies this vision of an ideal servant, and her enslaved lady's maid, Jenny, was her hand-picked favorite. In the home of a trustee family of Washington College this "old family servant" spent many years serving McDowell women from cradle to grave. Jenny was especially known in the college town for her talents at soothing the pains of overwrought minds and bodies. After a particularly jolting stagecoach trip, Sally was "glad to assign myself to the mesmeric passes of my little maiden." As she told her fiancé, a Princeton professor, "My little maid . . . did wonders for me." The "touch of her fingers" through her hair was "like dreamy music." When she felt pain that made her long "to lay my head in my Mother's lap & take hearty cry, whilst she stroked my hair in her gentle way," Jenny became a maternal substitute for Sally's dead mother. Sally teased her Princeton fiancé that she would never allow him to "colonize" Jenny; she was a slave too valuable and too essential to the workings of the college world to be sent to Liberia.[51]

Jenny was not a "little maiden," but well into her forties, and her soothing services had been in demand for years. Sally McDowell had lived through the early death of their parents, the western emigration of her brothers, and her own devastating divorce from an abusive husband. For years after her divorce Sally only appeared at events in her college town of Lexington, where college families understood why she had to escape from what they all considered a husband with an "unbalanced" mind. While her family's wealth and social status shielded her from much social ostracism, she preferred to live a retiring life. After purchasing the family home from her brothers, the thirty-year-old Sally became the mistress of Col Alto, a house with land on the outskirts of Lexington, Virginia. She lived in the house with her younger sisters and operated her farm through an overseer.

Sally's father had been the governor of Virginia as well as a trustee of Washington College. Her sister had married a professor. Sally had never considered remarriage until a Princeton professor, Samuel Miller, came to Lexington for a visit. Contemplating such a new connection, the trustee's daughter was fearful of marriage after her first painful experience with it. She was also worried about moving to a Northern region "inching to abolitionism." The future destination of her slaves became a problem that Sally needed to solve before her marriage. Miller suggested that she sell them, but imagining a future without her slaves brought Sally "real pain." She informed her future husband that she could not sell them (or colonize them) because of "family ties." She was "bound" to them, she believed, by a "strong tie of gratitude and affection." And for her it was Jenny who had the strongest claim.[52]

In her letters to Miller, Sally referred constantly to the nine house slaves at Col Alto—slaves who served her directly or who made her money by working for other whites in Lexington. Besides Jenny, there was Alfred, her coachman, who was the "servant whose business it is to take the mail & bring it every day," but who was also called to "scrape" snow and "do my bidding" around the house. Another man, Edward, ran errands while acting as a butler, "setting the dinner table & ringing the bell." He was a "delicate" house servant whose refinement attracted the proprietor of nearby Alum Springs, who hired him as a bath and dinner attendant. Sally received eighteen dollars a month for Edward's refined services. As for Malinda, she was a "confirmed invalid." Another slave woman, Mary, was "so frequently sick" that she could not be hired out "with convenience" to another Lexington family. These two women worked in the home. Mary had young children who were "too young to be subjected to such usage as generally falls upon hired little negroes." Sally, therefore, did not consider them worth much. They were "two little worries of children" who "irritate me incessantly like a pair of mosquitoes." Sally tolerated them, however, because she was busy refining them. They were made to "wait on the house," and she saw a future profit in them "growing in knowledge & skill." Two of Mary's other children were old enough to be hired out.[53]

As she informed Miller, Sally felt a "sort of care" for them "not to be transferred to another." When she bought the family property, there had been the usual "division of servants" and, as she informed her fiancé, this "set" preferred "a home with me" than "following the fortunes of any other member of the family." She believed no "white servants could be more reliable," or "half as much attached as these."[54]

Sally highlighted Jenny in her letters as the most effective and the most industrious of her slaves, and even more important, the slave woman showed an "earnest and real devotion" to her. Jenny's persistence in staying at Col Alto and serving Sally was remarkable. When Sally bought the family farm, she suggested that Jenny might prefer being owned by one of her younger sisters "whose long minority would secure her a home in the family for many years." Jenny objected strenuously and requested to stay at Col Alto serving Sally and being owned by her alone. She reminded Sally of her work as a "special nurse" to McDowell's mother during her last illness. As Sally remembered fondly, Jenny "shared with us in her dying injunctions." She decided to retain ownership of Jenny due to their shared collective family memories and her need for an effective nurse and housekeeper.[55]

With slaves often described as "delicate" and claiming "privileges" because of their condition, Sally complained to Miller that they were "valueless," but she cared for them anyway. This claim of self-sacrifice proved her virtuous membership in the college family circles of Lexington. As she lectured her Northern fiancé, when slaves were "old & worn out from faithful service," their owners were "bound to take care of them" because of "every sentiment of humanity & honor." When slaves were not of "special value for their industry & fidelity" or "have always been imprudent" like her "set," they proved "a great burden."[56]

To Sally, Jenny was different. She was of great value. As Sally began to envision her future college home at Princeton, she found it difficult not to consult with Jenny about this vision. One day, she "stepped out" where Jenny "was at work" to converse with her about her "fair chance for the future." She made Jenny a "confidante," revealing to her for the first time her plans to marry and move North, suggesting again that Jenny consider moving to her sister's home in western Virginia. To her "surprise," Jenny expressed "great pleasure" at the marriage and "most emphatically refused to leave me." She assured her mistress that she would go "anywhere I chose to go, and hoped if she outlived me" that she could then "belong to" one of Sally's sisters. If her Princeton suitor was "shocked" to hear of her "confiding" in a slave, Sally explained that Jenny had always been a "very kind and faithful friend" and "was entitled to such a mark of respect and attention." Jenny had fulfilled the conditions of being an ideal servant in the college world and to Sally was considered part of the college family.[57]

Jenny proved fascinated with Sally's lover and "very respectfully" began making her own study of his situation in life. She was "delighted" to hear he was a minister and a widower with children. The slave woman assured her mistress that she "always did love children; and I will love these." All of her affections seemed to "fix" on this little motherless family at Princeton up North. Daguerreotypes of the children, sent to Sally by Miller, became an intense object of Jenny's affection. She informed Sally that she could not help herself from "kissing" these images, she felt so naturally and affectionately drawn to them. She admitted they "aint nothing but pictures—but I just have to do that." Sally informed her suitor that Jenny was especially interested in his little son, who was "so sweet" that her affection seemed to spill over into the physical, passionate "animal spirits" that white families always ascribed to their slaves. As Sally reported, Jenny was so affected by the boy's sweetness that she wanted to "mash his eyes out & so on & so on" with her kisses and hugs. An expert nursemaid and an expert in the workings of the moral and intellectual order of the college world, Jenny knew how to perform ideal affection to the satisfaction of her college family, even if she did not truly feel it.[58]

Displaying her potential for new loyalty to the Princeton family, Jenny ensured a continuing display of old loyalties to Washington College and the McDowell family. She reminded Sally of how Governor McDowell himself had marveled at the deep bonds of attachment between his daughters and Jenny. One of Sally's youngest sisters loved Jenny so much, he always observed, that she would give up "her very skin" for her slave. This idea, that her sister loved Jenny so much that she would sacrifice her privileged white skin, persuaded Sally that her future happiness was impossible without Jenny. Whenever Sally "consulted" with Jenny, the "little maiden" shrewdly offered herself as the ideal servant, arguing that she was the natural choice to take care of Sally, her new college home at Princeton, and her stepchildren. She also participated in collective virtue, offering herself as a repository of family memories and stories for Sally to possess in her new home when she moved away from Lexington. Sally marveled later to Miller on "how I could have made up my mind" to give up ownership of Jenny. Portraying herself as the ideal servant, Jenny successfully made herself essential to the future workings of another college home. Even Samuel Miller included "our good old friend Jenny" in his vision of future happiness with Sally.[59]

After taking Jenny into her confidence Sally discovered that word had spread throughout the house that the mistress was going to marry and was thinking of selling up and moving out. Her slaves were "uneasy & anxious about their fate" and she did not "know what to do with them." She was long familiar with this sense of unease. The anxiety surrounding a slave sale was a "disagreeable proceeding" in Lexington. Whenever families began making decisions about their future, a series of "sudden and powerful changes" swept the college town like a revival, making "apparent to us" the "heavy evils of slavery." Having once inadvertently visited an aunt's home "on the eve of a sale," she had been horrified that her visit coincided with this "trying thing." The "college ladies" watched from a window as slaves they had known all their lives were "subjected to this trial." These slaves, she assured her Northern suitor, were all eventually bought "by the family," but she neglected to add that her family was moving west, out of Virginia, thus breaking the extensive black family ties in the Lexington region. While this "traffick in human beings" was "shocking," she could not see an end to it because "slavery will exist as long as the world." She viewed slaves as "poor creatures" whose "condition will never be remedied." In her opinion, colonization was good for some slaves but her college world was also expert at creating and maintaining a set of ideal slaves educated for loyal service, like the "efficient" Jenny, to keep society working smoothly.[60]

Efficiency was an important principal in Sally's life as she contemplated selling her property and remarrying. Tired of her "great scamp" of an overseer who she suspected was stealing from her, Sally hired a new man. He was "not a gentleman," but she admired his "great idea of retrenchment." He demanded that her profitless and "delicate" house slaves work in the fields alongside a set of cheap hired hands and she liked this collective labor ideal. As a college family member, she hoped the manual labor would "strengthen" the "delicate" Edward and improve the attitude of the coachman Alfred who "greatly annoyed" her. Alfred was "honest and faithful," she informed Miller, but also "sullen & simper truant to a degree that I found extremely hard to endure." She hoped her overseer's new system of labor would solve the attitude problem that was growing among her slaves. Jenny, however, seemed uncontaminated by these growing behavior problems and remained an ideal servant.[61]

Alfred was soon injured by the threshing machine, and Sally, "trembling at the news," visited him in his quarters. "With great solemnity" he informed her that he had been very close to death but he felt prepared to be "sent to judgment" and receive "my reward." As Sally observed to her suitor, Alfred was "what he calls a 'sufficient member' of the Methodist Church North" and was always "full of the phrases & peculiarities" of "his sect." By the 1850s, Alfred's "sect" was also moving stridently into the abolitionist camp, the Northern Methodists having split from the Southerners over the slavery issue in the late 1840s. While she allowed him to choose "his sect," Sally believed the slave had chosen wrongly. She doubted that her problematic coachman, who always refused to listen to the good news of Lexington's white Presbyterian ministers, was a "sincere Christian."[62]

Soon after his accident in the fields, Alfred attacked the new overseer. Writing to Miller, Sally explained in detail how she handled the problem as an "enlightened" college lady. "You Northern people can form only a faint idea of the panic created" when a slave is "bold enough to lift his hand against his Master, or his Master's white subordinate." She felt herself "in the midst of such a panic now." As a college lady, she moved to create order out of disorder. Her overseer reported that Alfred had "resisted his authority" and the men had fought with "heavy blows." Since the overseer was "not so strong as Alfred," the coachman had evidently won the fight. After speaking to the overseer, she summoned Alfred and "heard his story." He "wept profusely," but "felt that he had done no wrong." Sally assured her fiancé that she was "entirely self-collected and capable of giving all safe and proper directions." In spite of all the raised passions, she insisted that the incident be resolved the next day "when all parties would be calmer"—and she could "conveniently" summon her brother-in-law and the town constable. Sally immediately took advantage of this opportunity to correct some of the moral and intellectual errors she had discovered among her slaves.[63]

Although she informed her fiancé that this incident was her "first experience in such matters," Sally had lived in, benefited from, and supported the moral and intellectual order promoted in Lexington. She proved to be quite the authority on how to maintain it, at least among her slaves. The next day, Sally ordered the overseer to give the "whipping," the "town constable" to stand nearby "to assist him in case of repeated resistance," and her brother-in-law (a college professor) to also stand by to "see that the punishment was humanely given." She summoned all of her slaves to the back porch, where they observed the "white men" assembled "on the steps." They saw their white mistress standing "apart from any of them," but higher, "on the porch," looking "determined and composed." Sally described to Miller how she had to transform herself into a "Master" and "Judge" who announced Alfred's "fault & his punishment." She then lectured her slaves on their condition. They "must submit to me in the person of my Overseer" and "look to me as their protector." After the lecture, Alfred spoke up, asking if Sally would "allow me to speak a few words for myself?" Sally "consented," and Alfred objected to her theory of protection, arguing that his actions had been based on self-defense—"Am I to allow an Overseer to impose on me?" Sally reminded him of his dependent status and that he was not to "undertake to defend yourself" or "take the law in your own hands." Attempting to act like a free man in Lexington, Alfred had chosen his own religion and even grumbled about his job. His attempt at self-defense, however, went too far in threatening the "order of things" in the college world. Sally ordered the overseer to punish him, and the effect of the incident was immediate. "My whole household looks haggard. A tornado seems to have swept over us."[64]

As one of the house slaves, Jenny was present at Alfred's punishment and watched a college-world lesson she had learned time and again in Lexington. The speech, theories, and actions of white people defined the moral and intellectual order she served. Slaves could assert themselves and claim some economic or social power through luck or white neglect. Yet when they asserted too strongly, white logic always trumped black logic even if black men and women had the power of reason, justice, or even "common sense," on their side.

After she had resolved the "problem" of Alfred, Sally observed to her future Princeton family that the "Providence of God" had placed her "again & again" in "terribly trying circumstances." She wondered for a moment if she had received "scars" from her transformative experiences as a "lady" and a "slave owner." She decided that due to all her trials she was a "much improved person in many respects," but was "by no means perfect yet." She could not help adding, however, that the "heavy evil" of slavery would have been "managed better, if there had been no Northern interference." She suspected that Alfred's Northern-influenced Methodism was at the root of his rebellion rather than his own inclination to rebel. College servants were not expected to know their own minds.[65]

After a life of such lessons from the college world, Jenny also become a "much improved person." Like most college servants, she was an expert at navigating the moral and intellectual order of the college world. In 1860 she navigated herself right out of it, literally graduating herself. Sally McDowell finally married her Princeton professor, moving to New Jersey and bringing her loving and loyal "little maiden" with her. On a visit back to Lexington, she brought shocking intelligence to Washington College families. As one professor informed his wife, the Millers had appeared in town "minus their servant woman." Jenny had become, he noted sarcastically, "her own mistress." On a family trip to Philadelphia, Jenny had escaped the Millers and the college world. The news mystified the college families of Washington College. Jenny had been a "favorite servant," quite possibly the "most efficient one" that Sally had owned, and certainly a privileged one—a member of the family. It was also remarkable to this professor that Jenny was "rather advanced beyond the median of life" but made her escape anyway. All in Lexington assumed she could never have made such a choice by herself. She must have been tempted away from her virtuous mistress by another influence—"fanatical abolitionists." To white college families in Lexington, this privileged "servant" had acted against all logical reason. For Jenny, however, her escape to the free black community in Philadelphia (and perhaps to points farther north) was a move that made perfect sense. It marked the commencement of a life that she could finally shape for herself.[66]

As the experiences of John Russwurm and Jenny reveal, no "dark minds" were ever admitted to the privileges and advantages of the college world on an equal basis. John Russwurm received his "elevation" on the condition that he would never be free of racial prejudice or eligible for Bowdoin College benefits unless he left the republic. While trying to build a class of black leaders through the "business of instruction," Russwurm would always depend upon, and contend with, the patronizing supervision of the college world. While his fellow white college students had their own conditional duties and obligations to fulfill in order to receive benefits from the college world, young white men did not have to accept exile in exchange for supportive assistance. Aware that white supervision would never allow her true freedom, Jenny knowingly conformed to the demands of the college world, modeling herself as the ideal servant. Her conformity eventually allowed her to escape and, for once in her life, to define her own definition of freedom. In an expanding college world that celebrated eternal self-improvement, collective assistance, and the potent influence of virtue, students and servants judged "dark" were consciously excluded from the elevating influences of this dynamic environment.

Epilogue

BY THE 1840s, a series of "wild-goose-chase" projects, as one student called them, began to plague the college world and its inhabitants. They threatened to distract the minds of the colleges' refined, elevated beings from their ideals. Instead of relying on prudence and planning to plot out their future, many students began to embrace the notion of wild speculation, dreaming of adventures far from the college world and fortunes to be made overnight. College families had always identified the wider nation and its "erroneous" notions of virtue as a threat to their moral and intellectual order. This new worldly invasion into their virtuous world manifested itself in students and college "friends" contracting a variety of fevers that threatened to turn the republic upside down: "emigration fever," "gold fever," "Texas fever," "military fever," and "abolitionist fever."

A member of a Dickinson College family was able to observe "raging gould fever" in action as his Carlisle neighbors and a group of Dickinson graduates formed "companies" bound for California. One student marveled at the actions of student fortune hunters in Lexington, Virginia: "I did not think that men of their sense could be so easily deluded by such a palpable humbug" as "California fever." Like his instructors, he disapproved of such behavior. He worried that his friends were leaving the college world prematurely, having "staked their lives at a great hazard." A Washington College student monitored the similar career of his brother, who had left college without his degree determined only to "make money." Moving from Tuscaloosa to New Orleans to Texas, the brother had tried surveying, law, and cotton planting, driven by a "fever" for cash. Without the right infusion of virtue, his brother feared, his brother would become prey for bad company. Sure enough, he was swindled by gamblers, left alone and penniless in a distant Southern territory. These fevers infecting Americans young and old in the 1840s and 1850s reflected, to college families, a fearful threat to the moral and intellectual order they were trying to model and promote from their world.[1]

Passionate "fevers" also disturbed the culture of collective harmony promoted within the college world. When it began to infect college families, people took immediate notice. In 1858 a college lady from Lexington, Virginia, wrote to her brother about a "fever of excitement" gripping their college town. She had shocking news to report to him about the behavior of their Washington College president, George Junkin. The tensions between the college president and his colleague at the head of the new law school in town had become an "unfortunate and disgraceful affair." As Mary Davidson reported, the college president and a judge "had a fight on the street yesterday morning." It was well known that the two men held a grudge, since both wished to protect the interests of their separate institutions. Such bad blood between college officials was not unknown in college communities, yet college families usually fought each other through high-minded argument, wielding angry words in print or through public debate.[2]

The argument in Lexington proved "disgraceful" because the two men had exchanged loud insults and actual blows in public. Upon meeting one another on the street, the college president had criticized the law school and the moral behavior of the judge's students. The judge then demanded an apology from the president, calling him "a vile calumniator." The president refused and called the judge a "vile rum sucker," a reference to the judge's love of drink. The president's attack was so personal, or, as Mary described it, such a "tender point," that the judge, "in a great passion," struck the president in the face. The judge's law students, many graduates of Washington College, "set up a wonderful shout" as they watched these two self-appointed role models exhibit passionate, rather than prudent, behavior. Suddenly aware that the students were watching, or fearful that he was no match for the judge, the college president refrained from striking back and "very calmly walked away" in silence. So "what do you think of that?" Mary inquired of her brother, musing that the world was "coming to a woful end when right reverend Doctors are soundly boxed on the ears by dignified Judges of the Federal Courts." The incident, she suspected, would "cause trouble" for the future.[3]

This incident reveals how far the college world had weakened in its collective public calls for civility and order by the late 1850s. Even role models like college presidents found it hard to check their passions. The nation's ideal communities of virtue, created for the promotion of collective harmony, had themselves become infected by the extreme positions that were sweeping the nation as a whole. A few years later, President Junkin left his post and the town of Lexington and returned to his home state of Pennsylvania, his stand for national union drowned out by the local passion for secession. Like most college-family members, Junkin was no abolitionist: he was perfectly happy to retain slavery in the South (he argued that slavery accorded with biblical law), and he was also happy to promote colonization. But by 1860 there was no place for such calls for national union in a Southern state. As the Civil War ripped the young nation apart and destroyed a generation of young college-age men, the college world did not transcend the conflict or even call for peace or harmony. It divided along sectional lines. College families also divided. President Junkin's daughter Margaret remained behind in Lexington, married to a professor at the nearby Virginia Military Academy. She spent much of her later life championing the Confederate cause and Robert E. Lee's eventual ascension to the Washington College presidency, publishing an impressive amount of literary work, and memorializing the Confederate war dead, especially her slain brother-in-law, Professor T. J. "Stonewall" Jackson.[4]

As the daughter of the president at Dickinson College, Mary Johnson described the college world on the eve of the Civil War in this way: "Waves of fierce passion, running mountain-high in the fall of '60 over the coming elections, beat fiercely against the walls" of Dickinson College and its town of Carlisle. As she remembered, "Most of the students were from the South, and of course intense in their Southern sympathies; some were from the border, and tinged with the views of both sections; while a few were uncompromising abolitionists." As for the faculty at Dickinson, they "were almost as much divided as the students."[5]

For college families, the Civil War interrupted their carefully cultivated "business of instruction" as students turned into soldiers. College ladies North and South rolled bandages and sewed for the armies, their fundraising skills now channeled into financially supporting their respective armies, their literary skills now used to compose poetry, song, and story to bolster their side in the war. Southern college families saw their college structures burned and vandalized, their dormitories turned into barracks by "invaders" who were not "gentlemen." All worriedly read the newspapers and scanned the death lists, watching for the names of the young men they had known as students and who were dying too young. All pined for an end to war and looked forward to a time when "our college" would open again. Professors took up their own positions during the war, some on the battlefield leading students in war rather than recitation. College families lost many of their own. Isaac Jackson lost a son. So, too, did his scientific colleague, Albert Hopkins. The only son of Albert and Louisa Hopkins left student life at Williams to become a "gentleman" officer and died in battle in 1864. Albert determinedly went south to find his son's body and bring him home to Williams, assisted along the way by a network of college "friends," North and South. Hopkins returned with "Eddy" and buried him next to his mother in the college cemetery on campus. While Williams students after the war increasingly refused to view the pious Hopkins as a true scientist (he remained interested in sparking campus revivals and using the stars to prove the power of religion rather than in exploring the new, more-secular scientific methods), they and the college community itself certainly respected him as an example of virtuous self-sacrifice. As they strolled around campus after the war, Albert Hopkins and many of the faculty of his generation appeared to students as living models of traditional ideals and practices that were under debate in postwar America. To many college families, the Civil War proved that their carefully constructed world was not immune from the passions of the nation. Trying hard to transcend the republic in order to teach it, college families discovered in the 1860s just how deeply enmeshed they were in the nation and its troubles.[6]

As educational institutions reopened their doors in earnest after the war, college families North and South were some of the first to call for national unity, which was of course good for their "business of instruction." They provided advice and expertise, and many of their well-trained children now undertook to teach in a college world that spanned the continent and included more than just "small" colleges. After the Civil War, the college world filled up with new state universities, new women's colleges, and "negro colleges." These new institutions for ex-slaves and free blacks, often overseen by white trustees, promoted manual rather than mental instruction for these "dark" minds. Still, the growing numbers of black students and instructors took advantage of their new access to higher education, continually insisting to American society that there was no difference between the power of the black mind and that of the white mind. Even as they reached out to assist these new "Negro colleges" with their patronage, college families remained committed to the colonization ideal; they still believed that "dark" minds should always be educated in their own institutions, far away from white brilliance. Many continued to maintain racial segregation policies in their own institutions, and they also continued to support the new college in Liberia as the more-ideal destination for "negro" college professors and students.

The new state universities and their promoters offered another perspective on higher education. In contrast to the small colleges, by the end of the century the universities were accepting greater numbers of young white, middle-class men and women. They also tended to champion rather than condemn direct ties with the worlds of commerce and politics. After the Civil War, it was the universities that led the way in linking higher education with the growing world of the professions, introducing a new template for modern American education in which collegiate institutions sought to work *with* Wall Street and Washington. This new form of educational enterprise would prove to be both profitable and problematic. Yet the legacy of the older college world, that a higher education provided access to an exclusive set of contacts, opportunities, and privileges, remained—and this legacy increased in popularity as higher education became more and more accessible.

Some historians have argued that the universities blazed a new path into modernity and more-disciplined thought and professionalization, but I suggest that there was more continuity than difference between the early college world and the world of the university. The old practice of "claiming kin" still held firm and many of the children of the early college families were involved in founding and running the first state universities. One of Moses Waddel's sons remained at Franklin College as a professor, but his other son, John, after graduating and then spending time as a chaplain in the Confederate army, eventually took over the chancellorship of the University of Mississippi, where he worked to bring his state institution in line with the growing educational standards promoted by the state universities in Michigan and Wisconsin.[7]

Two graduates of Williams College provide further examples of how college families moved easily between the small colleges and the large universities. After graduating from Williams, Paul Chadbourne became a professor there before moving on to the presidency of the University of Wisconsin. He later returned to Williams to take over the presidency after Mark Hopkins retired in 1872. But Chadbourne finished out his career by leading the new state University of Massachusetts at Amherst. His colleague, John Bascom, was also a "Williams man" who graduated and would return to teach at his alma mater for over twenty years. When Chadbourne left Wisconsin, however, it was Bascom who took up his post there and helped develop the university at Madison. His rigorous improvements to the curriculum there were praised by trustees, his college-world advocacy of temperance not so much appreciated. College ladies and their organizational skills were also utilized in the new university system. The activities of John Bascom's wife, a local Williamstown girl named Emma Curtiss, reflected the expanding interests of a whole new generation of college ladies. As her family moved between older and newer institutions in the expanding college world, Emma expanded her "college work" to involve teaching, temperance work, and suffrage. She held positions in the Wisconsin suffrage associations and worked for the Woman's Christian Temperance Union. Her college-president husband supported her in both organizations and both Bascoms educated their children (male and female) with the expectation that they would take up posts in their family's expanding "business of instruction." All of the Bascom children would graduate from the University of Wisconsin and move on to professional posts, their daughter Florence receiving her Masters degree and then attaining a doctorate from Johns Hopkins. The first woman to work on a state geological survey, Florence Bascom would have a long teaching career that included terms at both the new Ohio State University and at one of the new colleges for women, Bryn Mawr.[8]

College families after the Civil War were highly active in founding and maintaining professional associations that would further institutionalize their "business of instruction." College presidents had their own associations. As a proven expert on how women could use education to further their influence on American society, Emma Bascom was one of the founders of the Association for the Advancement of Women, an organization that supported women interested in educational careers. Professors would also create organizations that would help define and justify their "disciplines," an especially urgent matter in large institutions like universities where academics continued to idealize their peculiar notion of family but behaved more like rival siblings in a competitive struggle to win funding, students, and hopefully, if some "friends of education" were especially generous, an impressive building to house their discipline.[9]

Historians have noted that numerous "models of intellectual citizenship," like early national debate societies, scientific groups, and literary organizations and "clubs," endeavored to model a different sort of thinker and citizen for the new republic. Many of these early associations certainly revealed the thirst for knowledge in early America and contributed to the creation of elite culture in the nineteenth century, but as one historian has noted, "the historical record does not favor them." Many of these elite clubs—with their conversations and circulating texts and their cliques of enthusiastic gentlemen, and some ladies—had faded within a generation. History reveals that theirs was but a brief moment of impressive intellectual work. Perhaps the public took some notice of their periodicals or books, but then the participants lost interest, moved away from each other, or simply moved on to other enterprises. Ultimately, however, when it came to leaving a lasting impression, they proved to be nothing more than an interesting example of "poignant, productive failure."[10]

In contrast, the first-generation of early national colleges founded along the frontiers of the new republic set in motion a number of associations that survive to this day. Most of these institutions are thriving today, promoting themselves on their websites for their expertise in training America's leaders and inculcating a "sense of tradition." Although the institutions survive, only traces of the actual college families remain.

Their names survive, adorning college landmarks from gates to gardens to administration buildings. One can still stroll by the Hopkins Observatory at Williams, wander around Jackson's Garden at Union College, admire the columned buildings at Athens and Lexington that were maintained and whitewashed by enslaved "college servants." Many of their family homes also survive, converted into dormitories, offices, or venues for social events. Most original-family members are buried in cemeteries on or near their campuses. Their portraits hang on the walls of administrative offices or may be found in the colleges' archives, their faces mostly unknown to present-day students, faculty, and staff. Their writings also survive, carefully preserved on the shelves of their college's archives and in numerous libraries, even if, like Phebe Upham's study of spiritualism, many were last checked out during the 1920s and are rarely consulted today.

It was their collective concern about how to direct the "business of instruction" in a virtuous manner that has made the most-lasting contribution to American society. This charter generation of educators began a series of debates with the new nation that still rage today. What are the ideal parameters of an American education? Is there still a need to teach a Revolutionary definition of virtue that calls for collective self-sacrifice? How do educators teach students to act with prudence rather than passion? What kinds of models of ideal behavior and thought do young minds need to achieve success? Are there differences between the female and male mind, and should that make any educational difference? What is the best balance between mental and manual labor? Should all Americans be eligible to receive the benefits of the elevated knowledge offered by the college world? How can an institution cultivate collective and affectionate cooperation between professionals?

Any discussion of the "issues at hand" in American higher education today engages with these questions first proposed and explored by the nation's first generation of college families. Whether these discussions take place at educational conferences or in the classroom, at political hearings or over a cup of coffee, the strategies employed by early college families and the blueprint they passed on to later generations of educators continue to spark debate about the precise "moral and intellectual" parameters that are needed to "train up" the next generation of Americans in virtue and knowledge. College families would be thrilled to learn that their "college work" continues on.

NOTES

Introduction

1. Longfellow, *Hyperion*, 1:83–84.

2. Junkin, "The Haunts of the Student." For the anonymous book review, see "Reviews and Notices," *American Annals of Education*, October 1839. For biographical background on Preston, see Coulling, *Margaret Junkin Preston*.

3. Junkin, "The Haunts of the Student."

4. In his study focusing on New England men socially and economically navigating their way through the early republic, J. M. Opal calls these evolving standards of success a "new sociology of ambition" (see Opal, *Beyond the Farm*, 101).

5. Joyce Appleby defines this generation as "agents of change in an era of change marked by the convergence of political revolutions, commercial expansion, and intellectual ferment that penetrated . . . the most mundane aspects of life" (Appleby, *Inheriting the Revolution*, 3).

6. See Cremin, *American Education;* Wood, *The Radicalism of the American Revolution;* Jaffee, "The Village Enlightenment in New England"; Bushman, *The Refinement of America;* and S. Martin, *Cultural Change and the Market Revolution in America.*

7. See Horn, Lewis, and Onuf, *The Revolution of 1800;* Frederickson, *The Black Image in the White Mind;* Howe, *The Unitarian Consciousness;* and Winterer, *The Culture of Classicism.*

8. The new republic inherited nine colleges from its former colonizer: Harvard (1650), William and Mary (1693), Yale (1745), Princeton (1746), King's College [Columbia] (1754), the University of Pennsylvania (1755), Brown (1764), Queen's College [Rutgers] (1766), and Dartmouth (1769). For legacies of leadership and public service in these original colonial institutions, see Robson, *Educating Republicans*, 3–28.

9. Junkin, "The Haunts of the Student." For the varying definitions of virtue during this era, see Kloppenberg, *The Virtues of Liberalism*. For early republican desires for collective harmony and "communion with others," see Burstein, *Sentimental Democracy*, xiv.

10. Lee, *Mary Austin Holley,* 118; Benjamin Vaughan to Jesse Appleton, 16 May 1808, Jesse Appleton Collection, George J. Mitchell Department of Special Collections and Archives, Bowdoin College Library.

11. For classic treatments of college history, see Hofstadter, *Anti-Intellectualism in American Life;* and Rudolph, *The American College and University.*

12. Roger Geiger's collection of articles, *The American College in the Nineteenth Century,* reflects this recent contextualizing. For works that link colleges to wider social and political, religious, and regional issues, see Novak, *The Rites of Youth;* Stevenson, *Scholarly Means to Evangelical Ends;* and J. Green, *Military Education and the Emerging Middle Class in the Old South.* For two important review articles on new educational scholarship, see Howe, "Church, State, and Education in the Young American Republic"; and Ogren, "Sites, Students, Scholarship, and Structures."

13. For both the social expectations and fears over these new colleges, see the example of the founding of Dickinson College in Carlisle, Pennsylvania, in Ridner, *A Town In Between,* 5-6.

14. Ibid., 4.

15. Philanthropos (pseud.), "On the Necessity of Disseminating Knowledge in America," *The American Museum, or Universal Magazine,* January 1789. For the transformation from patriarchal to paternal control, see Fliegelman, *Prodigals and Pilgrims;* and Yazawa, *From Colonies to Commonwealth.*

16. See Sizer, *The Age of the Academies,* chap. 1. See also Cremin, *American Education;* Kelley, *Learning to Stand and Speak;* and Opal, *Beyond the Farm,* chap. 4.

17. For a copy of the Yale Report, see Hofstadter and Smith, *American Higher Education,* 275-91. For further Yale faculty opinion about educational standards, see Stevenson, *Scholarly Means to Evangelical Ends.*

18. See Richard, *The Golden Age of Classics in America;* and Winterer, *The Culture of Classicism.*

19. Philanthropos (pseud.), "On the Necessity of Disseminating Knowledge in America," *The American Museum, or Universal Magazine,* January 1789. According to the historian Mary Kelley, academies generally imparted the "values and vocabulary of civil society" to students, urging young minds toward activity in the name of nationhood (Kelley, *Learning to Stand and Speak,* 32).

20. Junius Hillyer Memoir, p. 173, Hargrett Rare Book and Manuscript Library, University of Georgia.

21. See Ryan, *Cradle of the Middle Class;* Gay, *The Bourgeois Experience;* Davidoff and Hall, *Family Fortunes;* and Lewis, *The Pursuit of Happiness.*

22. Onuf, *Jefferson's Empire,* 2, 14.

23. See A. Hopkins, "Revivals of Religion in Williams College," 341.

24. See *The Seasons,* in Thomson, *Complete Poetical Works.* For Thomson as a well-known "Whig poet laureate," see Wood, *The Creation of the American Republic,* 92.

Chapter One. Cultivating the College World

1. For the early Presbyterian influence on higher education, see H. Miller, *The Revolutionary College.*

2. For the institutional history of Washington and Lee University, see Crenshaw, *General Lee's College.* For a version written by an early professor and president, see Ruffner, "Early History of Washington College."

3. Sellers, *Dickinson College,* 61; Wood, *The Creation of the American Republic,* 46–48.

4. Kloppenberg, *The Virtues of Liberalism,* 21–37.

5. George Baxter, "Letter from G. Baxter, on Revival in Kentucky," *The Western Missionary, and Repository of Religious Intelligence,* August 1803, 260–61. For the Kentucky revivals, see Boles, *Religion in Antebellum Kentucky.*

6. Crenshaw, *General Lee's College,* 36–37. For the wide-ranging influence of the "friends of education," see Cremin, *American Education,* 176–77.

7. George Baxter to Anne Baxter, 14 April 1805, 11 May 1805, Baxter Family Correspondence and Papers, Special Collections, Leyburn Library, Washington and Lee University.

8. Royster, *A Revolutionary People at War,* 360–68; Ferling, *The World Turned Upside Down;* Berlin and Hoffman, *Slavery and Freedom in the Age of the American Revolution;* and Norton, *Liberty's Daughters.*

9. [Noah Webster], "Education," *American Magazine,* February 1788. See also Appleby, *Capitalism and the New Social Order.*

10. MW, "On a Liberal Education," *Columbian Magazine,* February 1787, 263–66; Fenno (pseud.), "Importance of a Proper System of Education," *The American Museum, or, Universal Magazine,* October 1789, 290.

11. Philanthropos (pseud.), "On the Necessity of Disseminating Knowledge in America," *The American Museum, or Universal Magazine,* January 1789. Fortenbaugh, *In Order to Form a More Perfect Union,* 47; Hatch, *The History of Bowdoin College,* 2; Cleaveland and Packard, *History of Bowdoin College,* 5.

12. Butterfield and Rush, "Dr. Benjamin Rush's Journal of a Trip to Carlisle in 1784," 452–55.

13. For "informed citizenry," see R. D. Brown, *The Strength of a People.*

14. Butterfield and Rush, "Dr. Benjamin Rush's Journal of a Trip to Carlisle in 1784," 452–55.

15. Wood, *The Creation of the American Republic,* 426–27; Fortenbaugh, *In Order to Form a More Perfect Union,* 104.

16. Hampton McIntosh to Henry Jackson, 31 July 1819, Henry Jackson Papers, Hargrett Rare Book and Manuscript Library, University of Georgia.

17. Knight, *A Documentary History of Education in the South before 1860,* 4:5–8.

18. For a history of colleges and the state legislatures, see Herbst, *From Crisis to Crisis.*

19. Philo (pseud.), "The Nursery," *Boston Magazine,* August 1785; John Jay, "Report of the Regents of the University of the State of New York," *New York Magazine,* April 1796; Sellers, *Dickinson College,* 113.

20. Horace Holley to Mary Holley, 25 May 1818, Horace Holley Papers, William L. Clements Library, University of Michigan.

21. Benjamin Vaughan to Jesse Appleton, 15 June 1808, 3 August 1808, and William Vaughan to Jesse Appleton, 10 April 1810, Appleton Collection; Angelical Campbell to President Eliphalet Nott, 29 April 1805, Union College Letterbooks, Special Collections, Schaffer Library, Union College; Rev. Alfred Johnson to Joseph McKeen, 5 November 1801, Joseph McKeen Collection, Bowdoin College Library, Brunswick, Me.

22. Hannah M. Crocker to President Jesse Appleton, 23 July 1813, Appleton Collection; "From the National Intelligencer, Sept. 21," *New York Evening Post,* 23 September 1819.

23. George Baxter to Anne Baxter, 30 October 1805, 5 November 1805, Baxter Family Correspondence and Papers.

24. Daniel Dana to Jesse Appleton, 24 January 1809, Appleton Collection.

25. George Baxter to Anne Baxter, 11 April 1805, Baxter Family Correspondence and Papers.

26. George Baxter to Anne Baxter, 23 and 28 April 1805, ibid.

27. Elizabeth Tappan to Elizabeth Appleton, 22 October 1814, 7 March 1815, 1 December 1815, 12 February 1818, Pierce-Aiken Family Papers, Library of Congress. For husband Benjamin Tappan's biography, see Cleaveland and Packard, *History of Bowdoin College,* 149.

28. Andrews Norton to Jesse Appleton, 20 October 1810, Appleton Collection, Bowdoin College Library. Norton was a tutor from 1809 to 1810 (see Cleaveland and Packard, *History of Bowdoin College,* 148–49).

29. Horace Holley to Mary Holley, 27 May 1818, Holley Papers.

30. George Baxter to Anne Baxter, 11 April 1808, Baxter Family Correspondence and Papers; Rev. Alfred Johnson to Joseph McKeen, 5 November 1801, McKeen Collection.

31. George Baxter to Ann Fleming Baxter, 14 April 1805, Baxter Family Correspondence and Papers.

32. Louisa Baxter to W. Henry Foote, 27 September 1853, ibid.

33. Butterfield and Rush, "Dr. Benjamin Rush's Journal of a Trip to Carlisle in 1784," 452–55. For continuing problems at the College at Philadelphia, see Hessinger, *Seduced, Abandoned, and Reborn,* chap. 3.

34. "Commencement in Dickinson College," *Universal Asylum and Columbian Magazine,* July 1792.

35. Jenks, "The Inaugural Address, Delivered in Brunswick, September 9, 1802, By the Rev. Joseph McKeen."

36. Levi McKeen to Joseph McKeen, 8 January 1802, McKeen Collection.

37. For McKeen information, see Cleaveland and Packard, *History of Bowdoin College*, 2. See also Nehemiah Cleaveland's "Notes for History of Bowdoin," n.d., Nehemiah Cleaveland Papers, George J. Mitchell Department of Special Collections and Archives, Bowdoin College Library.

38. For Nott's inaugural, see "Union College," *Balance and Columbian Repository*, 6 November 1804, 256. For a study of how personal reputation and institution building were measured through speech and performance in the early republic, see Freeman, *Affairs of Honor*.

39. "L," "The Microcosm: Or Man As He Is," *The Nightingale*, 21 July 1796; "Extract from a Letter," *American Mercury*, 30 January 1816.

40. Levi McKeen to Joseph McKeen, 8 January 1802, McKeen Collection.

41. George Baxter to Anne Baxter, 14 April 1805, Baxter Family Correspondence and Papers.

42. George Baxter to Anne Baxter, 23 and 28 April 1805, ibid.

43. George Baxter to Anne Baxter, 11 May 1805, ibid.

44. George Baxter to Anne Baxter, 27 May 1805, ibid.

45. George Baxter to Anne Baxter, 30 October 1805, 5 November 1805, ibid.

46. George Baxter to Anne Baxter, 5 and 11 November 1805, ibid.

47. George Baxter to Anne Baxter, 18 November 1805, ibid.

48. George Baxter to Anne Baxter, 25 November 1805, 2 December 1805, ibid.

49. George Baxter to Anne Baxter, 3 December 1805, ibid.

50. Ibid.

51. Ibid.

52. George Baxter to Anne Baxter, 25 November 1805, ibid.

53. Cremin, *American Education*, 13.

54. Entry for 1 May 1818, Holley Travel Journal, Holley Papers; Horace Holley to Mary Holley, 2 May 1818, ibid. For Holley's problematic presidency, see Sonne, *Liberal Kentucky*.

Chapter Two. Organizing the College World

1. Abigail Morris to Martha Cleaveland, 16 February 1807, Cleaveland-Chandler Papers, George J. Mitchell Department of Special Collections and Archives, Bowdoin College Library.

2. For the Cleaveland family history, see Bowdoin College, *General Catalogue*, 23; Hatch, *The History of Bowdoin College*, 23–35; and Cleaveland and Packard, *History of Bowdoin College*, 126–29.

3. Hatch, *The History of Bowdoin College*, 212.

4. Martha Cleaveland to John Bush, 12 January 1808, Cleaveland-Chandler Papers.

5. For a similar form of elite networking based on exclusion and an "ideal of friendship" that "projected the existence of a hierarchy" and had to be "cultivated and earned," see Kaplan, *Men of Letters in the Early Republic*, 31–39.

6. Jonathan Ward to Jesse Appleton, 30 December 1807, Appleton Collection.

7. [Noah Webster], "Education," *American Magazine,* February 1788.

8. "A Dialogue between Solomon Spindle, a Country Preceptor, and His Son Jack, a College Blood," *The Massachusetts Magazine,* July 1796; "Studiosus," "History of a College Rake," *The Monthly Anthology and Boston Review,* February 1804. For the rise of the vice-ridden villain in early national literature, see Lewis, "The Republican Wife"; and C. Davidson, *Revolution and the Word,* esp. chaps. 1–3.

9. [Noah Webster], "Education," *American Magazine,* February 1788. For republican preoccupations with pastoralized virtue, see Wood, *The Creation of the American Republic,* 97–107. For the English legacy of country and court tensions, see Robbins, *The Eighteenth-Century Commonwealthman.*

10. T. C. Reed, "A Tribute to the Memory of the Late Edward Savage, Esq."; Francis Wayland to Alonzo Potter, 13 August 1821, Francis Wayland Family Papers, John Hay Library, Brown University, Providence; Conway, *Autobiography,* 65; A. Hopkins, "Revivals of Religion in Williams College," 342.

11. For studies of such cultural performances, see Halttunen, *Confidence Men and Painted Women;* Bushman, *The Refinement of America;* Thornton, *Cultivating Gentlemen;* and Boyer, *Ladies and Gentlemen on Display.*

12. For the subordination of the self and the redirection of passion, see Howe, *Making the American Self.*

13. Hatch, *The History of Bowdoin College,* 212.

14. Augusta and John McClintock to Jane McClintock, 10 and 16 January 1841, John C. McClintock Papers, Manuscript, Archive, and Rare Book Library, Emory University.

15. Parker Cleaveland Sr. to Parker Cleaveland Jr., 8 February 1807, Cleaveland-Chandler Papers.

16. This description of Parker Cleaveland's career is based on Hatch, *The History of Bowdoin College,* 28–35.

17. Cleaveland, *Elementary Treatise on Mineralogy and Geology,* 37–38.

18. C. Brown, *Benjamin Silliman,* 260. For sources on the emerging scientific community in the early republic, see Greene, *American Science in the Age of Jefferson.*

19. Parker Cleaveland to John Bush, 7 February 1818, Cleaveland-Chandler Papers.

20. Hatch, *The History of Bowdoin College,* 29.

21. For biographical information on Smyth, see Hatch, *The History of Bowdoin College,* 53–47, 212–13.

22. R.A.P to Miss Cornelia Lewis, 19 December 1844, Cornelia Lewis Papers, Special Collections, Leyburn Library, Washington and Lee University, Lexington, Va.

23. Horace Holley to Mary Holley, 15 June 1818, Holly Papers.

24. Ann Sudler to Eliphalet Nott, 22 April 1832, Union College Letterbooks; Hampton McIntosh to Henry Jackson, 31 July 1819, Henry Jackson Papers; Eliza

Maria Ross to Ann Smith, 20 January 1810, Ann Smith Academy Papers, Special Collections, Leyburn Library, Washington and Lee University.

25. Charles Hatch to Mark Hopkins, 28 May 1825, Mark Hopkins Papers, Massachusetts Historical Society.

26. Hall, *A Collection of College Words*, 24–35.

27. Fisher, *A Philadelphia Perspective*, 311.

28. M.W., "On a Liberal Education," *Columbian Magazine*, February 1787. For the relationship between the classical tradition, colleges, and the early American nation, see Eadie, *Classical Traditions in Early America*; Richard, *The Golden Age of the Classics in America*; and Winterer, *The Culture of Classicism*.

29. Martha and Parker Cleaveland to John Bush, 2 April 1808, Cleaveland-Chandler Papers; M.W., "On a Liberal Education," *Columbian Magazine*, February 1787. For a discussion of bodies "gendered" for the privileges of republican citizenship, see Landes, *Women and the Public Sphere in the Age of the French Revolution*, 152–68.

30. Samuel Phillips Newman to William Appleton, 17 April 1828, Pierce-Aiken Family Papers; Meyer, *The Instructed Conscience*, 129.

31. For contract relations, see Stanley, *From Bondage to Contract*.

32. Appleton, *Addresses . . . Delivered at the Annual Commencements*, 3–5.

33. John T. Kirkland to Jesse Appleton, 12 February 1815, Appleton Collection.

34. [Noah Webster], "Importance of Female Education and of Educating Young Men in their Native Country, Addressed to Every American," *American Magazine*, May 1788. For an analysis of how such elite white women's cultural power was based on male "consent" to their education and literacy, see Schloesser, *The Fair Sex*, 74–75, 191.

35. Benjamin Rush, "Of the Mode of Education Proper in a Republic," *New England Quarterly Magazine*, April–June 1802.

36. Martha and Parker Cleaveland to John Bush, 2 April 1808, Cleaveland-Chandler Papers.

37. Ibid.

38. "On the Advantage to be Derived by Young Men from the Society of Virtuous Women," *The Boston Magazine*, August 1785, 297; Hull, *Annals of Athens, Georgia*, 437; "A Letter from Edwin to His Sister," *The Medley, or, Monthly Miscellany*, August 1803.

39. "On the Advantage to be Derived by Young Men from the Society of Virtuous Women," *The Boston Magazine*, August 1785; Professor Alpheus Packard to Amos and Nancy Lawrence, 28 June 1839, Appleton-Aiken Family Papers, William L. Clements Library, University of Michigan; review of "Observations on Novel-Reading; in an Essay, Written by a Member of the Belles-Letters Society of Dickinson College," *Universal Asylum and Columbian Magazine*, October 1792.

40. Peyton, *Over the Alleghanies and Across the Prairies*, 112. For classical learning among early American women, see Winterer, *The Mirror of Antiquity*, 146–55; M. Kelley, *Learning to Stand and Speak*; and M. Nash, *Women's Education in the United States*, chap. 3.

41. Bryan, *A March Past,* 101; Elizabeth C. H. Seymour to "Georgianna," 10 February 1842, Miscellaneous College Files, Archives and Special Collections, Dickinson College.

42. Diary entries for 30 September 1839, 15 October 1841, 23 November 1839, 10 December 1839, and 14 May 1842, McClintock Papers.

43. Review of "Observations on Novel-Reading; in an Essay, Written by a Member of the Belles-Letters Society of Dickinson College," *Universal Asylum and Columbian Magazine,* October 1792.

44. Peyton, *Over the Alleghanies and Across the Prairies,* 112. For female academy students trained to control "unrestrained ambition" in themselves and society by thinking of themselves as "relational rather than individual," see Blauvelt, *The Work of the Heart,* 64.

45. Alderman and Gordon, *J. L. M. Curry: A Biography,* 57–58.

46. Maria von Phul to Miss Ann Gist, 8 April 1808, Henrietta Clay Collection, MSC 10, Transylvania University Library, Lexington, Ky.

47. Elizabeth Cleaveland to Ann Cleaveland, 14 October 1833, Cleaveland-Chandler Papers; Martha Cleaveland to Ann Cleaveland, 27 July 1831, ibid.

48. Abigail Morris to Martha Cleaveland, 16 February 1807, ibid.; Martha and Parker Cleaveland to John Bush, 2 April 1808, ibid.

50. Mary Appleton to Frances Appleton, August 1821, Appleton-Aiken Family Papers.

51. For similar examples of collective educational monitoring, see Blauvelt, *The Work of the Heart,* 50–81.

52. Parker Cleaveland to John Bush, 4 November 1808, Cleaveland-Chandler Papers.

53. Martha and Parker Cleaveland to John Bush, 12 January 1808, ibid.

54. Bowdoin College, *General Catalog,* 48; Parker Cleaveland to John Bush, 24 March 1819, Cleaveland-Chandler Papers.

55. Augusta and John McClintock to Jane McClintock, 16 January 1841, McClintock Papers.

56. Frances Packard to Mary Aiken, December 1837, Appleton-Aiken Family Papers; Martha Cleaveland to Parker Cleaveland, [February 1822], Cleaveland-Chandler Papers.

57. John Mills Brown to Parker Cleaveland, 16 November 1826, Cleaveland-Chandler Papers; Mary Brown to Parker Cleaveland, 2 September 1827, ibid. For another young woman exploring the "privileges" of the college world, see the writer Mary Terhune's season with a cousin near Hampden-Sydney College, in Kelley, *Private Woman, Public Stage,* 96–99.

58. Parker Cleaveland to John Bush, 4 February 1818, Cleaveland-Chandler Papers. In her work *Parlor Politics,* Catherine Allgor shows how the participation of ladies facilitated early American political culture. Indeed, many college ladies

married men who would participate in local and national politics, bringing their college-world training in the cultivation of virtue to varying political scenes.

59. Alice McKeen to Mary and Frances Appleton, 21 March 1822, Pierce-Aiken Family Papers.

60. Alice McKeen to Frances Appleton, 19 July 1820, ibid.

61. Hannah Bush to Martha Cleaveland, [23 July 1826], Cleaveland-Chandler Papers.

62. Susan and Joseph Baxter to Elizabeth Baxter, 17 March 1842, Baxter Family Correspondence and Papers.

Chapter Three. Building the College World

1. Waddel, *Memorials of Academic Life,* 110, 151. For university histories, see Coulter, *College Life in the Old South;* Brooks, *The University of Georgia under Sixteen Administrations;* and Dyer, *The University of Georgia.* For university buildings, see Boney, *A Pictorial History of the University of Georgia.*

2. I. Brown, *Biography of the Rev. Robert Finley, D.D. . . . ,* 176–77.

3. In this chapter I am indebted to those historians who have used buildings and spatial design in the interpretation of cultural transformation; see, e.g., Isaac, *The Transformation of Virginia;* Turner, *Campus;* Tolbert, *Constructing Townscapes;* C. Lewis, *Ladies and Gentlemen on Display;* and McNamara, *From Tavern to Courthouse.*

4. For analysis on the cultural representation of separate public and private spheres in the early republic, see Bloch, *Gender and Morality in Anglo-American Culture;* Wood, *The Creation of the American Republic,* 610–12; and Boydston, *Home and Work.*

5. Waddel, *Memorials of Academic Life,* 73–74; Hull, *Annals of Athens, Georgia,* 10; Augustin Clayton to Henry Jackson, 31 January 1819, Henry Jackson Papers.

6. For college builders "manipulating the environment in which human nature was shaped," see the discussion of Horace Mann in Howe, *Making the American Self,* 158–67. For Scottish thought as a "philosophy of containment," see T. Martin, *The Instructed Vision,* 11. For the mental universe of the college world, see Noll, "Common Sense Traditions and American Evangelical Thought"; Bozeman, *Protestants in an Age of Science;* Meyer, *The Instructed Conscience;* and Howe, *The Unitarian Conscience.*

7. Moses Waddel, "University of Georgia," *Weekly Recorder,* 22 August 1821; Putnam, *A Description of Brunswick, Maine,* 9–10; Van Vechten, *A Poem on Liberty;* Gilpin, *A Northern Tour,* 86. For the ideological positioning between wilderness and civilization as the "pastoral ideal," see Marx, *The Machine in the Garden.*

8. Waddel, *Memorials of Academic Life,* 101; diary entry for 28 June 1822, Moses Waddel Papers, Library of Congress.

9. Hull, *Annals of Athens, Georgia,* 25; Butterfield and Rush, "Dr. Benjamin Rush's

Journal of a Trip to Carlisle in 1784," 451; diary entry for 21 August 1822, Moses Waddel Papers.

10. For examples of the families that visited Athens and the college president's home, see diary entries for 15–31 August and 21 September 1822, Moses Waddel Papers; Hull, *Annals of Athens, Georgia*, 99, 180; Moses Waddel, "University of Georgia," *Weekly Recorder*, 22 August 1821; and "Athens University," *Weekly Recorder*, 23 July 1819.

11. Waddel, *Memorials of Academic Life*, 74; Hull, *Annals of Athens, Georgia*, 33–34; diary entries for 24 June 1822, 26 September 1822, and 30 December 1822, Moses Waddel Papers.

12. Hull, *Annals of Athens, Georgia*, 33–34. See also Coulter, *College Life in the Old South*, 81.

13. Coulter, *College Life in the Old South*, 28, 81; "Contributions from Athens," *African Repository*, October 1837. For colonization ideology, see Frederickson, *The Black Image in the White Mind*, chap. 1.

14. Coulter, *College Life in the Old South*, 79, 82; diary entries for 26 April 1824 and 26 July 1822, Moses Waddel Papers; diary entry for 1 May 1847, James P. Waddel Diary, Hargrett Rare Book and Manuscript Library, University of Georgia.

15. Waddel, *Memorial of Academic Life*, 107–8.

16. "Athens University," *Weekly Recorder*, 23 July 1819; Moses Waddel, "University of Georgia," *Weekly Recorder*, 22 August 1821.

17. Junius Hillyer Memoir, pp. 188–89, Hargrett Rare Book and Manuscript Library, University of Georgia. For Hillyer's bad behavior and Waddel's intervention, see diary entries for 8 June 1825, 20 September 1825, and 9–10 November 1825, Moses Waddel Papers.

18. Crooks, *Life and Letters of the Rev. John McClintock*, 193.

19. Diary entry for 12 September 1824, Moses Waddel Papers.

20. For news of Waddel's "Education Society," see *Pittsburgh Recorder*, 24 July 1823; see also diary entry for 26 November 1824, Moses Waddel Papers; and Evarts, *Through the South and West*, 101–2. For the sectarian alliance, see Boylan, *Sunday School*; Wosh, *Spreading the Word*, 62–88; and Foster, *An Errand of Mercy*.

21. Waddel, *Memorials of Academic Life*, 48; Hull, *Annals of Athens, Georgia*, 87–88; diary entries for 18 August 1822 and 12 May 1829, Moses Waddel Papers.

22. Waddel, *Memorials of Academic Life*, 154, 162, 112. College families initiated Sunday School systems for "town children" in many communities, contributing to the widening network of evangelical activity (see Boylan, *Sunday School*).

23. Diary entries for 17–25 July 1822, 11 September 1824, and 18 July 1829, Moses Waddel Papers; Hull, *Annals of Athens, Georgia*, 13–14

24. M. Hopkins, *Early Letters*, 214.

25. Diary entries for 2, 11, and 16 May 1829, Moses Waddel Papers.

26. Hawthorne, *Fanshawe*, 45–49, 50–51.

27. For public oaths and resisting tavern keepers, see Durbin Presidential File,

Archives and Special Collections, Dickinson College; and Atwater Presidential File, ibid.

28. "An Old Citizen" to President John P. Durbin, 1 January 1842, General Student Affairs File, Archives and Special Collections, Dickinson College, Carlisle, Pa.; Anonymous to Robert Emory, General Student Affairs File, Dickinson College; diary entry for 31 July 1822, Moses Waddel Papers.

29. For the Bowdoin Riot story, see Butler, *Education as Revealed by New England Newspapers Prior to 1850*, 104.

30. H. Brown, *The Sentimental Novel in America*, 22.

31. Anonymous to John Durbin, 6 May 1843, Durbin Presidential File, Dickinson College; Martha Cleaveland to Ann Cleaveland, [2 November] 1839, Cleaveland-Chandler Papers.

32. Eliphalet Nott and Sarah Potter to Clarkson Potter, 15 June 1835, Union College Letterbooks; diary entries from 12 September 1839 to 1 March 1840, McClintock Papers.

33. Diary entries from 12 September 1839 to 1 March 1840, McClintock Papers.

34. Coulter, *College Life in the Old South*, 95–96; Alpheus Packard to Daniel Goodwin, 1 August 1836, Alpheus Spring Packard Papers, George J. Mitchell Department of Special Collections and Archives, Bowdoin College Library; Aylett Alexander to William Alexander, 19 October 1831, 11 November 1834 and 28 February 1836, Anderson Family Papers, Special Collections, Leyburn Library, Washington and Lee University; Dr. John Bolton to Ann Harrison, 16 July 1838, Brock Collection, Huntington Library, quoted in Eaton, *The Freedom-of-Thought Struggle in the Old South*, 380.

35. Albert Hopkins to Harry Hopkins, [1828], Hopkins Papers.

36. Hislop, *Eliphalet Nott*, 122.

37. Merritt Caldwell to the Dickinson Board of Trustees, 29 July 1836, Durbin Presidential File, Dickinson College; Crooks, *Life and Letters of the Rev. John McClintock*, 241. For more examples of faculty complaints about the cramped, dilapidated, inconvenient, and haphazard state of college structures, see A. S. Packard and N. Cleaveland, "Biographical Notes," McKeen Collection; and John Price Durbin to Robert Emory, 18 September 1845, Durbin Presidential File, Dickinson College.

38. John McClintock to the Committee of Supervision, 22 July 1837, Durbin Presidential File, Dickinson College.

39. Smyth, *Reminiscences of My Life*, 24.

40. Diary entries for 1 and 28–29 December 1822, and 12 May 1829, Moses Waddel Papers; Waddel, *Memorials of Academic Life*, 94; Nehemiah Cleaveland to Leonard Woods, 24 December 1858, Parker Cleaveland Collection, George J. Mitchell Department of Special Collections and Archives, Bowdoin College Library.

41. The Cleaveland Family to Anne Cleaveland, 14 October 1833, Cleaveland-Chandler Papers.

42. Alpheus Packard to Daniel Goodwin, 1 August 1836, Packard Papers; Margaret

Graham to Mary Ann Alexander Anderson, 5 April 1845, Anderson Family Papers; G. Prentiss, *The Life and Letters of Elizabeth Prentiss,* 209.

43. Mark Hopkins to Mary Hopkins, 26 July 1841, Hopkins Papers; G. Prentiss, *The Life and Letters of Elizabeth Prentiss,* 398.

44. Waddel, *Memorials of Academic Life,* 119–20; diary entry for 8 September 1828, Moses Waddel Papers.

45. Diary entry for 29 November 1824, Moses Waddel Papers.

46. Augusta and John McClintock to Mrs. Jabez Wakeman, 29 June 1838, McClintock Papers; entry for 12 January 1857, Isaac Jackson Diary, Special Collections, Schaffer Library, Union College.

47. "Communication from P. M. Greenleaf & Others in Regard to Prayers," January 1839, General Student Affairs File, Dickinson College.

48. Mary Hopkins to Mary Hubbell Hopkins, 3 July 1843, Hopkins Papers; M. Hopkins, *Early Letters,* 270–71.

49. Mary Fenwick Kollock to George Kollock Jr., n.d., George J. Kollock Family Papers, Hargrett Rare Book and Manuscript Library, University of Georgia.

50. Diary entries for 23 November 1822, 4 December 1822, 13 December 1822, and 29 January 1829, Moses Waddel Papers.

51. Alpheus Packard to Daniel Goodwin, 1 August 1836, Packard Papers.

52. Diary entries for 10 March 1829, 24 March 1829, and 18 April 1829, Moses Waddel Papers.

53. Sidney Baxter to George Baxter, 9 February 1833, Baxter Family Correspondence and Papers.

54. Louisa Hopkins to Mary Hopkins, November 1843, Hopkins Papers.

55. "Franklin College," *Western Luminary,* 1 October 1828; Junius Hillyer Memoir, Hargrett Rare Book and Manuscript Library, University of Georgia.

56. Junius Hillyer Memoir, Hargrett Rare Book and Manuscript Library, University of Georgia.

57. Mark Hopkins to Mary Hopkins, 27 March 1840, Hopkins Papers.

58. Francis Henshaw Dewey to Charles Augustus Dewey Sr., 23 March 1840, Dewey-Bliss Family Collection, in *Women and Their Families in the 18th and 19th Centuries* [microfilm], reel 1.

59. Mary Graham to Mary Ann Anderson, 3 September [ca. 1830s], Anderson Family Papers; "Franklin College," *Western Luminary,* 1 October 1828.

60. Mary Fenwick Kollock to George Kollock Jr., n.d., Kollock Family Papers. Dancing was not an approved activity in college communities (see Mary Ann Anderson to Mary Ann Alexander, 11 July 1825, Anderson Family Papers; and Eliphalet Nott to Parents, 4 February 1847, Union College Letterbooks).

Chapter Four. Working in the College World

1. For biographical information on Louisa Payson Hopkins, see *Our Famous Women*, 541. See also the biography of her sister, *The Life and Letters of Elizabeth Prentiss*, written by George L. Prentiss.

2. G. Prentiss, *The Life and Letters of Elizabeth Prentiss*, 547, 204.

3. Ibid., 550, 546, 548.

4. Albert Hopkins to Mary Hopkins, 26 March 1841, Albert Hopkins Collection, Williams College Archives and Special Collections; Mark Hopkins to Mary Hopkins, 21 May 1841, Mark Hopkins Correspondence, Williams College Archives and Special Collections. For biographical information on Albert Hopkins, I drew primarily from Sewall, *Life of Professor Albert Hopkins*.

5. Sewall, *Life of Professor Albert Hopkins*, 189–90.

6. For the rise of the new brain-worker classes in the early republic, see Bledstein, *The Culture of Professionalism*; and Blumin, *The Emergence of the Middle Class*.

7. For white women's complicated relationship with "housekeeping" and the evolving market culture, as well as the important role of the "breadwinner," see Boydston, *Home and Work*.

8. For the transforming connection between masculinity and the "virtue" of agricultural and artisanal labor, see Roediger, *The Wages of Whiteness*, 19–64; Wilentz, *Chants Democratic*; and Laurie, *Artisans into Workers*.

9. "The Empire of Nothing," 5 November 1803, *The Port-Folio*, 354–55.

10. Manning, *The Key of Liberty*, 136–40.

11. Payson's unease is a reflection of what the historian Mary Kelley describes as the ambivalence of women writers (see Kelley, *Private Woman, Public Stage*, 177). See also G. Prentiss, *The Life and Letters of Elizabeth Prentiss*, 550.

12. G. Prentiss, *The Life and Letters of Elizabeth Prentiss*, 552–53.

13. Ibid., 551.

14. Junkin, *Silverwood*, 266–68. For a discussion of *Silverwood* as autobiography, see Mary Coulling's recent biography, *Margaret Junkin Preston*, 80–84. For earlier biographical material, see Allan, *The Life and Letters of Margaret Junkin Preston*.

15. Preston, "Elizabeth Barrett Browning."

16. G. Prentiss, *The Life and Letters of Elizabeth Prentiss*, 551–52.

17. Ibid., 552.

18. Ibid., 546–47.

19. The classic study of American intellectual women is Conrad, *Perish the Thought*. For individual studies, see Sklar, *Catherine Beecher*; Capper, *Margaret Fuller*; and Marshall, *The Peabody Sisters*.

20. G. Prentiss, *The Life and Letters of Elizabeth Prentiss*, 552.

21. Emerson, *The Early Lectures*, 79.

22. My discussion of the Hopkins brothers is drawn from Rudolph, *Mark Hopkins*

and the Log; M. Hopkins, *Early Letters;* Spring, *A History of Williams College;* and Durfee, *Williams Biographical Annals.* For additional narratives of New England men in search of success, especially the similar experience of Edward Hitchcock, a hatter's son turned Amherst College professor, see Opal, *Beyond the Farm.*

23. For the tradition of literary clubs for men in New York City, see Waterman, *Republic of Intellect.* Comprised of Williams College alumni and other young college-educated men exploring various professions in the city, this masculine collective for reading, debates, and "friendly" literary encouragement facilitated Mark's foray into periodical essay writing in the 1830s.

24. A.H. to H.H., 10 August 1829, and Albert Hopkins to Harry Hopkins, 2 June [1825?], Hopkins Papers.

25. M. Hopkins, *Early Letters,* 163.

26. Ibid., 163.

27. Jared Curtis to Mary Hopkins, 15 February 1830, Hopkins Papers.

28. M. Hopkins, *Early Letters,* 204–5.

29. Ibid., 237, 232.

30. Ibid., 220, 221–22.

31. Entries for 11–12 December 1854, Isaac Jackson Diary.

32. Crooks, *Life and Letters of the Rev. John McClintock,* 136, 200; diary entry for 19 June 1841, March 1841, and 27 January 1842, McClintock Papers.

33. Crooks, *Life and Letters of the Rev. John McClintock,* 200.

34. M. Hopkins, *Early Letters,* 269; Harry Hopkins to Mark Hopkins, 4 May 1829, Hopkins Papers.

35. M. Hopkins, *Early Letters,* 238, 240.

36. Albert Hopkins to Harry Hopkins, 14 April 1829 and 20 July 1837, Hopkins Papers.

37. M. Hopkins, *Early Letters,* 265–66.

38. Ibid., 271. Later in the century, this condition would be medicalized as "neurasthenia"—an illness that, according to David Schuster, victimized a middle class confronting changes brought about by modernization (see Schuster, *Neurasthenic Nation*).

39. Diary entries from 28 February to 7 March 1845, James P. Waddel Diary.

40. Mark Hopkins to Harry Hopkins, 27 April 1831, Hopkins Papers; "The Empire of Nothing," 5 November 1803, *The Port-Folio,* 354–55; Mary Hopkins to Mary Hubbell Hopkins, 3 July 1843, Hopkins Papers.

41. Diary entries from 28 February to 7 March 1845, James P. Waddel Diary.

42. For this general biographical information on Jackson, see Jackson Garden Vertical File, Special Collections, Union College.

43. For recent studies on the manual-labor movement, see Mullins, "In the Sweat of Thy Brow."

44. Agnes Branch to Elizabeth Baxter, 12 April 1842, Baxter Family Correspondence and Papers.

45. Mullin, "In the Sweat of Thy Brow," 147.

46. Rudolph, *Mark Hopkins and the Log*, 96, 142–45; Francis Henshaw Dewey to Charles Augustus Dewey Sr., 12 June 1837, Dewey-Bliss Family Collection, in *New England Women and Their Families in the 18th and 19th Centuries*, microfilm, reel 1; "Williams College," 21 August 1835, *Boston Recorder;* "Scientific Expedition," 18 September 1835, *Boston Recorder.*

47. M. Hopkins, *Early Letters,* 329, 333–34.

48. "Williams College," 1 September 1837, *Boston Recorder;* "Commencement at Williams College," 31 August 1838, *Boston Recorder;* "Williams College," 22 November 1839, *Boston Recorder.* (It is possible that Louisa Payson, acting as guest editor for the *Recorder,* was the author of this last article). For the history of the observatory, see Milham, *Early American Observatories.*

49. Albert Hopkins to Archibald Hopkins, 24 July 1833, Hopkins Papers.

50. Dall, *Spencer Fullerton Baird,* 140.

51. Ibid., 142

52. M. Hopkins, *Early Letters,* 280–81.

53. Ibid., 282–84.

54. Sewall, *The Life of Albert Hopkins,* 178.

55. Margaret Junkin, "The Reconcilement of the Real and the Ideal," *Sartain's Magazine,* January 1852.

56. For another example of a professor's wife who balances "domestic care and public duty," see the discussion of Orra White Hitchcock, a "college lady" managing Amherst College, in Opal, *Beyond the Farm,* 168–69.

57. Crooks, *Life and Letters of the Rev. John McClintock,* 118–19.

58. Dall, *Spencer Fullerton Baird,* 158. For more on academic households, see Lindsay, "Intimate Inmates."

59. Kelley, *Private Woman, Public Stage,* 168; Augusta McClintock to Mrs. Wakemen, 12 May 1839, McClintock Papers.

60. Augusta McClintock to Mrs. Wakemen, 12 May 1839, McClintock Papers.

61. For the conflicted relationship between women and their role in the male-dominated intellectual world, see Murray, *Genius;* Battersby, *Gender and Genius;* and Schiebinger, *The Mind Has No Sex.*

62. Preston, "Erinna's Spinning."

63. Smyth, *Reminiscences of My Life,* 39–40, 45.

64. Margaret Junkin Preston, "Elizabeth Barrett Browning," *Southern Literary Messenger,* 1 February 1860.

65. Review of *The Pastor's Daughter at School, American Biblical Repository,* October 1843. See also the assorted reviews in the back matter in Loomis, *The Elements of Geology.*

66. Upham, *The Crystal Fountain,* 49, 18, 60. For Upham's biographical information, see Cleaveland and Packard, *History of Bowdoin College,* 131–33; and Hatch, *The History of Bowdoin College,* 58–59.

67. Sewall, *The Life of Albert Hopkins*, 181; G. Prentiss, *The Life and Letters of Eliza-beth Prentiss*, 85.

68. Louisa Payson Hopkins to Mary Hopkins, November 1843, Hopkins Papers; C. Perry, *A Professor of Life*, 73.

69. Kitto, *A Cyclopaedia of Biblical Literature*, 1:571–74, 467–68. Hopkins's entries are signed "L.P.H."

70. Louisa Payson Hopkins to Mary Hopkins, November 1843, Hopkins Papers.

71. G. Prentiss, *The Life and Letters of Elizabeth Prentiss*, 547; Louisa Payson Hopkins to Mary Hopkins, November 1843, Hopkins Papers; and Mary Hopkins to Louisa Payson Hopkins, 4 October 1843, ibid.

72. For descriptions of the Hopkins property, see M. Hopkins, *Early Letters*, 258; and Sewall, *The Life of Albert Hopkins*, 196.

73. Albert Hopkins to Mary Hopkins, 8 May 1844, Hopkins Papers; Louisa Hopkins to Mary Hopkins, 4 August 1846, ibid.

74. Albert Hopkins to Calvin Durfee, 9 May 1849, Hopkins Collection.

75. Mark Hopkins to Mary Hopkins, 13 June 1843, Hopkins Papers; Sewall, *The Life of Albert Hopkins*, 178.

76. Review of *The Silent Comforter: A Companion for the Sick Room*, by Louisa Pay-son Hopkins, *Ladies Repository*, August 1848.

77. A. Perry, *Origins in Williamstown*, 47–50.

78. Prentiss, *The Life and Letters of Elizabeth Prentiss*, 209.

79. J. M. Opal argues that early American men who "departed from the labor ties and real estates that build reputations in the preindustrial hinterlands" felt they had a "tenuous claim to public spirit or manly status" (Opal, *Beyond the Farm*, 168). For college professors like the Hopkins brothers, or Edward Hitchcock in Opal's study, the dedication of their lives, fortunes, and families to their fledgling institutions strengthened such claims in their minds.

80. Preston, "Erinna's Spinning."

Chapter Five. Leaving the College World

1. "Mission to Hayti," *Christian Register*, 26 November 1824. For coverage of Russ-wurm's commencement speech, see "A Colored Graduate," *Christian Watchman*, 28 September 1826; *The Eastern Argus*, 12 September 1826; and the *Hartford Courant*, 25 September 1826. The *New Haven Journal* of 26 September 1826 also carried an item.

2. Boydston, "Gender as a Question of Historical Analysis," 574; Frederickson, *The Black Image in the White Mind*, 19.

3. For historians and theorists who call for the workings of racial systems to be placed in context with gender and class systems, see Boydston, "Gender as a Ques-tion of Historical Analysis"; Fields, "Slavery, Race, and Ideology in the Unites States of America"; Frankenberg, *White Women, Race Matters*; and Higginbotham, "African-American Women's History and the Metalanguage of Race." For a recent

review of literature on race, see Fishkin, "Interrogating 'Whiteness,' Complicating 'Blackness.'"

4. Cleaveland, *Elementary Treatise*, 37–38; Recipe Book, Baxter Family Correspondence and Papers.

5. Buckingham, *The Slave States of America*, 92–93.

6. Parker Cleaveland to Martha Ann Cleaveland, 2 July 1831, Cleaveland-Chandler Papers.

7. Martha Chandler to Martha Cleaveland, 12 April 1838, ibid. For this common white "revulsion" of black skin strengthening the promotion of colonization, see Frederickson, *The Black Image in the White Mind*, 17–18.

8. John Russwurm to Colonel John S. Russwurm, 9 January 1826, John Brown Russwurm Collection, Bowdoin College Library.

9. Ibid.

10. Eliphalet Nott, "Proceedings of the New York State Colonization Society," *African Repository and Colonial Journal*, November 1829. Nott's ideas reflect the exclusionary ideology behind the movement (see Frederickson, *The Black Image in the White Mind*, 12–21).

11. Margaret Junkin, "Departure of Emigrants for Liberia," *The African Repository*, April 1850.

12. Nancy Baxter to Louisa Baxter, 23 June 1849, Baxter Family Correspondence and Papers.

13. J. C. Cutler to Harry Hopkins, 26 August 1832, Hopkins Papers.

14. Alexander Hamilton Rice to Augusta McKim, 28 January 1844, Alexander Hamilton Rice Letters, Massachusetts Historical Society.

15. Russwurm's oration is in the John Brown Russwurm Collection at the Bowdoin College Library. But see also Philip Foner's biography of Russworm and his transcription of the manuscript in "John Brown Russwurm: A Document."

16. A. Ely, "African Free School," *Christian Watchman*, 20 May 1820. For the colonization movement, see Staudenraus, *The African Colonization Movement*; and Burin, *Slavery and the Peculiar Solution*. For colonists' perspectives, see Clegg, *The Price of Liberty*; Moses, *Liberian Dreams*; and Wiley, *Slaves No More*.

17. "Prospectus," 12 March 1827, *Freedom's Journal*.

18. "Letter from Bishop Allen," 2 November 1827, *Freedom's Journal*.

19. For John Russwurm's reasoning, see his articles in *Freedom's Journal*: "Liberia" (21 February 1829); "Our Vindication" (7 March 1829); "Colonization" (14 March 1829); and "To Our Patrons" (28 March 1829).

20. "Miscellaneous Items," *Western Luminary*, 16 September 1829; "Mr. Russwurm's Letter," *African Repository and Colonial Journal*, April 1830.

21. Russwurm's letters were excerpted and edited by the *African Repository* editor. No original letters seem to have survived. Quotations are from "Mr. Russwurm's Letter," *African Repository and Colonial Journal*, April 1830; "Liberia," *Philadelphia Recorder*, 8 May 1830; and "Letter from Liberia," *The Episcopal Watchman*, 15 May

1830. For John Russwurm's growing Africanist thinking, see Bay, *The White Image in the Black Mind*.

22. "Mr. Russwurm's Letter," *African Repository and Colonial Journal*, April 1830. For another example of a classically educated black Presbyterian trained at Athens, Georgia, see John M. Waddel, "Letter from John W. Waddel," *African Repository and Colonial Journal*, November 1846.

23. "Mr. Russwurm's Letter," *African Repository and Colonial Journal*, April 1830.

24. Ibid.

25. "Newspaper in Liberia," 29 May 1830, *Philadelphia Recorder*, 36.

26. "Liberia," *Genius of Universal Emancipation*, June 1830; C.D.T., "Mr. Russwurm," *The Liberator*, 30 April 1831, 70; "Z," "The Colony," *The Liberator*, 14 May 1831, 28.

27. John Russwurm to Francis Russwurm, 31 March 1834, John Brown Russwurm Collection, George J. Mitchell Department of Special Collections and Archives, Bowdoin College Library.

28. John Russwurm to Francis Russwurm, 31 March 1834, ibid.

29. John Russwurm to Francis Russwurm, 27 September 1835, ibid.

30. James H. Blanchard to General Russwurm, 14 June 1850, ibid.

31. "Newspaper in Liberia," *Philadelphia Recorder*, 29 May 1830.

32. "Trouble in Liberia," *The Liberator*, 9 May 1835.

33. Ibid.

34. For James Hall's perspective, see his "Voyage to Liberia," *The African Repository*, May 1858; and his "Liberia," 24 March 1837, *Christian Advocate and Journal*.

35. "Voyage to Liberia," *The African Repository*, May 1858.

36. "Intelligence," *Christian Register and Boston Observer*, 6 July 1839, 107.

37. For reports of Russwurm's travels around Liberia, see the following articles published in the *Christian Advocate and Journal*: "Trip to Dena," 25 June 1845; "Liberia," 27 August 1845; "Cape Palmas Station," 17 June 1846; and "Arrivals from Cape Palmas," 12 August 1846. See also "The Late Governor Russwurm," *Christian Advocate and Journal*, December 1851, 356.

38. See "Roman Catholic Establishment at Cape Palmas," *Christian Advocate and Journal*, 12 August 1846.

39. "Death of Governor Russwurm," *The African Repository*, November 1851; "Maryland in Liberia—A New State," *The African Repository*, October 1854; *The African Repository*, December 1851. For the end of Russwurm's colony and its annexation, see James Hall, "Voyage to Liberia," *The African Repository*, May 1858; and Penn, *The Afro-American Press and Its Editors*, 27–31. For the sense of betrayal among free blacks, especially in New York, see Alexander, *African or American?*

40. For the college world facilitating the founding of Liberia College, see Allen, *The Trustees of Donations for Education in Liberia*.

41. Hull, *Annals of Athens, Georgia*, 157–58.

42. Ann Eliza Leyburn to Alfred Leyburn, 22 December 1834, Alfred Leyburn Papers, Special Collections, Leyburn Library, Washington and Lee University.

43. Buckingham, *The Slave States of America*, 74, 87, 92–93; Marryat, *Diary in America*, 285.

44. Danforth, *Boyhood Reminiscences*, 170–71.

45. James, *Wales, and Other Poems*, 17–18.

46. Ibid., 2, 16–18.

47. Ibid., 163–64.

48. Danforth, *Boyhood Reminiscences*, 147; Nancy Means Lawrence to Elizabeth Appleton, 11 September 1834 and 12 September [1835], Appleton-Aiken Family Papers; Frances Packard to Elizabeth Appleton, 27 May 1836, ibid.

49. For an analysis of how the gender performances of "ladies" reinforced a specific class and racial order for the new republic, see Schloesser, *The Fair Sex*.

50. Frances Packard to Elizabeth Appleton, 8 December 1836 and September 1836, Appleton-Aiken Family Papers.

51. Buckley, *"If You Love that Lady, Don't Marry Her,"* 54, 66.

52. Ibid., 108, 100.

53. On the Col Alto slaves, see ibid., 68, 160–62, 485, 520, 333, 492, 735, 666.

54. Ibid., 100.

55. Ibid.

56. Ibid., 666.

57. Ibid., 182.

58. Ibid., 383–84.

59. Ibid., 182, 186.

60. Ibid., 388.

61. Ibid., 663, 666.

62. Ibid., 666–67.

63. Ibid., 815–16.

64. Ibid.

65. Ibid.

66. J. White, *Old Zeus*, 11.

Epilogue

1. Andrew Blair to J. A. Murray, 1 May 1850, Andrew Blair Family Papers, Archives and Special Collections, Dickinson College; Aylett Alexander to William Anderson, June 1835, Anderson Family Papers; Franklin Doswell to James Doswell, 22 April 1849, Benjamin Franklin Doswell Correspondence, Special Collections, Leyburn Library, Washington and Lee University.

2. Mary Davidson to Greenlee Davidson, 21 February 1858, James Dorman Davidson Scrapbooks, Special Collections, Leyburn Library, Washington and Lee University.

3. Ibid.

4. For Junkin family information, see Coulling, *Margaret Junkin Preston*. After

Robert E. Lee's death in 1870, the trustees of Washington College moved to rename the institution "Washington and Lee."

5. Dillon, *In Old Bellaire*, 188.

6. Albert Sewall, *The Life of Albert Hopkins*, 201–3. For the postwar generation's demand that new ideals of science and secularism should replace old ideals, see Menand, *The Metaphysical Club*.

7. Waddel, *Memorials of Academic Life*.

8. A. Perry, *Williamstown and Williams College*, 651–58; Bledstein, *The Culture of Professionalism*, 337; Willard and Livermore, *American Women*, 1:62.

9. Willard and Livermore, *American Women*, 1:62.

10. Kaplan, *Men of Letters in the Early Republic*, 232. See also Shields, *Civil Tongues and Polite Letters in British America*; and Waterman, *Republic of Intellect*.

BIBLIOGRAPHY

Archival Sources

Anderson Family Papers, 1755–1958. Special Collections, Leyburn Library, Washington and Lee University, Lexington, Va.

Ann Smith Academy Papers, ca. 1800s. Special Collections, Leyburn Library, Washington and Lee University, Lexington, Va.

Appleton, Jesse, Collection, 1791–1837. George J. Mitchell Department of Special Collections and Archives, Bowdoin College Library, Brunswick, Me.

Appleton-Aiken Family Papers, 1812–1900. William L. Clements Library, University of Michigan, Ann Arbor.

Atwater Presidential File. Archives and Special Collections, Dickinson College, Carlisle, Pa.

Baxter Family Correspondence and Papers, 1797–1918. Special Collections, Leyburn Library, Washington and Lee University, Lexington, Va.

Blair, Andrew, Family Papers, 1803–1861. Archives and Special Collections, Dickinson College, Carlisle, Pa.

Clay, Henrietta, Collection, 1793–1975. Special Collections, Transylvania University, Lexington, Ky.

Cleaveland-Chandler Papers, 1803–1937. George J. Mitchell Department of Special Collections and Archives, Bowdoin College Library, Brunswick, Me.

Cleaveland, Nehemiah, Papers. George J. Mitchell Department of Special Collections and Archives, Bowdoin College Library, Brunswick, Me.

Cleaveland, Parker, Collection, 1795–1994. George J. Mitchell Department of Special Collections and Archives, Bowdoin College Library, Brunswick, Me.

Davidson, James Dorman, Scrapbooks, 1832–1878. Special Collections, Leyburn Library, Washington and Lee University, Lexington, Va.

Doswell, Benjamin Franklin, Correspondence, 1847–1849. Special Collections, Leyburn Library, Washington and Lee University, Lexington, Va.

Durbin Presidential File. Archives and Special Collections, Dickinson College, Carlisle, Pa.

Garden, Jackson, Vertical File. Special Collections, Schaffer Library, Union College, Schenectady, N.Y.

General Student Affairs File. Archives and Special Collections, Dickinson College, Carlisle, Pa.

Hillyer, Junius, Memoir. MS 76A. Hargrett Rare Book and Manuscript Library, University of Georgia, Athens.

Holley, Horace, Papers, 1818. William L. Clements Library, University of Michigan, Ann Arbor.

Hopkins, Albert, Collection. Williams College Archives and Special Collections, Williamstown, Mass.

Hopkins, Mark, Correspondence. Williams College Archives and Special Collections, Williamstown, Mass.

Hopkins, Mark, Papers, 1790–1887. Massachusetts Historical Society, Boston.

Jackson, Henry, Papers, 1800–1840. Hargrett Rare Book and Manuscript Library, University of Georgia, Athens.

Jackson, Isaac, Diary, 1854–1860. Special Collections, Schaffer Library, Union College, Schenectady, N.Y.

Kollock, George J., Family Papers, 1815–1889. Hargrett Rare Book and Manuscript Library, University of Georgia, Athens.

Lewis, Cornelia, Papers. Rockbridge Historical Society Collection. Special Collections, Leyburn Library, Washington and Lee University, Lexington, Va.

Leyburn, Alfred, Papers, 1823–1899. Special Collections, Leyburn Library, Washington and Lee University, Lexington, Va.

McClintock, John C., Papers, 1828–1910. Manuscripts, Archive, and Rare Book Library, Emory University, Atlanta, Ga.

McKeen, Joseph, Collection, 1781–1966. George J. Mitchell Department of Special Collections and Archives, Bowdoin College Library, Brunswick, Me.

Miscellaneous College Files. Archives and Special Collections, Dickinson College, Carlisle, Pa.

Packard, Alpheus Spring, Papers, 1819–1886. George J. Mitchell Department of Special Collections and Archives, Bowdoin College Library, Brunswick, Me.

Pierce-Aiken Family Papers, 1797–1903. Library of Congress, Washington, D.C.

Rice, Alexander Hamilton, Letters, 1842–1844. Massachusetts Historical Society, Boston.

Russwurm, John Brown, Collection, 1819–2000. George J. Mitchell Department of Special Collections and Archives, Bowdoin College Library, Brunswick, Me.

Union College Letterbooks. Special Collections, Schaffer Library, Union College, Schenectady, N.Y.

Waddel, James P., Diary. 1845–47. Hargrett Rare Book and Manuscript Library, University of Georgia, Athens.

Waddel, Moses, Papers. 1793–1836. Library of Congress, Washington, D.C.

Wayland, Francis, Family Papers, 1754–1941. John Hay Library, Brown University, Providence, R.I.

Published Sources

Adams, O. Burton. "Yale Influence on the Formation of the University of Georgia." *Georgia Historical Quarterly* 51 (June 1967): 180–81.

Alderman, Edwin Anderson, and Armistead Churchill Gordon. *J. L. M. Curry: A Biography.* New York: Macmillan, 1911.

Alexander, Leslie. *African or American? Black Identity and Political Activism in New York City, 1784–1861.* Chicago: University of Illinois Press, 2008.

Allan, Elizabeth Preston. *The Life and Letters of Margaret Junkin Preston.* Boston: Houghton, Mifflin, 1903.

Allen, Gardner W. *The Trustees of Donations for Education in Liberia, A Story of Philanthropic Endeavor, 1850–1923.* Boston, 1923.

Allgor, Catherine. *Parlor Politics: In Which the Ladies of Washington Help Build a City and a Government.* Charlottesville: University Press of Virginia, 2000.

Allmendinger, David F. *Paupers and Scholars: The Transformation of Student Life in Nineteenth Century New England.* New York: St. Martin's Press, 1975.

Anderson, Patricia McGraw. *The Architecture of Bowdoin College.* Brunswick, Me.: Bowdoin College Museum of Art, 1988.

Appleton, Jesse. *Addresses by Rev. Jesse Appleton, D.D., Late President of Bowdoin College: Delivered at the Annual Commencements, from 1808 to 1818: With a Sketch of His Character.* Brunswick, Me.: Joseph Griffin, Printer, 1820.

———. *Lectures, Delivered at Bowdoin College, and Occasional Sermons.* Brunswick, Me.: Printed by Joseph Griffin, 1822.

Appleby, Joyce. *Capitalism and a New Social Order: The Republican Vision of the 1790s.* New York: New York University Press, 1984.

———. *Inheriting the Revolution: The First Generation of Americans.* Cambridge, Mass.: Harvard University Press, 2000.

Austin, Sarah. *Characteristics of Goethe.* Philadelphia: Lea and Blanchard, 1841.

Bailyn, Bernard. *Education in the Forming of American Society: Needs and Opportunities for Study.* Chapel Hill: University of North Carolina Press, 1960.

———. *The Ideological Origins of the American Revolution.* Cambridge, Mass.: Belknap Press of Harvard University Press, 1967.

Battersby, Christine. *Gender and Genius: Towards a Feminist Aesthetics.* London: Women's Press, 1989.

Bay, Mia. *The White Image in the Black Mind: African-American Ideas about White People, 1830–1925.* New York: Oxford University Press, 2000.

Baym, Nina. *American Women of Letters and the Nineteenth-Century Sciences: Styles of Affiliation.* New Brunswick, N.J.: Rutgers University Press, 2002.

Berlin, Ira, and Ronald Hoffman. *Slavery and Freedom in the Age of the American Revolution.* Charlottesville: University Press of Virginia, 1983.

Blauvelt, Martha Tomhave. *The Work of the Heart: Young Women and Emotion, 1780–1830.* Charlottesville: University of Virginia Press, 2007.

Bledstein, Burton J. *The Culture of Professionalism: The Middle Class and the Development of Higher Education in America.* New York: W. W. Norton, 1976.

Bloch, Ruth H. *Gender and Morality in Anglo-American Culture, 1650–1800.* Berkeley: University of California Press, 2003.

Blumin, Stuart. *The Emergence of the Middle Class: Social Experience in the American City, 1760–1900.* New York: Cambridge University Press, 1989.

Boatwright, Eleanor Miot. *Status of Women in Georgia, 1783–1860.* Brooklyn: Carlson Pub., 1994.

Boles, John B. *Religion in Antebellum Kentucky.* Lexington: University Press of Kentucky, 1976.

Boley, Henry. *Lexington in Old Virginia.* 1936. Reprint, Natural Bridge Station, Va.: Rockbridge Publishing Co., 1990.

Boney, F. N. *A Pictorial History of the University of Georgia.* Athens: University of Georgia Press, 1984.

Bowdoin College. *General Catalogue of Bowdoin College and the Medical School of Maine; A Biographical Record of Alumni and Officers, 1794–1950.* Portland, Me.: Anthoensen Press, 1950.

Boydston, Jeanne. "Gender as a Question of Historical Analysis." *Gender and History* 20 (November 2008): 558–83.

———. *Home and Work: Housework, Wages, and the Ideology of Labor in the Early Republic.* New York: Oxford University Press, 1990.

Boylan, Anne M. *Sunday School: The Formation of an American Institution, 1790–1880.* New Haven, Conn.: Yale University Press, 1990.

Bozeman, Theodore Dwight. *Protestants in an Age of Science: The Baconian Ideal and Antebellum American Religious Thought.* Chapel Hill: University of North Carolina Press, 1977.

Brooks, Robert Preston. *The University of Georgia under Sixteen Administrations, 1785–1955.* Athens: University of Georgia Press, 1956.

Brown, Chandos Michael. *Benjamin Silliman: A Life in the New Republic.* Princeton, N.J.: Princeton University Press, 1989.

Brown, Gillian. *The Consent of the Governed: The Lockean Legacy in Early American Culture.* Cambridge, Mass.: Harvard University Press, 2001.

Brown, Herbert. *The Sentimental Novel in America, 1789–1860.* 1940. Reprint, New York: Pageant Books, 1959.

Brown, Isaac V. *Biography of the Rev. Robert Finley, D.D., of Basking Ridge N.J., with an Account of His Agency as the Author of the American Colonization Society; Also a Sketch of the Slave Trade; a View of Our National Policy and That of Great Britain towards Liberia and Africa. With an Appendix.* Philadelphia: J. W. Moore, 1857.

———. *Memoirs of the Rev. Robert Finley, D.D.* New Brunswick, N.J.: Terhune and Letson, 1819.

Brown, Richard D. *The Strength of a People: The Idea of an Informed Citizenry in America, 1650–1870.* Chapel Hill: University of North Carolina Press, 1996.

Bryan, Janet Allan, ed. *A March Past: Reminiscences of Elizabeth Randolph Preston Allan.* Richmond, Va.: Dietz Press, 1938.

Buckingham, J. S. *The Slave States of America.* Vol. 2. 1842. Reprint, New York: Negro Universities Press, 1968.

Buckley, Thomas E., ed. *"If You Love that Lady, Don't Marry Her": The Courtship Letters of Sally McDowell and John Miller, 1854–1856.* Columbia: University of Missouri Press, 2000.

Burin, Eric. *Slavery and the Peculiar Solution: A History of the American Colonization Society.* Gainesville: University Press of Florida, 2005.

Burke, Colin B. *American Collegiate Populations: A Test of the Traditional View.* New York: New York University Press, 1982.

Burrowes, Carl Patrick. "Black Christian Republicanism: A Southern Ideology in Early Liberia, 1822 to 1847." *Journal of Negro History* 86 (Winter 2001): 30–44.

Burstein, Andrew. *Sentimental Democracy: The Evolution of America's Romantic Self-Image.* New York: Hill and Wang, 1999.

Bushman, Richard L. *The Refinement of America: Persons, Houses, Cities.* New York: Knopf, 1992.

Butler, Vera M. *Education as Revealed by New England Newspapers Prior to 1850.* New York: Arno Press, 1969.

Butterfield, L. H., and Benjamin Rush. "Dr. Benjamin Rush's Journal of a Trip to Carlisle in 1784." *The Pennsylvania Magazine of History and Biography* 74 (October 1950): 443–56.

Calhoun, Charles C. *A Small College in Maine: Two Hundred Years of Bowdoin.* Brunswick, Me.: Bowdoin College, 1993.

Camic, Charles. *Experience and Enlightenment: Socialization for Cultural Change in Eighteenth Century Scotland.* Edinburgh: Edinburgh University Press, 1983.

Capper, Charles. *Margaret Fuller: An American Life.* 2 vols. New York: Oxford University Press, 1992–2007.

Chitnis, Anand C. *The Scottish Enlightenment: A Social History.* London: Croom Helm, 1976.

Clark, Clifford. *The American Family Home, 1800–1860.* Chapel Hill: University of North Carolina Press, 1986.

Clark, Thomas D. *A History of Kentucky.* Lexington: University of Kentucky Press, 1954.

Cleaveland, Nehemiah, and A. S. Packard. *History of Bowdoin College, with Biographical Sketches of Its Graduates, from 1806 to 1879, Inclusive.* Boston: J. R. Osgood and Co., 1882.

Cleaveland, Parker. *Elementary Treatise on Mineralogy and Geology, . . . Illustrated by Six Plates.* Boston: Cummings and Hilliard, 1816.

Clegg, Claude A. *The Price of Liberty: African Americans and the Making of Liberia.* Chapel Hill: University of North Carolina Press, 2004.

Come, Donald R. "The Influence of Princeton on Higher Education in the South before 1825." *William and Mary Quarterly,* 3rd ser., 2 (October 1945): 359–96.

Conrad, Susan P. *Perish the Thought: Intellectual Women in Romantic America, 1830–1860.* Secaucus, N.J.: Citadel Press, 1978.

Conser, Walter H. *God and the Natural World: Religion and Science in Antebellum America.* Columbia: University of South Carolina Press, 1993.

Conway, Moncure Daniel. *Autobiography: Memories and Experiences of Moncure Daniel Conway.* 2 vols. Boston: Houghton, Mifflin, 1904.

Cornelius, Janet Duitsman. *"When I can read my title clear": Literacy, Slavery, and Religion in the Antebellum South.* Columbia: University of South Carolina Press, 1991.

Cottrol, Robert J., ed. *From African to Yankee, Narratives of Slavery and Freedom in Antebellum New England.* Armonk, N.Y.: M. E. Sharpe, 1998.

Coulling, Mary Price. *Margaret Junkin Preston: A Biography.* Winston-Salem, N.C.: John F. Blair, 1993.

Coulter, E. Merton. *College Life in the Old South, as Seen at the University Of Georgia.* 1928. Reprint, Athens: University of Georgia Press, 1973.

Crane, Theodore Rawson, ed. *The Colleges and the Public, 1787–1862.* Classics in Education, no. 15. New York: Bureau of Publications, Teacher's College, Columbia University, 1963.

Cremin, Lawrence A. *American Education: The National Experience, 1783–1876.* New York: Harper and Row, 1980.

Crenshaw, Ollinger. *General Lee's College: The Rise and Growth of Washington and Lee University.* New York: Random House, 1969.

Crooks, George R. *Life and Letters of the Rev. John McClintock.* New York: Nelson and Phillips, 1876.

Dall, William Healey. *Spencer Fullerton Baird: A Biography, including Selections from His Correspondence with Audubon, Agassiz, Dana, and Others.* Philadelphia: J. B. Lippincott, 1915.

Danforth, Keyes. *Boyhood Reminiscences: Pictures of New England Life in the Olden Times in Williamstown.* New York: Gazlay Bros., 1895.

Daniels, George A. *American Science in the Age of Jackson.* New York: Columbia University Press, 1968.

Dann, Martin E. *The Black Press, 1827–1890: The Quest for National Identity.* New York: G. P. Putnam's Sons, 1971.

Davidoff, Leonore, and Catherine Hall. *Family Fortunes, Men and Women of the English Middle Class, 1780–1860.* Chicago: University of Chicago Press, 1987.

Davidson, Cathy N. *Revolution and the Word: The Rise of the Novel in America.* New York: Oxford University Press, 1986

Davidson, Robert. *A History of the Presbyterian Church in the State of Kentucky.* New York: R. Carter, 1847.

Davis, David Brion. *The Problem of Slavery in the Age of Revolution, 1770–1823.* Ithaca, N.Y.: Cornell University Press, 1975.

Davis, Richard Beale. *Intellectual Life in Jefferson's Virginia, 1790–1830.* Chapel Hill: University of North Carolina Press, 1964.

Denison, J. H. *Mark Hopkins: A Biography.* New York: Charles Scribner's Sons, 1937.

Dillon, Mary. *In Old Bellaire.* New York: The Century Co., 1906.

Durfee, Calvin. *A History of Williams College.* Boston: A. Williams, 1860.

———. *Williams Biographical Annals.* Boston: Lee and Shepard; New York: Shepard and Dillingham, 1871.

Dwight, Timothy. *Travels in New England and New-York.* 4 vols. New Haven, Conn.: T. Dwight, 1821.

Dyer, Thomas G. *The University of Georgia: A Bicentennial History, 1785–1985.* Athens: University of Georgia Press, 1985.

Eadie, John W., ed. *Classical Traditions in Early America.* Ann Arbor: Center for the Coordination of Ancient and Modern Studies, University of Michigan, 1976.

Eaton, Clement. *The Freedom-of-Thought Struggle in the Old South.* New York: Harper and Row, 1964.

Ehrenberg, John. *Civil Society: The Critical History of an Idea.* New York: New York University Press, 1999.

Emerson, Ralph Waldo. *The Early Lectures of Ralph Waldo Emerson.* Edited by Robert E. Spiller and Wallace E. Williams. Cambridge, Mass.: Belknap Press of Harvard University Press, 1972.

Evarts, Jeremiah. *Through the South and the West with Jeremiah Evarts in 1826.* Edited by J. Orin Oliphant. Lewisburg, Pa.: Bucknell University Press, 1956.

Farnham, Christie Anne. *The Education of the Southern Belle: Higher Education and Student Socialization in the Antebellum South.* New York: New York University Press, 1994.

Ferling, John, ed. *The World Turned Upside Down: The American Victory in the War of Independence.* New York: Greenwood Press, 1988.

Fields, Barbara. "Slavery, Race, and Ideology in the Unites States of America." *New Left Review* 181 (May/June 1990): 95–118.

Fisher, Sidney George. *A Philadelphia Perspective: The Diary of Sidney George Fisher.* Edited by Nicholas Wainwright. Philadelphia: Historical Society of Pennsylvania, 1967.

Fishkin, Shelley Fisher. "Interrogating 'Whiteness,' Complicating 'Blackness': Remapping American Culture." *American Quarterly* 47 (September 1995): 428–66.

Fliegelman, Jay. *Prodigals and Pilgrims: The American Revolution against Patriarchal Authority, 1750–1800.* New York: Cambridge University Press, 1982.

Foner, Philip. "John Brown Russwurm: A Document." *Journal of Negro History* 54, (October 1969): 393–97.

Foote, William H. *Sketches of Virginia, Historical and Biographical.* 2 vols. Philadelphia: W. S. Martin, 1850–55.

Fortenbaugh, Samuel B. *In Order to Form a More Perfect Union: An Inquiry into the Origins of a College.* Schenectady: Union College Press, 1978.

Foster, Charles I. *An Errand of Mercy: The Evangelical United Front, 1790–1837.* Chapel Hill: University of North Carolina Press, 1960.

Fox, Early Lee. *The American Colonization Society, 1817–1840.* Baltimore: Johns Hopkins University Press, 1919.

Frankenberg, Ruth. *White Women, Race Matters: The Social Construction of Whiteness.* Minneapolis: University of Minnesota Press, 1993.

Frederickson, George M. *The Black Image in the White Mind: The Debate on Afro-American Character and Destiny, 1817–1914.* New York: Harper and Row, 1971.

Freeman, Joanne B. *Affairs of Honor: National Politics in the New Republic.* New Haven, Conn.: Yale University Press, 2001.

Gay, Peter. *The Bourgeois Experience: Victoria to Freud.* 5 vols. New York: Oxford University Press, 1984.

———. *The Enlightenment: An Interpretation.* Vol. 2, *The Science of Freedom.* New York: Alfred A. Knopf, 1969.

Geiger, Roger L., ed. *The American College in the Nineteenth Century.* Nashville: Vanderbilt University Press, 2000.

Gillespie, Michele. *Free Labor in an Unfree World: White Artisans in Slaveholding Georgia, 1789–1860.* Athens: University of Georgia Press, 2000.

Gilpin, Henry. *A Northern Tour.* Philadelphia: n.p., 1825.

Glickstein, Jonathan. *Concepts of Free Labor in Antebellum America.* New Haven, Conn.: Yale University Press, 1991.

Glover, Lorri. *Southern Sons: Becoming Men in the New Nation.* Baltimore: Johns Hopkins University Press, 2010.

Grandison, Kenrick Ian. "Negotiated Space: The Black College Campus as a Cultural Record of Postbellum America." *American Quarterly* 51 (September 1999): 529–79.

Gratz, Rebecca. *Letters of Rebecca Gratz.* Edited by Rabbi David Philipson. Philadelphia: Jewish Publication Society of America, 1929.

Green, Jennifer. *Military Education and the Emerging Middle Class in the Old South.* Cambridge, Mass.: Harvard University Press, 2008.

Greene, John C. *American Science in the Age of Jefferson.* Ames: Iowa State University Press, 1984.

Greven, Philip. *The Protestant Temperament: Patterns of Child Rearing, Religious Experience, and the Self in Early America.* Chicago: Chicago University Press, 1977.

Gutman, Herbert. *Work, Culture, and Society in Industrializing America: Essays in American Working-Class and Social History.* New York: Vintage Books, 1977.

Hall, Benjamin Homer. *A Collection of College Words and Customs.* New York: M. Doolady, 1859.

Halttunen, Karen. *Confidence Men and Painted Women: A Study of Middle-Class Culture in America, 1830–1870.* New Haven, Conn.: Yale University Press, 1982.

———. "Humanitarianism and the Pornography of Pain in Anglo-American Culture." *American Historical Review* 100 (April 1995): 303–34.

Hancock, Scott. "The Elusive Boundaries of Blackness: Identity Formation in Antebellum Boston." *Journal of Negro History* 84 (Spring 1999): 115–29.

Handlin, Oscar, and Mary F. Handlin. *The American College and American Culture: Socialization as a Function of Higher Education.* New York: McGraw-Hill, 1970.

Harris, J. William. *Plain Folk and Gentry in a Slave Society: White Liberty and Black Slavery in Augusta's Hinterlands.* Middletown, Conn.: Wesleyan University Press, 1985.

Hatch, Lewis C. *The History of Bowdoin College.* Portland: Loring, Short, and Harmon, 1927.

Hawthorne, Nathaniel. *Fanshawe.* In *Collected Novels,* edited by Millicent Bell. New York: Library of America, 1983.

Henry, James Buchanan, and Christian Henry Scharff. College As It Is: or, The Collegian's Manual in 1853. Edited by J. Jefferson Looney. Princeton, NJ: Princeton University Press, 1996.

Herbst, Jurgen. *From Crisis to Crisis: American College Government, 1636–1819.* Cambridge, Mass.: Harvard University Press, 1982.

Hessinger, Rodney. *Seduced, Abandoned, and Reborn: Visions of Youth in Middle-Class America, 1780–1850.* Philadelphia: University of Pennsylvania Press, 2005.

Higginbotham, Evelyn Brooks. "African-American Women's History and the Metalanguage of Race." *Signs: Journal of Women in Cultural and Society* 17 (Winter 1992): 251–74.

Higham, John, and Paul K. Conkin, eds. *New Directions in American Intellectual History.* Baltimore: Johns Hopkins University Press, 1979.

Hislop, Codman. *Eliphalet Nott.* Middletown, Conn.: Wesleyan University Press, 1971.

Hoeveler, J. David. *Creating the American Mind: Intellect and Politics in the Colonial Colleges.* Lanham, Md.: Rowman and Littlefield, 2002.

Hofstadter, Richard. *Anti-Intellectualism in American Life.* New York: Alfred A. Knopf, 1969.

Hofstadter, Richard, and Wilson Smith, eds. *American Higher Education: A Documentary History.* Chicago: University of Chicago Press, 1961.

Holley, Horace. "A Discourse Occasioned by the Death of Col. James Morrison, Delivered in the Episcopal Church, Lexington, Kentucky, May 19th, 1823, by the Rev. Horace Holley, President of Transylvania University." Lexington, Ky.: Printed by J. Bradford, 1823.

Hopkins, Albert. "An Address Delivered at the Opening of the Observatory of Williams College, 12 June 1838." Pittsfield, Mass.: Phineas Allen and Son, 1838.

———. "Revivals of Religion in Williams College." *Journal of the American Education Society* 13 (February 1841): 341–51.

Hopkins, Louisa Payson. *Henry Langdon, or, What Was I Made For?* New York: Gates and Stedman, 1846.

———. *The Silent Comforter: A Companion for the Sick Room.* New York: Gates and Stedman, 1848.

Hopkins, Mark. *Early Letters of Mark Hopkins.* Edited by Susan S. Hopkins. New York: John Day Co., 1929.

———. *Miscellaneous Essays and Discourses.* Boston: T. R. Marvin, 1847.

Horn, James, Jan Ellen Lewis, and Peter S. Onuf, eds. *The Revolution of 1800: Democracy, Race, and the New Republic.* Charlottesville: University of Virginia Press, 2002.

Horton, James Oliver, and Lois E. Horton. *In Hope of Liberty: Culture, Community, and Protest among Northern Free Blacks, 1700–1860.* New York: Oxford University Press, 1997.

Houghton, Walter E. *The Victorian Frame of Mind, 1830–1870.* New Haven, Conn.: Yale University Press, 1957.

Hovenkamp, Herbert. *Science and Religion in America, 1800–1860.* Philadelphia: University of Pennsylvania Press, 1978.

Howe, Daniel Walker. "Church, State, and Education in the Young American Republic." *Journal of the Early Republic* 22 (Spring 2002): 1–24.

———. *Making the American Self: Jonathan Edwards to Abraham Lincoln.* Cambridge, Mass.: Harvard University Press, 1997.

———. *The Unitarian Conscience: Harvard Moral Philosophy, 1805–1861.* Cambridge, Mass.: Harvard University Press, 1970.

Hudson, Winthrop S. *Religion in America.* New York: Charles Scribner's Sons, 1965.

Hull, Augustus Longstreet. *Annals of Athens, Georgia, 1801–1901, with an Introductory Sketch by Dr. Henry Hull.* Athens, Ga.: Banner Job Office, 1906.

Hynds, Ernest C. *Antebellum Athens and Clarke County, Georgia.* Athens: University of Georgia Press, 1974.

Isaac, Rhys. *The Transformation of Virginia, 1740–1790.* Chapel Hill: University of North Carolina Press, 1982.

Jaffee, David. "The Village Enlightenment in New England, 1760–1820." *William and Mary Quarterly*, 3rd ser., 47 (July 1990): 327–46.

James, Maria. *Wales, and Other Poems.* With an Introduction by A. Potter, D.D. New York: John S. Taylor, 1839.

Jenks, William, ed. "The Inaugural Address, Delivered in Brunswick, September 9, 1802, By the Rev. Joseph McKeen." Portland, Me.: Thomas B. Wait and Co., 1807.

Jennings, Walter Wilson. *Transylvania: Pioneer University of the West.* New York: Pageant Press, 1955.

Johnson, Walter. *Soul by Soul: Life Inside the Antebellum Slave Market.* Cambridge, Mass.: Harvard University Press, 1999.

Jordan, Winthrop D. *White Over Black: American Attitudes toward the Negro, 1550–1812.* New York: W. W. Norton, 1968.

Junkin, Margaret. "The Haunts of the Student." *Southern Literary Messenger* 16 (October 1850): 596–97.

———. *Silverwood: A Book of Memories.* New York: Derby and Jackson, 1856.

———. *See also* Preston, Margaret Junkin.

Kaplan, Catherine O'Donnell. *Men of Letters in the Early Republic: Cultivating Forums of Citizenship.* Chapel Hill: University of North Carolina Press, 2008.

Kearney, Hugh. *Scholars and Gentlemen: Universities and Society in Pre-Industrial Britain, 1500–1700.* Ithaca, N.Y.: Cornell University Press, 1970.

Keeney, Elizabeth B. *The Botanizers: Amateur Scientists in Nineteenth-Century America.* Chapel Hill: University of North Carolina Press, 1992.

Kelley, Mary. *Learning to Stand and Speak: Women, Education, and Public Life in America's Republica.* Chapel Hill: University of North Carolina Press, 2006.

———. *Private Woman, Public Stage: Literary Domesticity in Nineteenth-Century America.* New York: Oxford University Press, 1984.

———. "Reading Women / Women Reading: The Making of the Learned Women in Antebellum America." *Journal of American History* 83 (September 1996): 401–24.

Kelly, Catherine E. *In the New England Fashion: Reshaping Women's Lives in the Nineteenth Century.* Ithaca, N.Y.: Cornell University Press, 1999.

Kendall, Edward Augustus. *Travels through the Northern Parts of the United States, in the Years 1807 and 1808.* 3 vols. New York: I. Riley, 1809.

Kennon, Donald R., ed. *A Republic for the Ages: The United States Capitol and the Political Culture of the Early Republic.* Charlottesville: University Press of Virginia, 1999.

Kerber, Linda. *Toward an Intellectual History of Women.* Chapel Hill: University of North Carolina Press, 1997.

———. *Women of the Republic: Intellect and Ideology in Revolutionary America.* New York: W. W. Norton, 1980.

Kett, Joseph F. *The Pursuit of Knowledge under Difficulties: From Self-Improvement to Adult Education in America, 1750–1990.* Stanford, Calif.: Stanford University Press, 1994.

Kitto, John. *A Cyclopaedia of Biblical Literature.* 2 vols. New York: Mark H. Newman, 1846.

Kloppenberg, James T. *The Virtues of Liberalism.* New York: Oxford University Press, 1998.

Knight, Edgar W., ed. *A Documentary History of Education in the South Before 1860.* Vol. 4, *Private and Denominational Efforts.* Chapel Hill: University of North Carolina Press, 1953.

Koons, Kenneth E., and Warren R. Hofstra, eds. *After the Backcountry: Rural Life in the Great Valley of Virginia, 1800–1900.* Knoxville: University of Tennessee Press, 2000.

Landes, Joan B. *Women and the Public Sphere in the Age of the French Revolution.* Ithaca, N.Y.: Cornell University Press, 1988.

Lane, Christopher. *Hatred and Civility: The Antisocial Life in Victorian England.* New York: Columbia University Press, 2004.

Larkin, Jack. *The Reshaping of Everyday Life, 1790–1840.* New York: Harper and Row, 1988.

Laurie, Bruce. *Artisans into Workers: Labor in the Nineteenth-Century America.* New York: Hill and Wang, 1989.

Lee, Rebecca Smith. *Mary Austin Holley: A Biography.* Austin: University of Texas Press, 1962.

Lewis, Charlene M. Boyer. *Ladies and Gentlemen on Display: Planter Society at the Virginia Springs, 1790–1860.* Charlottesville: University Press of Virginia, 2001.

Lewis, Jan. *The Pursuit of Happiness: Family and Values in Jefferson's Virginia.* Cambridge: Cambridge University Press, 1983.

———. "The Republican Wife: Virtue and Seduction in the Early Republic." *William and Mary Quarterly,* 3rd ser., 44 (October 1987): 689–721.

Lindsay, Debra. "Intimate Inmates: Scientific Wives and Households in the Nineteenth Century." *Isis* 4 (December 1998): 631–52.

Litwack, Leon. *North of Slavery: The Negro in the Free States, 1790–1860.* Chicago: University of Chicago Press, 1961.

Locke, John. *Some Thoughts concerning Education; and, Of the Conduct of the Understanding.* Edited by Ruth W. Grant and Nathan Tarcov. Indianapolis: Hackett Publishing Co., 1996.

Longfellow, Henry Wadsworth. *Hyperion: A Romance.* 2 vols. New York: Samuel Colman, 1839.

———. *The Letters of Henry Wadsworth Longfellow.* Edited by Andrew Hilen. 6 vols. Cambridge, Mass.: Belknap Press of Harvard University Press, 1966.

Longstreet, Augustus Baldwin. *Georgia Scenes.* Edited by David Rachels. Athens: University of Georgia Press, 1998.

Loomis, Justin Rudolph. *The Elements of Geology, Adapted to the Use of Schools and Colleges.* Boston: Gould and Lincoln, 1852.

Lystra, Karen. *Searching the Heart: Women, Men, and Romantic Love in Nineteenth Century America.* New York: Oxford University Press, 1989.

Marryat, Frederick. *Diary in America.* Edited by Jules Zanger. Bloomington: Indiana University Press, 1960.

Marshall, Megan. *The Peabody Sisters: Three Women Who Ignited American Romanticism.* Boston: Houghton Mifflin, 2005.

Martel, James R. *Love Is a Sweet Chain: Desire, Autonomy, and Friendship in Liberal Political Theory.* New York: Routledge, 2001.

Martin, Scott C., ed. *Cultural Change and the Market Revolution in America, 1789–1860.* Lanham, Md.: Rowman and Littlefield, 2005.

Martin, Terence. *The Instructed Vision, Scottish Common Sense Philosophy and the Origins of American Fiction.* Bloomington: Indiana University Press, 1961.

Marx, Leo. *The Machine in the Garden: Technology and the Pastoral Ideal in America.* 1964. Reprint, Oxford: Oxford University Press, 2000.

Mathews, Donald G. "The Second Great Awakening as an Organizing Process, 1780–1830: A Hypothesis." *American Quarterly* 21 (Spring 1969): 23–43.

May, Henry F. *The Enlightenment in America.* New York: Oxford University Press, 1976.

McManus, Edgar J. *Black Bondage in the North.* Syracuse, N.Y.: Syracuse University Press, 2001.

McNamara, Martha J. *From Tavern to Courthouse: Architecture and Ritual in American Law, 1658–1860.* Baltimore: Johns Hopkins University Press, 2004.

Melish, Joanne Pope. *Disowning Slavery: Gradual Emancipation and "Race" in New England, 1780–1860.* Ithaca, N.Y.: Cornell University Press, 1998

Menand, Louis. *The Metaphysical Club: A Story of Ideas in America.* New York: Mac-Millan, 2002.

Manning, William. *The Key of Liberty: The Life and Democratic Writings of William Manning, "A Laborer," 1747–1814.* Edited and with an introduction by Michael Merrill and Sean Wilentz. Cambridge, Mass.: Harvard University Press, 1993.

Meyer, D. H. *The Instructed Conscience: The Shaping of the American National Ethic.* Philadelphia: University of Pennsylvania Press, 1972.

Meyers, Marvin. *The Jacksonian Persuasion: Politics and Belief.* Stanford, Calif.: Stanford University Press, 1957.

Milham, Willis I. *Early American Observatories.* Northfield, Minn.: n.p., 1937.

———. *The History of Astronomy in Williams College and the Founding of the Hopkins Observatory.* Williamstown, Mass.: Williams College, 1937.

Miller, Howard. *The Revolutionary College: American Presbyterian Higher Education, 1707–1837.* New York: New York University Press, 1976.

Miller, Perry. *Errand into the Wilderness.* Cambridge, Mass.: Harvard University Press, 1956.

Miller, Sally Campbell Preston McDowell. *Memoir of James McDowell, Governor of*

Virginia: Contributed to the Historical Series of Washington and Lee University by His Daughter. Baltimore: John Murphy and Co., 1895.

Mintz, Steven. *A Prison of Expectations: The Family in Victorian Culture.* New York: New York University Press, 1983.

Monroe, Joel Henry. *Schenectady, Ancient and Modern.* Geneva, N.Y.: W. F. Humphrey, 1914.

Moore, Arthur K. *The Frontier Mind: A Cultural Analysis of the Kentucky Frontiersman.* Lexington: University of Kentucky Press, 1957.

Morehead, Charles S. "An Address Delivered on the Second Anniversary of Van Doren's Collegiate Institute for Young Ladies: In the city of Lexington, Kentucky On the Last Thursday in July, 1833, to Which is Added a Prospectus of the Institute." Lexington, Ky.: Wm. M. Todd and Thos. T. Skillman, 1833.

Morgan, James Henry. *Dickinson College: The History of One Hundred and Fifty Years, 1783–1933.* Carlisle, Pa.: Dickinson College, 1933.

Moroney, Siobhan. "Birth of a Canon: The Historiography of Early Republican Educational Thought." *History of Education Quarterly* 39 (Winter 1999): 476–91.

Morse, Jedidiah, and Richard C. Morse. *A New Universal Gazetteer, or Geographical Dictionary: Containing a Description of the Various Countries, Provinces, Cities, Towns, Seas, Lakes, Rivers, Mountains, Capes, &c. in the Known World: . . . Accompanied with an Atlas.* New Haven: S. Converse, 1823.

Moses, Wilson Jeremiah. *Liberian Dreams: Back-to-Africa Narratives from the 1850s.* University Park: Pennsylvania State University Press, 1998.

Mullins, Jeffrey A. "In the Sweat of Thy Brow." In *Cultural Change and the Market Revolution in America, 1789–1860,* edited by Scott C. Martin, 143–80. Lanham, Md.: Rowman and Littlefield, 2005.

Murray, Penelope, ed. *Genius: The History of an Idea.* Oxford: Basil Blackwell, 1989.

Nash, Gary. *Forging Freedom: The Formation of Philadelphia's Black Community, 1720–1840.* Cambridge, Mass.: Harvard University Press, 1988.

Nash, Margaret A. "Rethinking Republican Motherhood: Benjamin Rush and the Young Ladies' Academy of Philadelphia." *Journal of the Early Republic* 17 (Summer 1997): 171–91.

———. *Women's Education in the United States, 1780–1840.* New York: Palgrave Macmillan, 2005.

New England Women and Their Families in the 18th and 19th Centuries: Personal Papers, Letters, and Diaries. Series A, Manuscript Collections from the American Antiquarian Society. Consulting editor, Ellen K. Rothman. Project coordinator, Randolph Boehm. Bethesda, Md.: University Publications of America, 1997–[2003].

Noll, Mark. "Common Sense Traditions and American Evangelical Thought." *American Quarterly* 37 (Summer 1985): 216–38.

Norton, Mary Beth. *Liberty's Daughters: The Revolutionary Experience of American Women, 1750–1800*. Boston: Little, Brown, 1980.

Novak, Steven J. *The Rights of Youth: American College and Student Revolt, 1789–1815*. Cambridge, Mass.: Harvard, 1977.

Oakes, James. *The Ruling Race: A History of American Slaveholders*. New York: Vintage Books, 1982.

———. *Slavery and Freedom: An Interpretation of the Old South*. New York: Knopf, 1990.

O'Brien, Michael. *Rethinking the South: Essays in Intellectual History*. Baltimore: Johns Hopkins University Press, 1988.

Ogren, Christine A. "Sites, Students, Scholarship, and Structures: The Historiography of American Higher Education in the Post-Revisionist Era." In *Rethinking the History of American Education,* edited by William J. Reese and John L. Rury, 187–222. New York: Palgrave Macmillan, 2008.

Onuf, Peter S. *Jefferson's Empire: The Language of American Nationhood*. Charlottesville: University Press of Virginia, 2000.

Opal, J. M. *Beyond the Farm: National Ambitions in Rural New England*. Philadelphia: University of Pennsylvania Press, 2008.

Painter, Nell Irvin. *Southern History Across the Color Line*. Chapel Hill: University of North Carolina Press, 2001.

Packard, Alpheus S. "Address on the Life and Character of Thomas C. Upham, Late Professor of Mental and Moral Philosophy in Bowdoin College. Delivered at the Interment, Brunswick, Me., April 4, 1872." Brunswick, Me.: Joseph Griffin, 1873.

———. "Address on the Life and Character of William Smyth, DD: Late Professor of Mathematics and Natural Philosophy in Bowdoin College; Delivered before the Alumni of the College, July 7, 1868." Brunswick, Me.: J. Griffin, 1868.

Parrington, Vernon L. *The Romantic Revolution in America, 1800–1860*. New York: Harvest Books, 1927.

Pasachoff, Jay M. "William College's Hopkins Observatory: The Oldest Extant Observatory in the United States." *Journal of Astronomical History and Heritage* 1 (June 1998): 61–78.

Penn, I. Garland. *The Afro-American Press and Its Editors*. New York: Arno Press, 1969.

Perry, Arthur Latham. *Origins in Williamstown*. New York: Charles Scribner's Sons, 1894.

———. *Williamstown and Williams College*. New York: C. Scribner's Sons, 1899.

Perry, Carroll. *A Professor of Life: A Sketch of Arthur Latham Perry of Williams College*. Boston: Houghton Mifflin, 1923.

Peyton, John Lewis. *Over the Alleghanies and Across the Prairies: Personal Recollections of the Far West, One and Twenty Years Ago*. London: Simpkin, Marshall, 1870.

Piersen, William D. *Black Yankees: The Development of an Afro-American Subculture* in *Eighteenth-Century New England*. Amherst: University of Massachusetts Press, 1988.

Potts, David. "American College in the Nineteenth Century: From Localism to Denominationalism." *History of Education Quarterly* 11 (Winter 1971): 363–80.

Prentiss, George L. *The Life and Letters of Elizabeth Payson Prentiss*. New York: Anson D. F. Randolph and Co., 1882.

Preston, Margaret Junkin. "Erinna's Spinning." In *She Wields a Pen: American Women Poets of the Nineteenth Century*, edited by Janet Gray, 88. Iowa City: University of Iowa Press, 1997.

———. *See also* Junkin, Margaret.

Pusey, William W. *Elusive Aspirations: The History of the Female Academy in Lexington, Virginia*. Lexington, Va.: Washington and Lee University, 1983.

Putnam, Henry. *A Description of Brunswick, Me. in Letters by a Gentleman from South Carolina to a Friend in That State*. Brunswick, Me.: Published by the author, 1823.

Rabinowitz, Richard. *The Spiritual Self in Everyday Life: The Transformation of Personal Religions Experience in Nineteenth-Century New England*. Boston: Northeastern University Press, 1989.

Rainsford, George N. *Congress and Higher Education in the Nineteenth Century*. Knoxville: University of Tennessee Press, 1972.

Reed, George Leffingwell, ed. *Alumni Record, Dickinson College*. Carlisle, Pa.: The College, 1905.

Reed, Thomas C. "A Tribute to the Memory of the Late Edward Savage, Esq." Schenectady: Printed by Riggs and Norris, 1840.

Reed, Thomas Walter. *"Uncle Tom" Reed's Memoir of the University of Georgia*. With an introduction by Ray Mathis. Athens: University of Georgia Libraries, 1974.

Reese, William J., and John L. Rury. *Rethinking the History of American Education*. New York: Palgrave Macmillan, 2008.

Richard, Carl J. *The Founders and the Classics: Greece, Rome, and the American Enlightenment*. Cambridge, Mass.: Harvard University Press, 1994.

———. *The Golden Age of the Classics in America: Greece, Rome, and the Antebellum United States*. Cambridge, Mass.: Harvard University Press, 2009.

Ridner, Judith. *A Town In-Between: Carlisle, Pennsylvania, and the Early Mid-Atlantic Interior*. Philadelphia: University of Pennsylvania Press, 2010.

Robbins, Caroline. *The Eighteenth-Century Commonwealthman*. Cambridge, Mass.: Harvard University Press, 1959.

Robson, David W. "The Early American College and the Wider Culture: Scholarship in the 1970s." *American Quarterly* 32 (Winter 1980): 559–70.

———. *Educating Republicans: The College in the Era of the American Revolution, 1750–1800*. Contributions to the Study of Education Series, no. 15. Westport, Conn.: Greenwood Press, 1985.

Roediger, David R. *The Wages of Whiteness: Race and the Making of the American Working Class.* New York: Verso, 1991.

Rorabaugh, William J. *The Alcoholic Republic: An American Tradition.* New York: Oxford University Press, 1979.

Rothman, David J. *The Discovery of the Asylum: Social Order and Disorder in the New Republic.* Boston: Little, Brown, 1971.

Rotundo, E. Anthony. *American Manhood: Transformations in Masculinity from the Revolution to the Present.* New York: Basic Books, 1993.

Royster, Charles. *A Revolutionary People at War: The Continental Army and American Character, 1775–1783.* New York: W. W. Norton, 1979.

Rudolph, Frederick. *The American College and University: A History.* Athens: University of Georgia Press, 1990.

——. *Mark Hopkins and the Log: Williams College, 1836–1872.* New Haven, Conn.: Yale University Press, 1966; Williamstown, Mass.: Williams College, 1996.

Ruffner, Henry. "Address to the People of West Virginia: Shewing that Slavery is Injurious to the Public Welfare, and that It May be Gradually Abolished, without Detriment to the Rights and Interests of Slaveholders. By a Slaveholder of West Virginia." Lexington, Va.: R. C. Noel, 1847.

——. "Early History of Washington College." Washington and Lee University Historical Papers, no. 1. Baltimore, Md.: John Murphy and Co, 1890.

Ryan, Mary P. *Cradle of the Middle Class: The Family in Oneida County, New York, 1790–1865.* Cambridge: Cambridge University Press, 1981.

Sandage, Scott. *Born Losers: A History of Failure in America.* Cambridge, Mass.: Harvard University Press, 2005.

Saum, Lewis O. *The Popular Mood of Pre-Civil War America.* Westport, Conn.: Greenwood Press, 1980.

Schiebinger, Londa. *The Mind Has No Sex? Women in the Origins of Modern Science.* Cambridge, Mass.: Harvard University Press, 1989.

Schloesser, Pauline. *The Fair Sex: White Women and Racial Patriarchy in the Early American Republic.* New York: New York University Press, 2002.

Schmidt, George P. *The Liberal Arts College: A Chapter in American Cultural History.* 1957. Reprint, Westport, Conn.: Greenwood Press, 1975.

Schuster, David. *Neurasthenic Nation: America's Search for Health, Happiness, and Comfort, 1869–1920.* New Brunswick, N.J.: Rutgers University Press, 2011.

Scott, Donald M. *From Office to Profession: The New England Ministry, 1750–1850.* Philadelphia: University of Pennsylvania Press, 1978.

Scott, Joan Wallach. *Gender and the Politics of History.* New York: Columbia University Press, 1988.

Sellers, Charles. *Dickinson College: A History.* Middletown, Conn.: Wesleyan University Press, 1973.

———. *The Market Revolution: Jacksonian America, 1815–1846.* New York: Oxford University Press, 1991.

Sewall, Albert Cole. *Life of Professor Albert Hopkins.* New York: A. D. F. Randolph and Co., 1870.

Sharp, Isabella Oliver. *Poems, on Various Subjects.* Carlisle, Pa.: A. Loudon, 1805.

Shields, David S. *Civil Tongues and Polite Letters in British America.* Chapel Hill: University of North Carolina Press, 1997.

Shteir, Ann B. *Cultivating Women, Cultivating Science.* Baltimore: Johns Hopkins University Press, 1996.

Sizer, Theodore, ed. *The Age of the Academies.* New York: Bureau of Publications, Teachers College, Columbia University, 1964.

Sklar, Kathryn Kish. *Catherine Beecher: A Study in American Domesticity.* New York: W. W. Norton, 1973.

Sloan, Douglas. *The Scottish Enlightenment and the American College Ideal.* New York: Columbia's Teacher's College Press, 1971.

Smith, Bonnie. *The Gender of History: Men, Women, and Historical Practice.* Cambridge, Mass.: Harvard University Press, 1998.

Smyth, George Adams. *Reminiscences of My Life.* Pasadena, Calif.: n.p., 1928. [typescript]

Solomon, Barbara Miller. *In the Company of Educated Women: A History of Women and Higher Education in America.* New Haven, Conn.: Yale University Press, 1985.

Sonne, Niels Henry. *Liberal Kentucky, 1780–1828.* New York: Columbia University Press, 1939.

Sprague, William B. *Annals of the American Pulpit.* New York: Robert Carter and Brothers, 1857.

Spring, Leverett W. *A History of Williams College.* New York: Houghton Mifflin, 1917.

Stanley, Amy Dru. *From Bondage to Contract: Wage Labor, Marriage, and the Market in the Age of Slave Emancipation.* Cambridge: Cambridge University Press, 1998.

Stanton, William. *The Leopard's Spots: Scientific Attitudes toward Race in America, 1815–1859.* Chicago: University of Chicago Press, 1960.

Staudenraus, P. J. *The African Colonization Movement.* New York: Columbia University Press, 1961.

Stearns, Peter N., and Jan Lewis, eds. *An Emotional History of the United States.* New York: New York University Press, 1998.

Stevenson, Louise L. *Scholarly Means to Evangelical Ends: The New Haven Scholars and the Transformation of Higher Learning in America, 1830–1890.* Baltimore: Johns Hopkins University Press, 1986.

Stone, Lawrence, ed. *The University in Society.* Vol. 2, *Europe, Scotland, and the United States from the 16th to the 20th Century.* Princeton, N.J.: Princeton University Press, 1974.

Stowe, Steven M. *Intimacy and Power in the Old South: Ritual in the Lives of the Planters.* Baltimore: Johns Hopkins University Press, 1987.

Streifford, David M. "The American Colonization Society: An Application of Republican Ideology to Early Antebellum Reform." *Journal of Southern History* 45 (May 1979): 201–20.

Tallant, Harold D. *Evil Necessity: Slavery and Political Culture in Antebellum Kentucky.* Lexington: University Press of Kentucky, 2003.

Taylor, Alan. *Liberty Men and Great Proprietors: The Revolutionary Settlement on the Maine Frontier, 1760–1820.* Chapel Hill: University of North Carolina Press, 1990.

——. *William Cooper's Town: Power and Persuasion on the Frontier of the Early American Republic.* New York: Alfred A. Knopf, 1995.

Taylor, William R. *Cavalier and Yankee: The Old South and American National Character.* New York: Harper and Row, 1957.

Thelin, John R. *A History of American Higher Education.* Baltimore: Johns Hopkins University Press, 2004.

Thompson, John Reuben. "Education and Literature in Virginia: An Address Delivered before the Literary Societies of Washington College, 18, June 1850." Richmond, Va.: H. K. Ellyson, 1850.

Thomson, James. *The Complete Poetical Works of James Thomson.* Edited by J. Logie Robertson. New York: Oxford University Press, 1908.

Thornton, Tamara Plakins. *Cultivating Gentlemen: The Meaning of Country Life among the Boston Elite, 1785–1860.* New Haven, Conn.: Yale University Press, 1989.

Tocqueville, Alexis de. *Democracy in America.* 2 vols. Edited by Phillips Bradley. New York: Vintage Books, 1990.

Tolbert, Lisa C. *Constructing Townscapes: Space and Society in Antebellum Tennessee.* Chapel Hill: University of North Carolina Press, 1999.

Townsend, William H. *Lincoln and His Wife's Home Town.* Indianapolis: Bobbs-Merrill Co., 1929.

Turner, Paul Venable. *Campus: An American Planning Tradition.* Cambridge, Mass.: MIT Press, 1984.

Union College. *A General Catalogue of the Officers, Graduates, and Students of Union College from 1795–1854.* Schenectady, N.Y.: S. S. Riggs, 1854.

Upham, Phebe. *The Crystal Fountain, or, Faith and Life: Personal Records from the Note-Book of Mrs. P. L. Upham.* Philadelphia: J. B. Lippincott, 1877.

——. *A Narrative of Phebe Ann Jacobs.* London: W and F. T. Cash, 1850.

Upton, Dell, and John Michael Vlach, eds. *Common Places: Readings in American Vernacular Architecture.* Athens: University of Georgia Press, 1986.

Van Vechten, Teunis A. *A Poem on Liberty: Delivered by One of the Graduates, at the Annual Commencement of Union College, on the 30th July, 1806.* Albany, N.Y.: Printed by Backus and Whiting, 1806.

Waddel, John Newton. *Memorials of Academic Life: Being an Historical Sketch of the Waddel Family.* Richmond, Va.: Presbyterian Committee of Publication, 1891.

Washington and Lee University. *Catalogue of the Officers and Alumni of Washington and Lee University, Lexington, Virginia, 1749–1888.* Baltimore: John Murphy and Co., 1888.

Waterman, Bryan. *Republic of Intellect: The Friendly Club of New York City and the Making of American Literature.* Baltimore: Johns Hopkins University Press, 2007.

Watkins, Robert, and George Watkins. *A Digest of the Laws of the State of Georgia.* Philadelphia: R. Aitken, 1800.

Wayland, Francis. *Thoughts on the Present Collegiate System in the United States.* Boston: Gould, Kendall and Lincoln, 1842.

Welch, Claude. *Protestant Thought in the Nineteenth Century.* Vol. 1, *1799–1870.* New Haven, Conn.: Yale University Press, 1972.

Wells, David Ames. *Sketches of Williams College.* Springfield, Mass.: H. S. Taylor, 1847.

Weston, Edward P. *The Bowdoin Poets.* Brunswick, Me.: J. Griffin, 1840.

White, Henry Clay. *Abraham Baldwin, One of the Founders of the Republic, and Father of the University of Georgia, the First of American State Universities.* Athens, Ga.: McGregor Co., 1926.

White, James J. *Old Zeus: Life and Letters of James J. White.* Edited by Charles W. Turner. Verona, Va.: McClure Press, 1983.

Whitehead, John S. *The Separation of College and State: Columbia, Dartmouth, Harvard, and Yale, 1776–1876.* New Haven, Conn.: Yale University Press, 1973.

Wilentz, Sean. *Chants Democratic: New York City and the Rise of the American Working Class, 1788–1850.* New York: Oxford University Press, 1984.

Wiley, Bell I. *Slaves No More: Letters from Liberia, 1833–1869.* Lexington: University Press of Kentucky, 1980.

Wilkeson, Samuel. *A Concise History of the Commencement, Progress, and Present Condition of the American Colonies in Liberia.* Washington, D.C.: Madisonian Office, 1839.

Willard, Frances, and Mary Livermore, eds. *American Women: Fifteen Hundred Biographies with Over Fourteen Hundred Portraits; A Comprehensive Encyclopedia of the Lives and Achievements of American Women during the Nineteenth Century.* 2 vols. New York: Mast, Crowell and Kirkpatrick, 1897.

Winterer, Caroline. *The Culture of Classicism: Ancient Greece and Rome in American Intellectual Life, 1780–1910.* Baltimore: Johns Hopkins University Press, 2002.

———. *The Mirror of Antiquity: American Women and the Classical Tradition, 1750–1900.* Ithaca, N.Y.: Cornell University Press, 2007.

Wood, Gordon S. *The Creation of the American Republic, 1776–1787.* New York: W. W. Norton, 1969.

———. *The Radicalism of the American Revolution.* New York: Alfred A. Knopf, 1992.

Woody, Thomas. *A History of Women's Education in the US.* 2 vols. New York: Science Press, 1929.

Wosh, Peter J. *Spreading the Word: The Bible Business in Nineteenth-Century America.* Ithaca, N.Y.: Cornell University Press, 1994.

Wright, John D. *Transylvania: Tutor to the West.* Lexington: University Press of Kentucky, 1975.

Yazawa, Melvin. *From Colonies to Commonwealth: Familial Ideology and the Beginnings of the American Republic.* Baltimore: Johns Hopkins University Press, 1985.

INDEX

with, 88–89; visits to Athens merchants, 97

Waddel, Sarah, 96, 112

Waddel, William, 96

Ward, Jonathan, 51

Washington (D.C.): Baxter's fundraising in, 41, 43–44; white buildings of, 158

Washington, George, 15–16, 20, 29, 40

Washington College (Lexington, Va.): buildings, 158; charter, 25; circle of support and connections, 18–21, 29–30, 59–60; colonizationist views, 162; faculty and fighting, 196–97; faculty homes, 107; fundraising, 10, 15–16, 28–29, 38–39; graduates mentioned, 59–60, 81, 163–64, 196; as ideal space for scholars, 1–2; as moral and educational hub, 45–46; origins, 15–16; presidents (*see* Baxter, George; Junkin, George); religious revival, 112–13; renamed Washington and Lee University, 221–22n4; slaves as workers and servants, 179; temperance views, 102–3; trustee (*see* McDowell, James); trustees' limited attention to, 32

Webster, Noah, 19–20, 51, 52

Whig ideology, 12–13, 37, 52–53, 134

white male elites: admissions limited to, 6–7, 156–57; critique of, 19–20, 121; democratization of, 3; expected power of, 6

whiteness: celebrations of, 156–58

Willard, Emma, 7

William and Mary College (Williamsburg, Va.), 203n8

Williams College (Williamstown, Mass.): approach to studying, 11; Civil War's disruption of, 198; faculty self-assessment based on college's success, 141–42, 151–52, 154; faculty's local village connections, 97; faculty's mental and manual labor regimen, 138–39; faculty teaching and self-accounting, 129–33; faculty wives' freedom of intellectual pursuits, 146, 147–48; graduates mentioned, 62, 115, 127–28, 164, 199–200; Hopkins brothers, 127–28; as ideal space for schol-

ars, 2; individual growth possibilities, 147–48; living spaces, 107, 108; Lyceum of Natural History, 138; mathematics and science professor (*see* Hopkins, Albert); moral philosophy professor (*see* Hopkins, Mark); observatory, 139–40, 152, 201; presidents (*see* Hopkins, Mark); professor-student relationship, 62; religious revival, 113, 114–15; servants, 180–81, 183; temperance views, 103–4

Williamstown (Mass.): ABCFM founded in, 95; chapel for poor, mixed-race district, 152; as "society in miniature," 53; temperance views, 103–4. *See also* Williams College

women and girls: academic household duties, 55–56, 76–78, 107, 108; Browning as heroine, 124; collective scrutiny and discipline, 73–75; complementary roles, 70–71; conversational skills, 72–73; education for, 7, 67–70, 117–18; feminine ideal, 121; freedom in intellectual pursuits, 146–55; household and educational activities intertwined, 76–80; intellectual work and housekeeping combined, 143–46; parents' concerns for, 61–62; search for vocation, 124–25, 127; sectarian alliances, 95–96; social advice and direction from, 66–68, 71–75; as tutors for male students, 69, 70, 71, 74

women writers and translators: ambivalence of, 215n11; college-world freedom in intellectual pursuits, 146–55; intellectual work and housekeeping combined by, 143–44; literary market and, 121–25. *See also specific writers*

Woods, Leonard, Jr., 150

work: agricultural vs. academic, 130, 131, 133–35; manual vs. academic, 119–21; mental and manual labor combined, 136–39. *See also* college work

Yale College (New Haven, Conn.), 7, 26, 37, 45–46, 51, 203n8

youth. *See* graduates; students

Douglas Bradburn
The Citizenship Revolution: Politics and the Creation of the American Union,
1774–1804

Clarence E. Walker
Mongrel Nation: The America Begotten by Thomas Jefferson and Sally Hemings

Timothy Mason Roberts
Distant Revolutions: 1848 and the Challenge to American Exceptionalism

Peter J. Kastor and François Weil, editors
Empires of the Imagination: Transatlantic Histories of the Louisiana Purchase

Eran Shalev
Rome Reborn on Western Shores: Historical Imagination and the Creation of the
American Republic

Leonard J. Sadosky
Revolutionary Negotiations: Indians, Empires, and Diplomats in the Founding
of America

Philipp Ziesche
Cosmopolitan Patriots: Americans in Paris in the Age of Revolution

Leonard J. Sadosky, Peter Nicolaisen, Peter S. Onuf, and Andrew J.
O'Shaughnessy, editors
Old World, New World: America and Europe in the Age of Jefferson

Sam W. Haynes
Unfinished Revolution: The Early American Republic in a British World

Michal Jan Rozbicki
Culture and Liberty in the Age of the American Revolution

Ellen Holmes Pearson
Remaking Custom: Law and Identity in the Early American Republic

Seth Cotlar
Tom Paine's America: The Rise and Fall of Transatlantic Radicalism in the Early
Republic

John Craig Hammond and Matthew Mason, editors
Contesting Slavery: The Politics of Bondage and Freedom in the New American
Nation